meeting your

Half-Orange

meeting your Half-Orange

AN UTTERLY UPBEAT GUIDE TO USING

DATING OPTIMISM

TO FIND YOUR PERFECT MATCH

AMY SPENCER

RUNNING PRESS
PHILADELPHIA · LONDON

Printed in the United States

*This book may not be reproduced in whole or in part, in any form or by any means,
electronic or mechanical, including photocopying, recording, or by any information storage and retrieval system now known or hereafter invented, without written permission
from the publisher.*

9   8   7   6   5   4   3   2   1
Digit on the right indicates the number of this printing

Library of Congress Control Number: 2009938134

ISBN 978-0-7624-3774-0

Design by Joshua McDonnell
Edited by Jennifer Kasius
Typography: Archer, Bembo, and Wendy

Running Press Book Publishers
2300 Chestnut Street
Philadelphia, PA 19103-4371

Visit us on the web!
www.runningpress.com

CONTENTS

8 PREFACE:
One Thing, Before You Plant—
Are You Being Too Picky?

10 INTRODUCTION:
What Is Your Half-Orange?

20 PHASE ONE:
Get Your Soil Ready: Believe You Can Have It

43 PHASE TWO:
Hit the Garden Shop: Admit You Want It

67 PHASE THREE:
How to Choose your Seed: What Do You Want?

84 PHASE FOUR:
How to Plant the Seed: Focus and Imagine Feeling It

129 PHASE FIVE:
Nurture Your Sapling to Bloom: Live a Happy Life

196 PHASE SIX:
Know When to Pluck:
How to Recognize Your Half-Orange

219 BONUS APPENDIX A:
Dating Strategies of Operation Optimism

226 BONUS APPENDIX B:
The OrangeAid Handbook

234 Acknowledgments

For my husband—my true other half

half-orange (haf or'inj) n., translation of the Spanish phrase *mi media naranja*, which means "my half-orange"; used to describe, in love, one's sweetheart, one's beautifully perfect other half.

PREFACE:

One Thing, Before You Plant . . . Are You Being Too Picky?

I just have to get one thing out there, because it is an emotional prerequisite to appreciating and successfully using this book. If you, in the last days, weeks, months, or years of your dating life, have asked yourself the following question: "Am I being too picky?" I have an answer for you: No.

No, no, no, no, no. You're not being too picky!

Just because you want to be with someone you feel a real, true connection with does not mean you're being too picky. Just because you don't want to spend your time on dates with guys you don't find interesting or physically attractive or compelling or funny or smart or compatible in any way does not mean you're shallow or asking for too much. You know yourself better than anyone else, and you know what kind of connection you want. You're allowed to want what you want. So stop listening to all the voices telling you otherwise.

I say this because if you're at all like me, you've probably heard every accusation in the book about why you're still single: "You know what you're doing wrong? You need to give guys a chance." "You have to widen the net." "There's no such thing as a perfect man." By this point, one of those voices might even be yours, saying, "Well maybe, just maybe . . . it's time to settle."

Believe me: It's not.

As far as I'm concerned, you can never be too picky when it comes to finding the love of your life. If you want a real, true, magical, loving relationship, you can have it. Here, let me put it in perspective for you:

You're allowed to be picky about the dessert you order (a ten-minute commitment), the movies you see (a two-hour commitment), the shoes you buy (a six-month commitment) and the jobs you take (a one-year commitment). So for goodness' sake, shouldn't you be picky about the fifty-year commitment you're looking for?

This book is all about being picky. You're allowed to want what you want, and you deserve to get it! And if you agree with that premise, then you will do just fine.

INTRODUCTION:

What *Is* Your Half-Orange?

Well, it's your ideal partner, the person you're meant to share your life with. But it's also a hope *so* optimistic that just knowing your other half is coming your way will change your life completely

Picture this: Let's say you visit a fortune teller, a woman famous for owning the world's only crystal ball that predicts the future with 100 percent accuracy. Now, what if this woman told you that in your future, you do find the love that is meant for you—an incredible, mind-blowing, magical, adoring, and life-altering love? What if she said that in, say, eight months, you were going to meet *the* perfect man[1] for you?

Now, we're talking about a guy who makes you laugh so hard it hurts. A guy who's so attractive, you feel lucky walking beside him. A guy who thinks you're smart, hip, hilarious and sexy as hell. A guy you could be stuck at the end of the DMV line with and still have fun. A guy who adores you and treats you like gold. A guy your friends love *so* much, they hug him as quickly as they hug you when you walk into a party—then tell you all

---

[1] For the sake of consistency, I'm going to address you, my beautiful reader, as a "she," and the half-orange you're seeking as a "he." But my words are intended for every person who wants to fill his or her life with love. This advice works just as well if you're a "he" seeking a "she," a "she" seeking a "she," a "he" seeking a "he," or someone keeping the gender checkbox blank to see who shows up! We all deserve a great love in our lives—a partner who brings out our best. So, please, adjust the pronouns as you need so you can still follow the path to your very own half-orange.

night, "I want a boyfriend like yours!" How would you feel if you knew, *with 100 percent certainty*, that whether you socialized or not, whether you dated or not, whether your traveled or stayed in, *that guy* would just land on your doorstep at the end of those eight months?

Probably a sense of relief. Some giddy excitement. And most likely, it would give you a freedom and lightness to your step that you—as a single woman who has been pounding the pavement for love with heavier and heavier steps—haven't felt in a long time.

It would mean that now, as you exit that fortune teller's studio and walk back into the world, you can live up your last few months as a single woman! It would mean you could go out with the girls and relax instead of scanning the room every six seconds for a possible guy. It would mean you could hit the town with some cute not-the-marrying-type guys without putting pressure on yourself to move on and get serious. It would mean you could relax at home and watch reality show marathons without feeling guilty that you're wasting time that could be spent meeting a man. It would also mean you could take a big trip, start writing the novel about your life, or learn French in case *that guy* you're going to meet in eight months wants to whisk you off to Paris. The point is, your life would be a playground full of possibilities again.

Well, that's the feeling dating optimism can give you. Once you start using the powerfully optimistic techniques I will describe here for you, you will start to feel free and genuinely happy and not have a fear in the world about your future because you *know* it's all going to work out. How do you know? Because you'll be focusing your energies on what you want in such a powerful way, it will affect your body and the world around you, so that the only place *that guy* can come is straight to you. When you're happy in your own skin, someone who is right for you will be naturally drawn to you, just the way it's supposed to be.

I wish I knew this sooner when I was single. God, I cringe when I think about the guys I pushed to like me, the dates I pushed to happen, the parties I waded through in desperation, asking all my girlfriends, "Is anyone single here?" and "Have you seen any cute guys?"

I remember once hounding my sister to arrange a set-up with her friend Rachel's brother, who was mentioned to me in passing. (See Amy. See straw. See Amy grasping at straw.) I'd call my sister every day asking, "Did you talk to Rachel about her brother yet? Have you heard anything?" Three weeks later, the brother passed on a message to Rachel, who told my sister, who delivered it to me. "I hear she's a brunette," he moaned. "I don't date brunettes."

I felt like a fool. Not only was I trying too hard, but I was doing it for a superficial jerk. The point is, that experience was *not* good for my self-esteem. I felt like a desperate single woman on the prowl, willing to do anything to find a partner. And though I never admitted it, my desire to find love was affecting every second of my life: I saw weekends out of the big city as time I should have spent in it trying to meet a man. I saw my friendships with married couples as wasted valuable time away from the singles crowd. And I saw the time I spent with my best gay friend and hairdresser Todd—the Will to my Grace—as possible self-sabotage: If I wanted a relationship, why was I going for dinner every night with him?

Why is it, I wondered, *that living life the way I want and finding a life partner are mutually exclusive?* I didn't want to make a choice, and I didn't want to settle. I wanted it all! I wanted the life I had, and I wanted real, true love to go with it. Not just an average, "Yeah, sure, I love him" arrangement, but a deep, soul mate kind of love. A love that made me shine. A partner in crime. A real *other half.*

But I was losing hope. In fact, I remember the night I was ready to give up all of it when it came to dating in New York City.

It was a warm September night. Two dozen people were lined up outside the sushi restaurant across from my place; a flock of perfumed, giggling girls was clicking down the sidewalk in sync like toy soldiers; and the lounge on the corner opened its French doors to inhale the balmy air the way we all were. And as for me? I was about to meet Jason[2] for a drink. Before I left my apartment, I told my married friend I was determined to make it work. Because my life, at the moment, needed a seriously big upper.

I had worked as a magazine editor for ten years at magazines including *Glamour* and *Maxim*. But one year before, I decided I was ready for a new challenge. So I jumped off the safety dock of the "regular paycheck" to try to survive in the sea of freelance writing. By that warm night in September, I was struggling with work and I was struggling with love. And since much of my work involved interviewing women, couples, and experts about love and relationships, well, it all seemed like a cruel joke.

I looked for solace from the stress and loneliness in an overactive social life, but that was only costing me more money. And since the last few dates I had dragged myself on turned out to be big, boring no-gos, I was only becoming more depressed. I was on a merry-go-round that was sucking up my money, my energy, and my optimism. Translation: I really *really* didn't want this guy to be another waste of time.

Jason was someone I'd met at my friend's fashion show party a week before. When we met, he bumped his head into the low-lying clothing rack hanging from the ceiling and yelled at it saying, "Yo, bad rack!" It reminded me of how my mom used to scold inanimate objects when I'd bang into them, so of course my mind raced ahead, oh, a decade or so, thinking: *Aw, what a good dad this guy would be.* (That's how my single mind worked, by the way; *everything* was a sign of what a good dad a guy would be.) Jason and I chatted for twenty minutes, he called four days later, and now, as I spread on my lucky I-blew-$25-on-Chanel-lip-gloss, we were minutes away from meeting again.

---

[2] For the sake of their privacy, or by request, I have changed some people's names throughout the book.

Please just let this guy be normal, I thought, as I clomped down my walk-up. I just want one nice date. Well honestly, I was also thinking, *Oh my God, this could be it! Maybe he's the One! Then we'll fall in love and fly somewhere fabulous for New Year's and then we'll have kids and he'll be such a good dad . . .*

Jason was already there when I arrived and was cuter than I remembered. Wow, I thought, this really could be the last first date I'll ever have.

Our drinks extended into dinner, and just as I started falling for how charming, smart, and clever he was, he chuckled and said, "Do you know what a sociopath is?"

"I guess," I said. "Why?"

"No, it's just funny," he said, "because—well, maybe I shouldn't tell you this—but that's what my roommate calls me. He says I'm a sociopath."

"Oh." I reviewed the little I actually knew about sociopaths: They have a professionally diagnosed disorder. They're interested in their selfish desires without concern for the effects of their behavior on others. And, um, weren't they the ones who turned out to be serial killers?

"I just think that's funny," he said.

"Yeah, sure," I said. "I guess maybe that's funny."

Not funny ha-ha; like funny *American Psycho*. Still, we finished our drinks on a high note, and he even offered to pay. I was feeling so good about it, I was careful to make the right move so he'd want to go out with me again. So I kissed him goodnight and said goodbye to him on my doorstep. Well. That's when he lost it.

"Are you [bleep]ing kidding me?" he said. "You're seriously not inviting me upstairs? What the [bleep]? What a [bleep]ing waste of my time!" Then Jason stormed off, never to be heard from again.

I was stunned. And confused. And bummed as all hell. So I called my married friend as soon as I got upstairs to tell her about it.

"Oh my god," she said. "Your love life is always so hilarious!"

Once again, not hilarious ha-ha; like hilarious pathetic. Because after I hung up, I cried my way through a *Saved by the Bell* rerun in which the goofy, balding school principal character, Mr. Belding, fell in love. I couldn't handle it. "Mr. Belding found love?" I whimpered. "Why not meeeee?"

That was the night I decided I was through being dragged down by my datelessness. For months—years—I'd been forcing myself to go on dates with guys I only half-liked, dragging myself to singles parties, signing up for every online matchmaking service in my zip code, and taking writing assignments about being set up by everyone from my high school friend to my mother all in the name of finding Mr. Right. I was scanning the city like a search-and-rescue dog, and no man was going unturned. But the guy of my dreams was nowhere to be found. And all I could think about was how I was going to end up old, crotchety, barren, and alone. Sure, hilarious.

Now, here's where the magic comes in. A few years ago, my sister Liz had an itch to travel. She'd been living in New York City for eight years and—thanks to the ridiculous cost of rent—could count on one hand the trips she'd taken out of town. As a still-single woman herself, she realized that if she was ever going to feed her travel bug and escape the city, this was a perfect time. So she started making plans for a cross-country drive.

As helpful inspiration, she and her friends formed a small group of girls called "The Goalies." They met each week to talk about the goals they'd set and to pump each other up with positive thoughts and optimistic thinking.

My sister's plan was that in four months, she would take a break from her work schedule as a massage therapist: "I'm going to buy a cheap used car and drive from New York to California and back," she said. Liz planned to stop at all the big spots: the Badlands, the Grand Canyon, New Orleans, and L.A. And when she talked about her plans, she described with gusto how she could picture herself driving in her car, feeling free, the wind on her cheeks, the future through her windshield. She couldn't wait to see the world beyond New York she'd never seen before.

Three months later—*just* before she was planning to make arrangements to quit her job and buy her used car—she called me with some news.

"I'm changing my plans," said Liz. "I just got offered a great job, and I'm going to take it."

"Oh, shoot." I said. "A *job?* I mean, that's great I guess . . . but won't that ruin your plans to travel?"

"Actually . . . no," she said. At which point I could *hear* her smile. "Because, uh, well, I'd be working as the massage therapist for a rock band on their world tour for a year and a half."

Instead of traveling alone in a used car, she'd be traveling in a famous entourage by private jet. Instead of hopping from one Motel 8 to another, she'd be sleeping in five-star hotels in Rome, Paris, Brussels, New Zealand, Australia and Tokyo. It was, quite simply, a dream come true. It was everything she was looking for and *then* some. She wanted to see the world, right? Well, now she was going to do it in the grandest way.

That's when my sister gave me a pep talk about how thinking positively can get you somewhere. She had dreamt it, focused on it, felt what it was going to be like to get it—and now she had more of her dream than she'd even thought to ask for in the first place. And then she told me exactly how to do it for myself.

I made it my love experiment: I was going to use what my sister used—what I call optimistic magnetism—to meet the big love of my life in one year. But I wasn't going to *find* the man of my dreams; in my plan, the man of my dreams was going to find *me*. Instead of me hitting every singles' event in town in search of him, I was going to focus every cell in my body on attracting this guy—whoever he was—*to me*. My sister got her big dream trip, and I was going to get my big dream love. And I was going to do it within the confines of just twelve months. I knew, after all, that the key to making dating optimism work for me was to have complete, absolute confidence that it *was* going to work. I had to visualize the outcome the way Lance Armstrong pictured himself crossing the Tour de France finish line each impossible time. I knew I had to be that bold about it.

I told all of my friends and family my plan. Some thought I was a little nuts (the hope was one thing; the timeline another!) and some gave me those pity-the-single-girl grimaces and enough "Awwws" to make me crazy. Well, this time I knew I would find someone, so I let the pity slide. The beauty was, I no longer cared what people thought of the single girl looking for love. Because this time, I was determined.

I created some positive visualization techniques (some I did once, others every other day). I devoted all my senses to what I wanted, from sight to sounds to smells. I did some physical tricks, smiling and breathing a certain way at important times. I flipped my point of view about formerly depressing situations into seriously great ones. And I began to do things that had nothing to do with dating—all the while keeping my focus on the end result: how I was going to feel when I found my perfect match.

And it worked. It actually *worked.*

The man I met was the one who taught me the Spanish term *mi media naranja.* (Not that I speak Spanish, mind you. My vocabulary barely extends past the terms he's taught me: "Hello. I'm hungry. My husband is intelligent. Goodbye.") But this term really meant something. *Mi media naranja* translates literally as "my half-orange." It's an endearing term his Argentinean parents use to describe one's other half: that sweet, beautiful, perfectly fitting partner, the object of every hopeful young lover's dreams. When I heard him explain this, I melted with appreciation. A half-orange, to me, is not someone who completes you in life, but who complements you in love. Sure, I had a full, happy life of my own, but I wanted someone to share my love with and all that goes with an equal partnership: One person drives while the other navigates; one does the dishes while the other does the laundry; and both share their hopes and fears and hugs and hard times and happiness as a team. Hold up two half-oranges in front of you and you can see how they meet perfectly in the middle: Neither side is bigger or bolder or pushing or pulling more than the other; they unite in the center, separate but equal, and together form a bright full circle. *That's* how my soul felt deep-down, having gotten what I'd held out for all those years, and it's what every woman deserves: her very own half-orange.

I began to tell every single woman I knew about my experiment. Within six months, some had found their other halves and were on the road to marriage. Last week, a friend who'd read the early draft of this book as a single woman asked me how I'd like my name phrased on her wedding invitation. And I've spoken to hundreds of other women in happy relationships who say they've used many parts of this process themselves and they, too, are convinced it led to them to meeting their other halves.

I know it works. I've seen it work. And I want *you* to be able to reach that same level of hope and certainty for love in your future, which will ultimately lead you to your big love, too. There are no guarantees on how fast it works, of course. But whether it's eight months or eight days, your life will improve along the way. Because instead of devoting your days to the drudgery of sifting through dates, logging your matchmaking hours, or meeting every single man in a thirty-mile radius, you can live your life *living* it. And *loving* it.

In the pages that follow, I'm going to walk you—step by step— through the same exact process that worked for me and for other women. If you try my dating optimism techniques and get good at making them second nature for you (in a drinking-a-few-glasses-of-water-a-day kind of way) you will feel *so* good about your dating situation and *so* hopeful about your chances of meeting someone amazing for you that you'll actually *create* the perfect state of mind for your ideal love to grow. And you're going to do it like you're planting an orange seed: Just as you'd prepare the soil, plant the seed, and nurture your sapling into a healthy, full orange tree, you will do the same with yourself. In doing so, you will become your happiest, favorite version of yourself—the perfect half-orange—fully prepared to attract and meet your other half.

The process of using dating optimism to bring you true love centers on a few simple steps:

1. Believe you can have it. (Because, I'm telling you, you can.)
2. Admit you want it, to yourself and others. (Yes, out loud.)
3. Visualize and imagine feeling yourself in the relationship you want.
4. Openly hope for it like you've never hoped for anything before.
5. Live a happy life. Sleep and repeat.

I promise you: This is *not* some schmaltzy, gooey, New Age, chakra-based plan for tuning into your spiritual being. This is a real-world guide for a real woman like you. I'll be suggesting things you can do while you get dressed for work, on your lunch hour reading *Us Weekly*, at Starbucks while you wait for your latte, over cocktails with your best friends—and most importantly on those frustrating dating down-days spent watching forensic shows on cable for eight hours straight when you feel like your chance at love is equally D.O.A.

Using the simple techniques outlined in this book, you will soar from where you are emotionally to a place between hope and *absolute certainty* that your love life is going to be as amazing as you want it to be. And here's the best part: The optimistic energy you create by feeling this way is exactly what will bring the one thing you want most in your life right now: your own half-orange.

PHASE ONE:

Get Your Soil Ready: Believe You Can Have It

HOW THE ORANGE SEED WORKS

The dating world, like life, is made up of optimists and pessimists. Where do you fit in? Are you a glass half-full, who can see the positive side of being stuck with a boring date . . . fixing a flat tire in the rain? Or are you a glass half-empty, who can meet a handsome, well-adjusted guy who thinks you're cute . . . and decide there must be something wrong with him? Maybe, after years of being disappointed in dating, you've become a little bit of both—what you'd consider a "realist." Well, if you want to attract that big amazing love, it's time to adopt dating optimism in a big way.

The good news is, optimism *can* be learned. Like any skill that relies on focused thought—like crossword puzzles, Scrabble, and sudoku—the better you get at training your brain to think the right way, the further you'll get in the game. And that means that those of you who are admittedly pessimistic about dating can change (and so can those of you who *used* to feel like optimists but have begun doubting your hope). All it takes is a commitment to flipping your attitude in such a way that you are thinking and feeling so positive about your love life, you end up attracting exactly what you want. **You know that happy, smiling fulfilled and confident person you want to be in a relationship?** *You're going to learn to be that person now.* Because if you can feel it, you can attract it into your life.

Optimism, you see, is simply a belief that your life is going to work out for the best, explains Suzanne Segerstrom, Ph.D., associate professor of psychology at the University of Kentucky in Lexington, and author of the book *Breaking Murphy's Law: How Optimists Get What They Want From Life—and Pessimists Can Too.* So, as a dating optimist, you must simply believe that your *love* life will work out for the best. That's it! With that confidence, you'll be more motivated to make it happen, and you'll work harder at focusing your thoughts on meeting your other half—all the things that I did to find mine. Plus, I know you have potential to be a dating optimist. How? Because dating pessimists are so convinced love is *not* going to work out, they think, *Why bother trying?* And if you believed that deep down, you wouldn't have read this far. If you believe there is even the smallest chance your love life will work out and you have a desire to persist until it does, then you, my friend, have optimism in your blood!

That's not to say that as a dating optimist, you have to be positive every single second and post Cupid calendars around your desk. It's normal to have ebbs and flows of your mood. You're allowed to cry into your cocktail when the occasion calls for it. Optimism isn't about ignoring the tough parts. It's about facing the tough parts head on, owning your feelings, and choosing to battle your bad days when you want to feel better about yourself. Even after you get good at some of the techniques I'll suggest for you, it's normal to be on a high for a week or two and then have a day where you're flat-out, kill-me-now, bummed out. And that's okay! This isn't about a short-term happiness fix. Your positive thoughts aren't like sewing a Prada label onto a cheap shirt and calling it quality. Your positive thoughts will change the quality of the shirt—your dating future—altogether.

THE BRAINPOWER BEHIND POSITIVE THINKING

In the last few years, you've probably heard something about the profound power of using positive thought. Well, you're now going to direct your thoughts for a new and absolutely positive purpose: to bring you a big, beautiful relationship. "Our thoughts are not merely reactions to events; they change what ensues," writes Martin Seligman, Ph.D., the father of positive psychology, in his book *Learned Optimism: How to Change Your Mind and Your Life*. That's right: Your thoughts can change your future.

The overall idea of dating optimism is based on what I call optimistic magnetism, which, in its simplest form, means that we attract what we think about, focus on, and feel. The general concept has been around for ages, and it's been rendered as everything from a therapeutic technique to a spiritual belief to a scientific principle. Yet all of these views—as contrary as they may seem—all come back to that same basic idea. How is that so? Perhaps because you can't fight the laws of nature. There's obviously more going on in our brains, bodies, and in the world around us than we've so far been able to "prove." Let's start with that therapeutic approach first.

The first piece of the positivity puzzle is how therapeutic research fits in, based on the field known as "positive psychology," co-founded in 1998 by University of Pennsylvania psychologist Martin Seligman, Ph.D. and psychologist Mihaly Csikszentmihalyi. It is, in essence, a study of optimism and happiness. While traditional psychology focuses on our painful emotions (fears, anxiety, or depression), positive psychologists—while not discounting negative issues—also work with clients on the affirmative aspects of their lives, all the good stuff. While certainly addressing painful issues, patients are also encouraged to discuss what they're grateful for, what makes them laugh, what they're good at. When Seligman founded the Positive Psychology Center at the University of Pennsylvania, he launched a movement.

In 2005, following in Seligman's footsteps, psychologist Tal Ben-Shahar,

Ph.D., began doing lectures in positive psychology at Harvard University, which became the most popular elective class in the school's catalog. Positive psychologists believe that we as people are not helpless; we have some control over the outcome of our future by virtue of the way we *think*. And they've discovered that encouraging people to think about and act upon the things that make them happy actually brings *more* happiness into their lives. In essence, then, we attract what we think about, focus on and feel.

But focusing on the positive isn't a new concept by any means. People from Hindus to current day believers in New Thought have seen humans as beings who are vibrating with energy—we're either vibrating with positive energy or with negative energy. And unlike refrigerator magnets, in which unlike polarities attract, whatever we think about and focus on we attract more of: Like attracts like. If you smile or laugh or greet someone with affection, you create ripples of positive emotion throughout your body and become, as a person, a positively charged one who will attract other positively charged people and things: an available taxi, a winning lottery scratch card, a call from a friend you haven't seen in years, a wink from a cute guy. Of course the same goes for negative thoughts. If you groan or complain or curse someone out, you create ripples of negative emotion throughout your body and become a negatively charged person who will attract other negatively charged things: parking tickets, jammed printers, spilled drinks, rejections from guys you like. From this spiritual standpoint, what you focus on is vibrating within you and around you every step you take.

A great way to think about it is the "good hair day." When you're having a good hair day, doesn't your whole entire day seem to shine? Well, it's not because the world is kind to people with good hair. It's because *you* feel good about your hair, which makes you feel good overall. So good, in fact, that you smile more—in the elevator and in the coffee shop; on the road, you get a few green lights in a row. When you get to work, you have more ideas for the meeting. Lunch tastes better and you eat less of it because you feel so good you don't want to ruin your good mood. And on and on and on. What's happening is that your positive emotions are creating positive feelings throughout your body that attract other positive things. You are virtually a *magnet* of positive things.

But it's not a phony mystical notion, which is where the science comes in. Based on third grade science, we know that everything in life—from our bodies to the grass to the computers we work on—are made of matter. All matter is made of atoms, and all atoms are made of subatomic particles of energy. But as Austrian physicist Niels Bohr, who was key in the development of quantum physics, once said, "Nothing exists until it is measured."

Well guess what? **Your thoughts can be measured**. Your thoughts are integral, moving, measurable pieces of electrical energy. And energy, we know, can be moved and changed and transferred. Which means that, through the use of your thoughts, you have more control of the energy within and around you than you realize. In recent years, scientists have even been able to pick up human brain cell electrical activity of thought through fMRIs (functional Magnetic Resonance Imaging), ultimately "reading" the thoughts and intentions of participants, with goals of, say, helping paraplegics use their thoughts to control computer devices that would act as arms, hands, and legs. That's pretty powerful stuff: thoughts that can pick up a glass of milk.

Similar types of brain scan research are also making huge headway in the world of cognitive psychology. "You can actually now do MRIs and track personal growth in people by watching the neuronal connections change in the brain," says psychologist Peter Pearson, Ph.D., cofounder of The Couples' Institute in Menlo Park, California. "Personal growth is no longer woo-woo," says Pearson, "you can see the growth in the brain." Clinical neuroscientist Daniel Amen, M.D., founder of the Amen Clinic in Newport Beach, California, has turned to SPECT imaging (Single Photon Emission Computed Tomography) to measure cerebral blood flow and brain activity of thoughts. "SPECT studies actually show which parts of the brain are activated when we concentrate, laugh, sing, cry, visualize, or perform other functions," he writes in *Change Your Brain, Change Your Life*. In his practice, Dr. Amen has been able to pinpoint areas of brain activity responding to anxiety, depression, OCD, aggression, substance abuse, and, of all things, love. Because when you are in love, the feel-good, dopamine-rich areas of your brain light up like a pinball machine.

How Your Biggest Dating Tool Works

At the center of dating optimism, then, is the tool we will turn to for this change in your thoughts: your brain. I'm going to get slightly technical for a minute, but hang in there, because it will help you grasp the core of optimistic magnetism and how powerful a change it can make in your life.

In short, your emotional brain is made up of numerous systems working together to process your thoughts, both conscious and unconscious. Below the cortex lies an area usually referred to as the limbic system, a set of brain structures that stores and processes emotional memory. Scientists say that the actual storehouse for our emotional memory is a set of two small almond-shaped neural structures called the amygdala, which holds these memories as subjective experiences—just feelings of sorts.

So let's say you walk into a party and you see a handsome man standing by the vegetable dip. The process in your brain works like this: When sensory data comes into your brain, after moving through the immediate sensory areas of, say, sight and sound (ooh look—a smile and a sexy laugh from the handsome man), the data heads to your limbic system and through the amygdala, which scans your database of emotional memories (all the handsome men who've loved you, and the handsome fools who haven't), and then works with other structures to direct a signal to the body on what to do next. (Should you stay cool? Smile back? Make a beeline for the ladies' room?) Some researchers refer to the entire system that processes emotions as the deep limbic system, or the emotional brain. It's this area—your emotional brain—that is going to respond when you start changing your thoughts from negative to positive ones. It's your emotional brain that will turn your choice to become a dating optimist into a shift of mental and physical energy that will draw your half-orange straight to you. That's because directly correlated to your emotional brain is the physical response in your *body*.

"The response of the body is an integral part of the overall emotion process," explains neural scientist Joseph LeDoux in *The Emotional Brain*. If we look at the effect of your thoughts on your body, the payoff of positive thinking is vast: By virtue of your thoughts alone, you change your body's physical energy within and around you. Think about it: When you're stressed about finding a guy, or anxious or panicked that you never will, your body translates these feelings physically. Your face falls, your shoulders hunch, your neck gets tense. And what seems to happen to you in this negative state? Negative things. And when you're feeling positive about your love life, your body translates that, too: Your shoulders loosen up, your brow relaxes, your presence softens, your smile grows, and you are drawn to and attract more positive things.

That's exactly what happened for Kerry, a thirty-two year old business owner in Los Angeles, at an outdoor music party one July night in the Angeles Crest mountains. After a few years living the single life, Kerry was feeling great about life—but had met plenty of single girls who weren't as positive as she was. "They would walk around with scowls on their faces and their arms crossed, and would be bummed out that they never met anyone." On the night of the party, Kerry was determined to do the opposite. She agreed to help a friend hand out some business cards, and took off on her own to explore the crowd, focusing on how grateful she was to be outdoors on a warm evening. "At one point, I was standing in the clearing looking out over the city, with my chin up, and a very contented smile on a face, just dancing by myself to the DJs, feeling really happy," says Kerry. Five minutes later, a handsome guy stepped right into her path. "I looked him in the eyes and handed him a card," says Kerry, "but when he grabbed it, neither one of us let go! We just stood there holding it, smiling at each other, and I haven't let go since." That was eleven years ago. Kerry and Angelo are now married and running a company together—and it was the smile on her face, the dance in her step and the contentment of her being that drew Angelo right to her. Your thoughts change your body language and your energy, and your body language and your energy can change your life.

Luckily, science is on our side, because by changing your thoughts in a determined way, you can actually create a *permanent* change in your brain, which can effectively change your entire emotional experience with dating and love! This is based on the fascinating and still-fresh research of neuro-plasticity—the idea that the neuronal pathways in your brain can be un-wired and re-wired to ultimately change how your brain responds to sensory data. "When we learn something new, neurons fire together and wire together," writes psychiatrist Norman Doidge, M.D., in *The Brain That Changes Itself,* citing a theory developed by neuroscientist Donald Hebb. This is great news for any of you who feel you have emotional damage or bag-gage, because by adding or removing connections you have about your past experiences within your brain, you can re-mold the brain as if it were a piece of warm plastic, effectively making changes in your everyday life.

If you assume, for instance, that every cute man who talks to you is just killing time until he finds someone better, you can work to change the knee-jerk reaction your emotional brain triggers and learn to be more open—and self-confident!—in the future. What you're changing is the way your emo-tional brain (mainly the emotional memory storehouse of your amygdala) reacts with your thinking brain (the one that analyzes every move you make) to form new positive neuronal pathways, and override negative ones. Jeffrey Schwartz, M.D., a research professor of psychiatry at the UCLA School of

Medicine explains what's behind the science of dating optimism this way in *The Mind and the Brain: Neuroplasticity and the Power of Mental Force:* "The brain's ensembles of neurons change over time, forming new connections that become stronger with us, and letting unused synapses weaken until they are able to carry signals no better than a frayed string between two tin cans in the old game of telephone." Which is to say that for you to grasp onto the hope and optimism that you will find your other half, you must let those negative thoughts—how you'll "never find a great guy"—wither and fray like old string. Overall, this act of consciously changing the neural activity underlying your emotional processes is known as "emotional regulation," and it's at the heart of what you'll be doing through dating optimism.

In essence, then, all this research on positive psychology, spiritual "vibrations" and brain neuroplasticity points to this: By changing your thoughts, you change your brain activity, which leads to a change in how your body physically responds, which creates an energy within and around you that changes how you perceive the world and how the world perceives you. At its core: You attract what you think about, focus on, and feel.

Positive "energy" is a real thing. Like a poker player's tell or a liar's giveaway, your thoughts affect the very essence of your being: How you stand, how you walk, how your face rises or falls, how you greet your date, how you hold your hands, how you speak. You are what you eat, and you *are* what you think. It's important to remember, however, this doesn't just work in a "positive" way. You can also attract negativity by focusing on negative thoughts.

Take Shayanne, a twenty-nine-year-old sexy blond chef I know who loves throwing parties and telling zany travel stories and who always has a to-do list four pages long. One afternoon, we made plans to meet for lunch at a café in Hollywood. On my drive over, I was thinking about how lucky I was to be away from my desk for a few hours, and how good it was going to be to catch up with Shayanne. As I approached the café, I considered parking a few blocks away in a one-hour spot; but then I thought, "Nah, I'm feeling lucky. Maybe

I'll get one of those two-hour spots right in front of the café." As I turned the corner in front of the café, there it was: a car pulling out of a two-hour parking spot. I pulled in and entered the café grinning.

Ten minutes later, Shayanne walked in like she'd just put out a fire in her chef's hat: Her hair was tousled, her face was twisted, and her bag was falling open as she plopped down into the chair beside me. "Oh my God, I have had the *worst* day," she said. Then she hilariously listed the many things that had gone wrong: "I woke up late, didn't get a single email about new jobs, and banged my knee on the coffee table so hard I have a huge bruise. And then I get here and every spot I pull into has a broken parking meter." (Which, in California, cruelly means you *can't* park there; it doesn't mean you get a free ride.) "I mean, what's next?"

Shayanne wasn't just having a bad day—she was *attracting* a bad day by practically asking for the next worst thing that was going to come to her. Did she get a ticket at the end of that lunch? You bet she did. And she couldn't, for the life of her, understand why.

In terms of dating and love, the same holds true: You attract what you think about and focus on. But here's the thing, and it's a *big* thing: The world around you doesn't know the difference between what you say you want and what you say you *don't* want—those are just semantics. The universe just knows what you're giving your attention to. And this is so important when it comes to love, since, as a single woman, you're probably used to talking about what you don't *yet* have. If you're single and find yourself saying, "I don't want to be single anymore!" the world will bring you what you're focusing on: *being single.* If you find yourself saying, "I don't want to be alone," the world will bring you what you're focusing on: *being alone.* If you find yourself saying, "How come all the guys I like are selfish and commitment-phobic?" the world will bring you what you're focusing on: selfish and commitment-phobic guys. You see where this is going?

When you focus on the *lack* of something, that's exactly what you'll get more of. So if you can't help but list the litany of problems you find along the way—the bad dates, the incompatible matches, the lame guys, the pointless set-ups—then the universe will bring you more of the same: bad dates and incompatible guys. Don't let your lack get you down. It's vital that you think about and focus on what you *do* want, rather than what you don't. In this case, you probably want something like, say, an incredible, fulfilling, magical, compatible, loving, adoring relationship. Sound good? I hope so. Because while you're going to come up with your own specific dream relationship, those ideas will start you off with a pretty good one for now—so *that* is what you're going to start thinking about and focusing on.

Sure, there are times when you're in a crappy mood or you're having a crappy day or you feel like giving yourself a single pity party. And that's allowed. I've had some damn good times with a six-pack and a game of solitaire. But over time, in the grand scheme, guess what? You can learn to control what you think about and how you feel in order to create optimism and feelings of positivity in your body. And that means you can change what you attract. Instead of attracting jobless schlubs or smarmy players or men who can't commit to anything longer than a game of Keno, you can attract the healthy relationship you've always deserved.

If you're still trying to decide whether or not you should start trying to make dating optimism work for you, let me tell you this: **This is not something you choose to start using. Like gravity, it is already happening, all the time**. It's happening to you *right now*. What you can choose is how to make the good stuff swing your way.

THE BONUS OF YOUR FOCUS

There's another benefit to your optimism, and that comes with your focus. Let's say you need a car, and after much research, decide you'd really love a Toyota Prius. Now, suddenly, everywhere you drive, they're all you see:

Priuses turning every third corner, sputtering past you on the freeway, parked in your work parking lot. Have you attracted the Priuses to you? Perhaps. But you've also created such a deliberate focus, it has allowed you to *see* the Priuses that were already all around you.

When you start thinking about what you want—in this case, the incredible, fulfilling, magical, compatible, loving, adoring relationship of your dreams—your mind will be so focused on what you want that you will start to *see* the steps toward it in ways you never did before: You'll see more nice guys, you'll see more couples in love, you'll meet more men who share your beliefs and values, you'll feel more lucky and grateful to be surrounded by people who love you, and you're start to feel your cravings for a great relationship can be satiated. What you think about and focus on you attract, plain and simple.

I had to be convinced. When I first heard about the power of positive thought, it seemed too good to be true. So I started small. Do you remember earlier when I mentioned that at the time of my date with the sociopath, I had just gone freelance and was having trouble paying the bills? Well, I was also worried I'd no longer be able to afford my rent in Manhattan. My friend Yvonne suggested we share a place together over the bridge in an off-the-beaten path part of Brooklyn. I hadn't had a roommate in five years and didn't particularly want one, but I was trying to be practical. Plus, Yvonne was my accomplice in the art of being single, so I knew we'd have a blast together. But after seeing the apartment's shared hallway, bathroom and kitchen, I longed to keep living and writing on my own.

Later that night, in a cab headed home, I nearly got teary-eyed as I pictured what I *really* wanted: me, in my apartment, paying my rent, having extra cash in my bank account at the end of the month. *I just need to know the money will come*, I thought. *If some money comes soon, everything will be alright.*

Just then, in the middle of the bridge, as I reached to get my phone out of my purse, I touched something stuck by the seatbelt buckle in my bucket seat. It was a crumpled $1 bill. *Huh, a dollar bill.* I reached down again to check, and there was another one. Then another. Then *another.* By the time we reached the end of the bridge, I had pulled $11 in crumpled singles out of the seats! That is an absolutely true story. I have no idea how a random pile of singles ended up stuffed in that seat, but I used that money to pay the cab driver and shut the door stunned: *I had asked for money, and there it was.* The coincidence blew me away, and I took it as a sign: Things were going to be okay, I just knew it. This, of course, led me to focus even more on how badly I wanted to make more money. A few days later, a check for a story I wrote finally arrived, and I began paying my bills with ease.

You get the idea: This stuff works.

Here's the best and final word I have on optimistic magnetism for now: It is kind. It won't require you to do much physical work. It's like the lazy exerciser's best friend: It is, literally, the thought that counts! Just do *your* part thinking, focusing, and feeling, and let the energy you create in your body and the world around you do the rest.

See, it's not your job to figure out *how* you're going to get the relationship you want. It's your job to *want* it. This is important, because it lets you off the hook for having to figure out the how, which just seems so impossible sometimes. ("How, in a city this big or a town this small am I going to stumble upon the love of my life?") Well from now on, that's not your concern! You don't need to come up with a scheme to meet a man. You don't have to treat love like it's a job. You don't have to go on a third date with a nice guy you met just because you feel like you "should" be out there dating. I'll say it again because it's important: **It's not your job to figure out *how* you're going to get what you want.** It's your job to want it. Simply want it badly enough, focus on it with the most positive feelings you can muster, and the energy you create within and around you will bring it straight to you.

YOU DID IT WITH YOUR CAREER AND LIFE, YOU CAN DO IT WITH LOVE

Nearly every unattached woman I know has it going on in some other area of her life, so I'm sure you're no different. You're a cool, smart, independent woman with a good life and a great future ahead. You've made opportunities happen for yourself. You can put up your own shelves or check your own oil or find your way around any city in the world if you feel like it. And maybe, instead of a thriving love life, you have a thriving career—or at least a job you're damn good at, or a vision for your future that you want to make happen. In paramount ways like this, you've made your life happen, so you can make your love happen, too. Yeah, you may think, but love depends on someone else, I can't make *other* people happen. Guess what? You *can*. Just take the efforts and confidence you put into your career or job ambition, and turn it into love ambition.

My friend Lily is a great example. At thirty-eight, she has a kickass life: She's a freelance writer with her own big apartment in Brooklyn. She is on contract with a national magazine that flies her from New York to Los Angeles every few weeks to sleep in a suite in the Chateau Marmont and interview celebrities over expensive meals. She's publishing her very first novel, which has always been a dream of hers. And she has a cute little dog that doesn't bark, like, ever.

How did Lily achieve this great life? By believing she would. "I have never, for a second, doubted that I would get what I want in my career," says Lily. "I just *knew* that I would be a writer, that I would get a contract, and that I would get a book deal. But for some reason," she told me several months ago, "I don't feel the same confidence about finding the right guy."

Ah yes, it's a familiar predicament. I know a lot of women like Lily. In this post-feminist era, most of us were raised determined to prove we can have the same jobs as men, make the same money, and break the glass that held our grandmothers back decades ago. That determination and belief that we could do it is what has led so many of us to pursue higher education or careers we're passionate about. But, in turn, it has also led a lot of us to put off focusing on love. Just know you're not alone. Our entire society is shifting.

The U.S. Census reports that the median age women and men tie the knot has risen steadily in every racial, ethnic, and socioeconomic group. Currently the age is twenty-six for women and almost twenty-eight for men, and though the actual ages may not *seem* too up-there, they're the oldest they've been since the polls began in the 1890s! The reason: Our priorities have changed drastically.

In fact, ask college students about their life priorities today, and their answers are quite shocking. In 2007, clinical psychologists Catherine Mosher of Duke University Medical Center and Sharon Danoff-Burg at the University of Albany, conducted a study about college students' life priorities. They asked 237 male and female undergraduates to rate their life goals, which included concrete achievements (financial success, home ownership, career, and education), as well as relational achievements (romantic relationships and marriage). They also asked both men and women about their willingness to sacrifice some goals for others (i.e., a willingness to sacrifice career achievements for a romantic relationship).

As I first read the study, my spine straightened, hoping that the women in the study would make it clear that no female should sacrifice her career for love and marriage, right? Well, that *is* what the women said. And the men? "Contrary to predictions," the study reads, "results suggested that men were more willing than women to sacrifice some achievement goals for a romantic relationship." Wait, the *men* said this? Yep. It turns out that 61 percent of men said that romantic relationships were more important than financial stability, compared with only 51 percent of women. And that's when it hit me: Our recent generations of women have been so innately trained to pursue independence and ambition, many of us waved away the silly love part until we got ourselves sorted. But men, on the other hand—men who get to stay the path of expecting success in both work and love—are allowed to admit what their hearts want: "Hell yeah," they can say, "of course I want love!" Well, maybe it's time we women looked at what *our* hearts want as well. If men are able to say they consider romantic relationships vitally important in their lives, then heck, we women should be able to say it, too!

Because so far, instead of admitting we want love, we've learned to do the next best thing, which is exactly what *Sex and the City* taught us to do: to date like men, to keep striving in our careers, and have casual sex instead of asking to be wooed by romance. The problem for some of us has been that in wanting to get our independent lives or our careers off the ground first, our goals of dating and finding "the One" were put off. Or, perhaps, the fact that we hadn't yet found the right relationship gave us an excuse to take on extra hours at work, to dive into our jobs or our hobbies, and end up with a fulfilling life on our own.

Let's look at the career angle specifically for a minute. I told Lily that because she was able to make her career happen by unwittingly using optimistic magnetism—believing she would have it and focusing on it—she would also be able to use that intense focus and hope to find love. But here's where Lily and many of you try to poke a hole in the plan: "My career was all me," says Lily. "I made it happen. Love is different because it involves someone else."

A-ha, good point. But guess what? All those other areas of your life in which you've succeeded—especially in your career—you haven't done that alone either! You have relied on other people, just like love does.

Think about it: Unless you're a wunderkind who's been her own boss since the age of fourteen, someone had to hire you for your first job—a decision you couldn't control. Someone promoted you—again, out of your hands. And eventually, once you found the career you wanted, someone had to agree you were right for the gig and hire you again. Then, people had to like or believe in you enough through the meetings you attended, the emails you sent, the sales you made, the marketing ideas you pitched, the efforts you made to do better, or the deals you closed to approve of you enough to promote you or pay you a bit more. At some point, it was *other* people who had to sign off on things, approve things, print things, or buy things that you arranged. Until you become (or became) your *own* boss, every hour you've punched has involved jobs opening up and *someone other than you* giving you the nod. In other words? A path full of *other* people and things out of your control. Just like love.

In order to gain the confidence that you can attract love to you, you need to be reminded that while some things certainly are out of your control (say, hurricanes and economic recessions), other parts of your life *are* in your control. You need to internalize what psychologist Julian Rotter in the 1950s named your "locus of control." Let me ask you this: Do you believe you're controlled by someone else's remote, that you have no power over your own future and that outside forces completely devise your destiny? That's considered having an external locus of control, and I hope you don't believe that. Especially now, knowing how the orange seed works—that you can change your thoughts, which changes your brain, which changes your physical energy, which changes how you are perceived and what you can attract. Knowing that, you have to admit, you do have *some* control over your future, right? Well, you can apply this "internal locus of control" to your love life, too: You can say yes to a date or you can say no; you can meet up with your date smiling and feeling positive about your life, or with a frown on your face; and dinner conversation can consist of all the things that went wrong during your day or all the things that went right. Every single one of those decisions is going to affect your dating destiny, right? So obviously, you *do* have some power over what happens in your love life. Take charge and own some locus of control the way you have in other areas of your life.

I hit that crossroads of control myself. I was a woman in my thirties who wanted to find a wonderful man and raise a family with him. Yet if I wasn't confident I would find him, what was my other option? Being bummed out, depressed, disappointed, bitter, lonely—you get the idea. I had spent years going through moments like that already, and I was tired of it. So I *chose*, instead, to feel hope, optimism, and excitement about my future. Instead of saying, "Life sucks; I'll never meet anyone," I decided to say, "Wow, life is so fun. I wonder who I'll end up with. I can't wait to find out!" That's what I used to say about my career, so why not say the same about love?

DRESS THE PART FROM THE INSIDE OUT

They say that if you want to move up in your career, you should dress for the job you want, right? Which means if you're an assistant answering phones, you should start dressing like your boss, wearing sharp clothes and nice shoes. That way, when a position opens up, who are they going to hire? The girl who's wearing ratty jeans and flip-flops or the one who's spruced up enough to attend a meeting with a higher-up the way the new job requires?

You know how to dress the part at work, so why not dress the part for love? Now, I don't mean changing the wardrobe in your closet—I mean dressing yourself from the inside out. If you want to find a guy who makes you feel calm and happy and naturally glowing, you have to *become* that person first. Chances are, the guy you are looking for wants a calm and happy and naturally glowing girl, too, right? Well, how else is a guy going to know that this is the woman you can be if you're not emotionally "dressed" that way to begin with? If you're not feeling happy and fulfilled and hopeful and calm and smiling on your own before you meet a man, you're no better than an assistant wearing ratty jeans and flip-flops. You can shout to the rooftops that "No, but I can change later, once I have what I want!" but no one is going to hire you or want you if you don't look the part *now*.

Dress for love from the inside out. Become the woman *now* who you want to be in your relationship later. If you want to feel calm, smart, pretty, loved, adventurous, confident, and cared for in your dream relationship, become a calm, smart, pretty, adventurous and confident woman who loves and cares for herself. Go places and put yourself in situations that challenge your intellect, make you feel beautiful, fuel your adventurous spirit, and bring out your confidence among people who love and care for you. **Become the happy woman *now* who you want to be in your happy relationship later**. Dress for love from the inside out.

BELIEVE YOU CAN HAVE IT

Dating optimism, as you now know, is based on the belief that your love life is going to work out for the best. But my friend Parker, the proudest pessimist I know, is really struggling with this part. "I mean, I *want* to believe it," she says, "but I can't." I told her what I've been telling you: If you don't believe it can happen, you're holding yourself back from *letting* it happen.

Granted, Parker has reason to be wary about love. She was dating her boyfriend for seven years before they got married; six months later, when she'd turned thirty-nine and was just about to start their family, her husband asked for a divorce. Two years later, she's living on her own in the apartment they rented together, working from home as a graphic designer. I mean, my God, I get her uneasiness about diving back into love. After being hurt, it's hard to imagine feeling eager and hopeful ever again. But the fact is, for dating optimism to work, you need to be able to imagine a happy ending. I'm not minimizing the struggle it takes to get back your self-confidence and a desire to gamble with your heart again. All I'm saying is that, in looking toward your future, you must tap the cells you have left inside you that are still full of hope and romance, the ones that still sigh at cute scenes in Drew Barrymore movies, believing that maybe, sure, I mean, possibly . . . that *could* be you.

So do that: Reach down into your soul for a second, and find that part of you that practicality hasn't touched yet. Can you imagine what it would be like if you ever did meet someone perfectly right for you? Can you imagine —*even for a split second*—what it would feel like to stand next to *that guy* who you can love and trust, who is so incredibly, obviously right for you? That microscopically small smidgen of belief that you can get the love you want is going to be your biggest tool as we go through this process.

YES, HE EXISTS

When I first got my driver's license, my mom would hand me the car keys, begging me to be alert. "I'm not worried about your driving," she'd say. "I'm worried about the *other* people on the road." And I know for some of you, that's where your doubts about love lie: outside of you. Maybe it doesn't seem possible the *partner* you want exists.

Megan Marlena, thirty, the morning traffic reporter for ABC news in San Francisco says she was certain she would never find the right guy for her, either. "You know when you get with girls and you analyze your love life?" asks Megan. "I would look at friends getting engaged and getting married, and it bewildered me how they could find someone they wanted to be with forever. I didn't understand it. I thought I would *never* find someone. I had never met a man I could commit to, so I thought that maybe I was a girl that didn't apply to that rule."

Ah yes, the "maybe I'm just not the committing type" fear. Well guess what? It's baloney. You *can* tap the vein of commitment in your blood if you meet the right guy. Actress Maria Bello spent ten years saying she simply didn't believe in marriage. "The whole idea of monogamy is nonsensical to me," she told *Esquire* in 2006. Yet two years later, she was telling me over chips and salsa during a magazine interview that she'd met someone who made her re-evaluate her stance. "I was always anti-marriage," she said. "I couldn't figure out how that could last. And then I met Bryn and I started to understand the beauty of constancy and history and change and going on the roller coaster with someone—of having a partner in life." At age forty-one, Maria got engaged for the first time and basked in the feeling of commitment she thought she'd never have. You can, too. So knock commitment-phobia off your worry list once and for all. It's not that you don't have it in you to commit; you just haven't found the guy you want to commit *to*.

When Megan was ready to find her great relationship, she decided it was time to believe he existed. "I've always believed in the idea of affirming your own destiny," says Megan. So she made a list of her perfect guy that included things like "educated," "great sense of humor" and "likes to salsa dance," as well as the ever-important "no back hair," and "no man jewelry." Sometimes, she admits, laughing, "I'd look at my list and think, 'Maybe I am being too picky!'" But she was resolute. "Life's too short to settle," she says.

Megan re-read her list at night a few times a month, and in the meantime, she focused on having fun. If she was going to be with the love of her life soon, she may as well live it up now, right? So she spent time out with her girlfriends, entertained herself by dating a few Mr. Right-Nows, and took pride in her career. "I'm a strong, confident woman, and I liked being alone," says Megan. "I wanted a partner to enhance my life, but not to complete me. Sometimes things are just more fun with someone else."

A few months later, Megan spied a cute guy at a bar, and—against every traditional bone in her body—approached him. They went out a few times, and she was thrilled to learn he hit a number of items on her list—but before she found out about the salsa dancing, they parted ways; the relationship just wasn't clicking. Still, Megan never forgot her bar find and was grateful to know that at least a guy she could like existed. "My friends used to say, 'Well, there was that *one* guy you liked . . .'" laughs Megan. Now, at least, she could believe.

Two years and a few months later, Megan noticed "that *one* guy" in line in Costco, and he—Mike Scott—called her a few days later. "He had my number handy because, for some reason, in those two years, he never took my business card out of his briefcase." They started dating so seriously that she relocated from L.A. to San Francisco to be near him. And not only was he free of back hair and man jewelry, but yes, he loved to salsa dance! "We go dancing all the time," she says, with sheer joy in her voice. A year and a half into their relationship, Mike pulled out a ring and proposed in a park facing the Golden Gate Bridge. The couple is now buying a house as they plan their wedding, and are looking ahead to more than just the fairytale. "We are taking marriage seriously," says Megan. "We had a lot of long conversations to make sure we had the same expectations and were on the same page, and we are really trying to focus on a long-lasting marriage, rather than going crazy planning the wedding day."

For Megan, sure, there was only "that *one* guy" she liked enough to commit to, but one guy is all you need! "I wanted to really desire someone because I'd never felt that," says Megan. "So I didn't settle, and I waited until I could find that feeling. And it's a *great* feeling. Life's too short to go without it." Megan's right. She was all about being picky and all about asking for the love she wanted. Sure, she had her doubts it was out there, but she held onto the most important tool in dating optimism: She believed she could have it. And she got it in Mike. Remember, one guy—the right guy—is all you're looking for.

Parker, on the other hand, has convinced herself that no man will like her unique combination of strength and sarcasm, mixed with artistic tendencies and an uncanny ability to quote *South Park* on demand. "I want someone who sees me for who I am and sees my flaws and finds them charming," says Parker. Yet so far, she says, she simply "can't fathom" that there's a guy out there who will.

I assure you, we all have fears that guys will take a nibble of us and put down the fork, that no one will have a taste for a full plate of our kind. I had more than a few moments of fear for that myself. I thought I was too strong. Too jokey. Too bold for mens' tastes. And, of course, too picky to like any guy who *did* like me for those things. My friend Crazy Dave tried to cheer up my sorry self one night when he said, "It's not your fault you're single. I've never met a guy who's good enough for you." At first I was flattered, but as I lugged my clothes to the laundromat alone again the next day, I felt worse. *My biggest fear is true,* I thought, *there's just no match for me.*

But it turns out there was a match for me. An incredible match! And the partner you are looking for? He exists too. And the reason you haven't recognized him yet is that the man you want is special. I mean, come on, they don't churn out the guy you want like cans of aerosol cheese. The guy who's right for you is as special a combination as you are, and it's just going to take the world a minute to get you in the right place at the right time for the relationship you want. Instead of seeing it as an impossible mission, believe that the love of your life is out there! I don't believe, by the way, there is only one person on this whole Earth for each of us. I think we can make it work with a number of people, albeit in different ways and varying levels of suitability. Your half-orange, remember, isn't someone who completes you, but someone who complements you. And your chances of finding him are better than you think.

Your success in love depends on how you see your search. And from now on, I don't want you thinking about how unlikely it could be that you'd find a guy who's right for you. I want you to focus on the fact that while you don't know where he is now and when exactly he's coming, he is out there! Do you have one microscopic smidgen of belief that a guy who is meant for you might possibly exist? A smidgen is all you need. So if you have it, say it now. Or just say it in your heart: "I believe."

PHASE TWO:

Hit the Garden Shop:
Admit You Want It

ADMIT IT: YOU WANT AN ORANGE!

Pretend you're looking at one of those standardized tests in which you have to fill in the little oval with a number 2 pencil. The only question on the paper says:

I . . .
(a) love being single.
(b) really want to be in a relationship.

Obviously, if you fill in both ovals on that test paper, you'll make it void. You can't answer a "this one or that one" question both ways, just like life. You can't have a Four Seasons dinner *and* pay McDonald's prices. You can't have a rustic Ford Lariat that runs like a new Jaguar. You can't wear sexy spiked heels that feel as comfy as Uggs. And you can't say "I love being single!" but also really want to be in a relationship.

So, which is it?

I'll be honest: If you mentally checked that you (a) love being single, then I'd walk this book back to the place you bought it and ask for a refund. Because if you want to be single, then this strategy for putting yourself in the path of a relationship is not going to work. Seriously, it's not.

Don't get me wrong: You're allowed and encouraged to enjoy being single—for now—while you look for a relationship. (In fact, if you're *miserable* being a single, it's going to be even harder to find a relationship.) But for dating optimism to work, you have to really, honestly, *truly* want the thing you're hoping to get. You need to *really* want a healthy relationship.

I, for one, was trying to live it both ways. Deep down, when I was single, I wanted a relationship. But I never *admitted* that. What I said was, "Oh my God, being single is the best ever! I love it!"

In public, I embraced my badge of singleness with pride. "I love that I'm not tied down," I'd tell people who'd ask. My friend Yvonne and I would go out at night, dance barefoot on banquettes, and shout, "Being single is the best!" in time to the thumping music. But then I'd go home alone, as usual, and wonder why no one wanted me. Being single definitely wasn't always "the best," but I felt I had to say that. Why? *Because*, I thought, *there's nothing sorrier than a single girl who wishes she wasn't*. Goodness no. I was a modern girl who didn't need a man to make her happy. I was independent! I was awesome! I loved my life! But after a while, I felt like I was wearing someone else's badge and being called the wrong name all night.

I didn't understand it. There I was, being positive and optimistic and happy about being single, but it wasn't getting me any closer to finding love. *Why isn't some guy absolutely crazy about me?* I thought. *Why aren't I in a relationship?*

I'll tell you why. It's because **I was wishing for two entirely opposite things at the same time**. One, I was saying I wanted a relationship, and two, I was saying I wanted to remain single as all get-out. In effect, I was canceling out my own wishes. I say this because I meet so many single women who echo those things I used to say, and it's not bringing them—or maybe you—any closer to finding love.

I met a girl a few years ago named Francine. She's a thirty-six-year-old financial broker at a huge bank in New York City, where she lives in an apartment with floor-to-ceiling windows overlooking Central Park. For work, she travels to London and Tokyo. For fun, she uses her vacation time diving in Australia and surfing in Hawaii. And her love life is just as high-octane. One night, she told me about the two guys she was dating at the same time.

"One is this really cute model that lives in Miami and likes to fly me down to visit him," she said. "And the other is a French guy who visits me every month and wants to take me to Bali."

"Oooh," I told her, "they sound great!" Then I asked, "So would you want to get serious with either one of them?"

"Oh, please," she said. "I'm not looking to settle down. I love being single! This is all just for fun."

I believed her. Because after all, that's what being single and loving it is really all about: dating, experimenting, and getting the most out of life. She sure was doing it better than I ever had. But then Francine explained more.

"Well, actually . . ." she said, "the Miami model has a girlfriend, so I just fly in when she's out of town. It gets complicated because we'll make plans and then he has to cancel to see her. But that's cool by me. I mean, it's *better* for me that he has a girlfriend because I don't want to get serious either."

And the French guy?

"Well, he's a total player," she said. "Apparently, he flew some other girl to Bali with him earlier this year. But it's fine, because I'm not looking for a relationship right now either."

I wondered how much of this was true, and how much was rationalization. Maybe Francine really *did* prefer her life as a single woman with no attachments. My friend Kimberly also balances a few men at a time, but I believe her when she says she wouldn't want it any other way. When I last asked her if she was bringing a date to an event that would be crawling with men, she laughed, "Oh please, you don't bring a sandwich to the picnic!" But there was something in Francine's voice—I want to say it was like a big sigh—that made me wonder the ol', "Are you trying to convince *me* of this . . . or are you trying to convince yourself?" I felt like Francine wasn't being entirely truthful, and then it hit me: I *recognized* it, because I had heard myself using those very words before.

The message Francine was sending out to the world was one I used to send out, too: "I'm cool. I don't want a relationship right now. Things are great the way they are." And if you *really* mean it, hey, that's terrific.

Anne Violette, a writer and wedding photographer raised in Maine, was a self-proclaimed "serial dater" for eleven years (who spent half of her photography job fighting off brides who wanted to set her up). Yet after a marriage that went sour, she questioned the idea of a soul mate. "Instead," she chuckles, "I dated the same types of guys over and over. And every year or so I would trade one in for another 'model.'" But when Anne looked at why she was doing this, she realized there was a clear and perfectly *positive* reason: "I really liked being single," says Anne. "I think I attracted relationships that were destined to fail because, deep down, I didn't really *want* a commitment or to get remarried quite yet." The point is, if you have your own reasons for living the single life a little longer, great. In fact, if your goal *is* to be committed forever someday, you may only have a short window of time to fulfill a few crazy-single experiences, so live it up.

But if deep down you feel *differently,* admit it. Eventually, when I decided I wanted something more, I didn't realize I had to change my "Being single is great!" mantra. It was all I knew how to say. But if you want a relationship, you have to admit it. So back to that question I asked earlier:

I . . .

(a) love being single.

(b) really want to be in a relationship.

If you want a relationship, then choose (b) with all your heart.

What about just being "open" to love? Well, I'm asked that a lot. But the whole "I love being single, but I'm also open to finding a relationship" isn't enough. Why not? Because the universe will bring you what you are giving most of your focus and more of emotion to. Whatever you feel *most* passionately about, you will attract. So look at that sentence again: "I love being single, but I'm also open to finding a relationship." What you're saying is that you—whoa, totally—"loooove" being single, but you're—ya know, kinda sorta—"open" to a relationship. And that means you're putting your strong emotions onto the wrong part! Instead, flip it: "Sure, being single is good, but I really *really* want to find a loving, fulfilling, adoring relationship."

I know why you're doing it—because saying you're "open" gives you an out. That way, if you don't get what you want, you can say, "Well, that's okay, I didn't expect it. But I'm still open to it." Screw that. You didn't pick up this book because you are "open" to a relationship. You picked it up because you *want* one! You want it full on, all the way, a deep, true, real love. And you should expect it. In fact, for this to work, you *have* to expect it. Then and only then will you get it.

About a month after that dinner, Francine and I were out for drinks when she told me the fun factor was wearing thin. The truth was, she said, "I wish I could find a guy who lived in the same town as me for once and who doesn't have a girlfriend . . . or three." And I told her what I'm telling you: You're not going to get it by telling yourself and others those "I'm so happy being single!" stories. Because those stories send a very clear message into the universe that say: *I don't want a relationship right now.* If you want a relationship, admit it to yourself and the world that you're ready.

The *Sex and the City* problem

Socially, it's no surprise that some modern women, like Francine, get stuck in this staunchly solo rut. I blame the women's movement. I also blame, as I mentioned earlier, *Sex and the City*. As much as I loved the show (and sobbed my way through the movie), it abetted the women's movement in ruining romance for a lot of us. Yes, both events were potently imperative in forming the smart, strong women we are today and have profoundly impacted how we strive for equality in our careers and relationships—as we should! But they also swung the pendulum too far the other way when it came to love.

Women today have somehow gotten the idea in our heads that we're on one side of the equation or the other: We're either a 1950s housewife who accepts the stereotype of a man bringing home the bacon, or we're a twenty-first century independent career woman who doesn't need a guy to be happy. Some of you single women feel like you can't admit you want romance, because, well, you *shouldn't* want romance.

Gloria Steinem, along with other powerful leaders of the women's rights movement like *The Feminine Mystique* author Betty Friedan, encouraged women that we could have life both ways—that we could have marriages and families *and* we could have careers. But when that pendulum swung from the home to the office, it got stuck behind the copy machine; women started striving to become independent career women who simply didn't need men. So instead of *just* being married with no career, women began *just* having careers with no relationships. Over time, women filtered the feminist message as one that eschewed romance in favor of success. As Steinem herself once said, "Some of us are becoming the men we wanted to marry." In other words: Some of us became like characters from *Sex and the City*.

Samantha and Miranda were the epitome of that tough chick who says she doesn't need love and feels she should be allowed to have sex like a man—no commitments, no romance, no love. (The only character who insisted on romance was Charlotte, and any time she said so, she got eye rolls and "Awws" in return.) And single women all over the country who felt burned by men started waving the "Sex Like a Man" flag. Now, I'm all for the message of equality: I think women *should* be allowed to have sex without commitment, to seek pleasure without the romance. I mean, hey, we all need to turn on the engine now and then to keep the battery charged. But, my dear friends, you do know that casual sex is like initialing the sign-in sheet for short-term pleasure, right? Casual sex leads to casual relationships, plain and simple. If that's all you want, fine. But if you want a meaningful, serious relationship, I think it's time you started looking at your sex life more seriously, too. And yes, I've heard stories of one-night-stands turning into love; it even happened for a good friend of mine (after a year of her enduring the "Where is this going?" drama, they eventually got married and had two kids). So I know it *can* happen. But far more often, those one-night-stands become numbers on a notches list or turn into ten-night-stands peppered with mixed messages. If you're finally ready for the guy who not only wants you to stay the night, but wants to make you breakfast the next morning and meet your mother, then stop having uncommitted short-term sex and start asking for a committed long-term kind of relationship.

The problem is that women like Francine who have kicked butt in their careers and are feeling empowered through casual sex aren't about to flip the script and say, "No, on second thought, I want a guy in my life to lean on and commit to me," which almost feels like betraying how far women have come. By this point, Francine and lots of single women have trained themselves like Samantha to say, "I'm fine on my own. In fact, I'm happier *without* a man!" Saying otherwise feels a little outdated and old-fashioned. Now, add to the flame our love of feisty feminists like Katharine Hepburn, who didn't believe in the "bloody impractical" institution of marriage: "I often wonder whether men and women really suit each other," Hepburn once said, adding, "Perhaps they should live next door and just visit now and then." And what do you have? A generation of women who equate single-ness with strength and romance with weakness.

Do you recognize yourself in any of this? Perhaps, after years of chant-ing, "I don't need a man to make me happy!" it feels like a step backward to admit that, well, yeah, you do. "Need" of course is the wrong word. No, you don't *need* a man to survive—you can feed and clothe and shelter yourself just fine yourself, thank you very much. But it's okay to admit that you *want* a man to be your happiest self.

Because guess what? It's *biologically natural* to seek connection with other human beings. Many women today think they want total independence, but we're biologically geared toward wanting connection. It's not independence we want; it's *interdependence*: a state in which two people are each independ-ent on their own, but who are dependent on one another for a few of their needs. Even Stephen R. Covey, who wrote *The 7 Habits of Highly Effective People*—a career bible for high achievers—recommends a move from inde-pendence to interdependence. Covey proposes that learning to work with and rely on others is a necessary tool for effectiveness.

Psychologist Sue Johnson agrees, due to a principle she calls "attachment theory." She explains that the need for connection is innate, that what begins with the security a baby feels with its mom evolves into a continual search for a basic, human connection with someone else. "Attachment is an innate and primary motivating force," says Johnson, author of *Hold Me Tight*, in her workbook for therapists. "Seeking and maintaining contact with significant others is essential for human beings across the life span." Don't look at the bond you want to foster with a man as taking away from your strength. Look at it as a fortifying tool. "Secure dependence is a sign of health and comple-ments autonomy," explains Johnson. "Secure dependence *fosters* autonomy and self-confidence...The more securely connected we are, the more sepa-rate and different we can be."

And as much as women might want to date like a man or have sex like a man, let's face it women, most of us are not good at doing this—and there's a physiological reason for it: Our bodies are simply wired too differently for this to work in the long-term. When a man feels stressed, for instance, it activates testosterone in his body, making him want sex, action, and aggression. And when a woman feels stressed, it activates oxytocin, a hormone that makes you want to hug, bond, and connect. We are born to want *more* than good careers and great sex. We are sociologically, emotionally, and physiologically meant to connect, so stop feeling bad about wanting to.

Gloria Steinem found a man, by the way. At the age of sixty-six, she married David Bale (father of actor Christian Bale) through vows in which they called one another partners. "He had the greatest heart of anyone I've ever known," she said of him. Bale passed away three years later of brain lymphoma, but it sounds like Steinem found her half-orange.

And remember, lots of other bold, iconic, glass-ceiling stomping women have signed on the dotted line of the marriage license, too: Barbra Streisand, Diane Sawyer, and former Paramount Pictures chairman Sherry Lansing are a few. First female Speaker of the House Nancy Pelosi has been married to her husband Paul for more than forty-six years. Even strong and sassy Katharine Hepburn found true love with Spencer Tracy; their love affair (while he was still married) lasted twenty-seven years, until his death in 1967. And there are plenty of younger kick-ass, successful women showing that they want love to go with their triumphs, too. Golden Globe-winning actress Kyra Sedgwick has been married to Kevin Bacon for more than twenty years now. And former volleyball pro Gabrielle Reece has been married to big-wave surfer Laird Hamilton for twelve. The list goes on, but the point is simple: You can be a strong, independent woman and want a loving relationship, too.

If you want a man to love you, admit it. Don't feel ashamed or lame or pathetic saying so, because part of the reason you don't have a relationship yet is that you haven't *said* you want it. And, as Sue Johnson adds, all this beating yourself up for wanting a romantic connection is not helping your case! "A single person might say, "I'm depressed because I'm lonely, and I know I shouldn't be lonely; I know I should be independent," Johnson wrote in *Psychology Today*. "Well, of course you're depressed if you're feeling lonely, and then you turn around and beat yourself up for it!" This, says Johnson, is the beginning of a vicious cycle that nearly ensures you won't find the connection you need. In fact, you may inadvertently be projecting to men who potentially do want a relationship with you that a connection is the last thing on your mind.

MISS INDEPENDENT

Ask yourself this: Have you ever found yourself telling a man how independent you are? Or how accomplished you are? Or how you don't need anyone to pay your rent or put up your shelves or to take care of you? I used to say things like that a lot. I was proud of what I'd been able to do on my own in my life, but the effect of saying so wasn't what I intended. I remember, for example, telling one of my male coworkers at *Maxim* years ago that I'd cried while watching a movie.

"Yeah, right!" he said, laughing.

"What's so funny about that?" I asked.

"You don't cry," he said. "I bet you've never cried a day in your life!"

All I could think was, *What on earth am I putting out there that people think this of me?* Well, I was putting out so much I-can-do-it-alone energy, there wasn't an I-need-nurturing bone being seen in my body. "Sure," I told guys, "I installed my own air conditioner by myself." What I didn't say is that I wished I didn't *have* to.

It's exactly what happened with Bobbi Palmer, a Long Beach resident with a booming career as a manager in the technology sector. She was dating a lot of really nice guys, but not getting any phone calls afterward. "I was absolutely sure it was because I was not thin and tall and blond that I wasn't getting second dates," says Bobbi, who is 5'11" with a medium-build and brown, curly hair. "But I had an epiphany one day that it really had nothing to do with what I looked like. It had to do with what I brought to the table. I was being inauthentic." How?

"I think that those of us who have a level of success in a man's world feel we have to act like them and wear this tough badge," says Bobbi. "You spend ten hours a day behaving a certain way at work, so to soften up on your way home is hard to do!" Instead, Bobbi wore her badge to dinner, telling dates, "I'm independent, I can take care of myself." And if they didn't call her the next day, she'd act like it was perfectly okay and then do just that: take care of herself. "I think it's a wall we women put up, like, 'If you don't like me, it's okay. I'm fine by myself,'" says Bobbi. "Or maybe we're testing them, like, 'I dare you to like me, but I don't *need* you.' Either way, it's so insidious," she says, "it gets into the core of your being."

The more confident Bobbi became in the business world, the less confident she felt about herself in the relationship world. "I was able to finally see how I presented myself to men, and how disingenuous it was. In reality, I had so much fear: fear of being rejected, fear of making bad decisions, fear of losing myself in a man—you name it. All those guys who never called me back weren't responding to the real me—the open, warm, positive, compassionate me—but to that scared woman who fundamentally didn't believe there was someone out there for me or that I was worthy. I was judging myself by what I perceived *they* would think of me. When I decided I was a good person based on my *own* rules, I decided I was worthy."

It was then that Bobbi brought her true self to the dinner table, fears and all. "I kid you not, after my next five dates, I had second and third dates," she says. "I absolutely changed how I presented myself, and admitted what I wanted." She's talking about admitting you're scared a work deal might not work out, or telling a man that although you live alone now, you would love to have a partner to share your life with. "I realized that allowing a man to make me happy doesn't diminish me," she says, "it makes me stronger."

Two months after her epiphany, Bobbi met Larry. And six weeks later, they were planning a wedding. She says he's the nicest man she's ever known, and he brings out the soft side of her she needed. But she admits it took the journey to appreciate what she has. "Five years ago, I would have said, 'Oh, he's *too* nice,'" laughs Bobbi. "It's so crazy. If a woman is telling herself that, I think she needs to work on herself!" She's right. If you're not attracted to him because he's too meek or too awkward or too into *Star Trek*, that's one thing—but too nice? We should all be so lucky.

Let the nice in and let the vulnerable part of you out. Remember, males and females both produce testosterone *and* estrogen. If you're used to using your testosterone, give in to your estrogen. Let it play its part. Let yourself be loved.

The deal is this: You have a good job, ambition, and a plan for the future to take perfectly good care of yourself. In fact, if you want to, you could have a baby on your own and take care of the both of you all by yourself. And then you could have everything you want: A job, a future, a nice home, a baby, great friends, confidence, pride, all that good stuff—all by yourself. Hear you roar.

But be honest. You've read this far because you don't *want* to do it all by yourself. And it doesn't mean you're not a strong woman. It doesn't mean you don't stand behind feminism and want to prove to the world that women can do it all. It means that you want to share your life with somebody. And that's not a bad thing. It's a beautiful thing. Once you've admitted this to yourself, you're going to tell the people you're close to the same thing.

TELL EVERYONE YOU WANT ONE

A baby cries when it's hungry. Why? Probably because wiggling its toes isn't going to send you racing for the baby food quite as fast. A baby knows what it wants and it's—"Wahhhhhhh!"—far from shy about telling you. I suggest you think a little more like Junior about going after love. See, you know you're hungry for love, and because you're reading this book I know you're hungry for love. But if you don't tell anyone other than us about it, how the heck is the world going to know? The time has come to vocalize that you're ready for your dream relationship.

Two years ago, I interviewed Richard Bolles, the author of *What Color Is My Parachute*, for an article I was writing about how to unearth and pursue your dream career. What he said first was, "Picture yourself in a bookstore. What section do you go to?" Bolles said that by identifying your interests in your off-hours—History? Gardening? Photography?—you're helping to pinpoint specifically what category your dream career might fall under. Then, write your dream career down, he explained, "and show it to every friend and person you run into during the week." Not only does this help to get the word out there that you have a particular career in mind, but talking about it helps to focus *you* as well. All in all, *this same process works for love*. If you want dating optimism to work for you, you have to know what you want—*specifically*—and then tell people who ask what you're looking for. This gets your desires out there in the universe, and it reminds you what *you* want.

So, how are you going to tell them? Well, here's what I told my friends: "I've decided I'm going to bring myself a real relationship."

"Good for you," they said. Many left it at that. The ones who seemed amused or asked more questions got more from me.

"No, I'm serious about it," I'd say. "I'm going to bring an amazing relationship into my life."

"Oh really?" they asked. "How are you going to do that?"

"By focusing on it, and letting the universe know I'm ready for it. That's why I'm telling you, so you know."

Now, a fair warning: Be prepared for some people to give you those awful pity faces and "Awwws" we talked about. "Awww, it's okay, you'll find someone!" and "Oh, sweetie, there's a guy out there for you, I just know it!" The good news is, they'll only say this once. So you might feel stupid or lonely or sad for a moment, but then it will be gone. (As far as I'm concerned, though, the crazier they think you are, the better you're creating your own energy shift!) So tear off the Band-Aid, and tell your friends and family that you're taking control and finding love. Let them feel sorry for you for a second, then move on. Just think how little you'll really care when you're sitting next to your half-orange on your honeymoon, sipping Piña Coladas and gazing into each other's eyes as you thank the universe for bringing you both together.

The first time I told someone this, I felt a little corny. I mean, come on, "I've decided I'm going to bring myself my dream relationship" is quite a pronouncement on the sandwich line at the deli. But the more people I told, the more naturally it came out, and the more confident and optimistic I felt that I really *was* going to bring my dream guy to me. It's similar to what you do when you want to get in shape: If you tell your best friend you're doing Pilates for four weeks to fit into your for-that-price-they-should-be-gold-plated jeans, you're not only mad at yourself if you fail, but you dread having to face your friend in your fat jeans! Telling your friends or family makes it more real.

Take it from the master of "the man mix," Patty, a twenty-six-year-old from Chicago who kept her friends posted on the progress of her single life. "All my friends joked about how I always had 'a mix' of people I dated," says Patty. "They'd say, 'Patty's doing her rounds, she has her mix.' It's true, I was always with someone. I don't know if it was a power thing or that I was keeping my options open so I could always have someone to run to. But they were right, I always had my 'mix.'"

When Patty decided she wanted more, she told her friends. "I was really intentional about how I wanted to fall in love with the right one—not just anyone. And I told them I was willing to be alone and single in order to wait for that."

A year later, while Patty worked on creating her own company that provides businesses with team-building experiences through doing community service, she went to a lunch event for people who work at home. That's where she met David; he asked her out soon after. And though she liked him, she felt, for some reason, she didn't need to over-prepare for him like she did with other guys—and she means it literally. "For our first date, I was still wearing makeup from the day before. I figured, take it or leave it, here I am!" Within the month, Patty and David were saying, "I love you," and when Patty talks about their coupling, she keeps using the same words over and over: "awesome," "natural," "easy" and "fun." And while her friends miss her stories about "the mix," they know it's for the best, says Patty. "There's no need to analyze things with your friends when things are this good!"

For me, the watershed moment was telling my mother what I wanted. We were standing in the kitchen in my parents' house over the holidays. As we loaded the dishwasher, I told her that I'd recently gone out for coffee with an old boyfriend who lived a few towns away. Dmitri was handsome, intelligent, and funny and a guy I desperately *wished* I liked. But our chemistry was off. Way off. He kissed a bit like a drooling Bulldog might, and as much as I tried teaching him what I liked, our dates got awkward over time because I was always inventing ways to avoid kissing him. My mother, however, liked the idea that Dmitri came from an area nearby. And as a couples therapist, she had the insight to back it up.

"You'd be surprised how many people find love right back where they came from," she said that day. "A shared background is a wonderful beginning to a relationship." She wasn't being pushy about it, but I knew that deep down, she was desperate for her daughter to find a great guy and start a family. But now that I was using dating optimism—now that I was determined to find the best guy for me—I knew she didn't need to worry about me. I was confident that I would find the right man, and this seemed as good a time as any to tell her just that.

"Mom," I said, "I just want you to know that I've made a decision about my love life. I've decided that I'm not willing to settle for anything less than my dream relationship."

Uh-oh, I saw her face say. Because that's a married person's least favorite phrase: "I'm not willing to settle." After all, they love to say, marriage is all *about* compromise and settling for things you don't agree with sometimes. But here's what I say to that: Yes, marriage is all about compromise and settling ... eventually. And at first, only on the *little* things. You know, on who's going to pay which bills, on who's going to do which housework around the house, on who has to take on more or less hours at work. You compromise on day-to-day living, on surviving with one another, on combining two opinions and lifestyles into one. But I don't believe in settling on the big things. You shouldn't settle for someone you don't respect or someone who makes you feel you have to change to be with them. You shouldn't settle for someone with a gravely different world view or someone you spend your days trying to cheer up one minute and calm down the next. And for goodness' sake, you shouldn't settle for a relationship with someone you'll bob back and forth to avoid kissing for the rest of your life! And that's what I wanted my mother to know. I wasn't going to settle for anything less than someone who I felt, in a marriage, was *worth* compromising for.

"I've decided," I said, "that I'd rather wait ten more years for my dream relationship than settle for someone who's not right for me now. And if it means I have to have kids some other way, then that's what I'll do. Because I don't want to be with just anyone. I want to be with the right person for *me*." I think she was a little disappointed—ten years is a long way away—and she probably felt I needed some sense kicked into me. But she said neither. "Alright," she said, "good for you."

I asked her recently if she remembered that conversation, and she answered with a resounding yes. So, what *was* she thinking when I told her all this? "Well," she said, "I was thinking, 'How brave.'" Of course this brought tears to my eyes. Here I was, thinking my mother was disappointed in me, but what she saw—and what other parents and friends might see in you, too—is bravery. After a few seconds of silence while I held the feeling like a mighty sword, she broke in again. "I guess," she added. "I also thought you were being a little picky." A-ha! But you know by now how I feel about being picky: You have every right to be picky if it's for *your* benefit and what *you* want. So when you tell your friends and family about your new plan to stick to your guns and bring yourself a loving, adoring, incredible relationship, feel brave. They may think you are various levels of staunch, stubborn, idealistic, and unrealistic. But this isn't anyone else's life you're living, this is *yours*.

I was so confident in my plans, I didn't care what anyone thought anyway—I was going to get my dream relationship, whether others believed me or not. And to be honest, I also felt stronger in their doubt. I was going to find love and prove them all wrong, they'd see! And the more people I told, the more I believed it myself. It's a magical shift, and you'll feel it when it happens to you.

For one woman, telling her mom what she wanted was the best thing she could have done! A few weeks before turning twenty-five, Wendi Forrest decided she was done "dating for the sake of having a date." She had just finished grad school, was living alone for the first time, and was gloriously happy with who she was: "I got to the point where I would rather spend the night at home alone than on a random date that meant nothing. It had to be quality or I had better things to do with myself!" Now, ready to find the man she'd marry, she said just that to her friends and to her mom.

"I told her, 'I'm ready to find whoever it is. I'm not depressed and cynical, I'm not 'woe is me.' I can get a date if I want to. And if all I wanted was to be married, I could have been married.' But," says Wendi, "I told her, 'I'm just ready. I'm not worried if it takes six months or a year, I just don't want to waste time hanging out with people who aren't that.'"

A week later, Wendi's mother called from her Las Vegas home to say, "I've met the man you're going to marry!" Earlier that day, Wendi's parents had been paired with a handsome young man named Nate for a round of golf; eighteen holes later, Wendi's mom asked for his number to give her daughter. Wendi's first thought when she heard this: "*What kind of crazy guy would give a 50–year-old woman his number?*" Her second thought: "*Well, I said I was ready so I may as well give it a shot. If this guy is awesome, great! If not, I'll cross him off the list. The worst thing that could happen is I'll play a round of golf, and that's fantastic.* I just had an optimistic mind frame."

One month later, Wendi drove from her L.A. home to Las Vegas for a double date with Nate . . . and her parents. "Our tee-time was at 3 p.m. on Saturday, and Nate and I did not leave each other's sides until 7 a.m. Monday morning when I had to drive back to Los Angeles," says Wendi with giddiness in her voice. She moved to Nevada three months later and they just celebrated their third wedding anniversary. They even launched a dating service that helps people find love on the links, based on their personal success! "Nate makes me laugh every day. And rest assured," she laughs, "my mother is ridiculously proud of herself."

But Wendi should also be proud of *her* self, for she feels that telling her family and mom that she was ready for her big love is "*absolutely*" the reason she got it. She says she spent a few months thinking about what she wanted, but not saying it out loud. Then, when she was really ready, "I audibly put it out there," says Wendi. "I was casting that net. We never would have found each other if my mom didn't ask him out for me!" She's right. She was casting her net. And it's time that you do the same.

CAST YOUR NET ONLINE, TOO

When I first tried online dating, I wanted to seem like a cool, hip chick open to all sorts of relationships: casual, activity partner, just friends. "Hey," I asked Yvonne days later, "why do guys keep writing to me saying they're looking to 'have fun' instead of looking for serious relationships?" Oh.

Because I told them that's what I wanted, too.

If you have any profiles up online, I suggest you make sure that each and every one of them reflects one thing and one thing only: That you are "looking for a serious relationship." That's all, nothing else. If you're committed to meeting your very own half-orange, then your profile should reflect that.

The minute my single friend Lily unchecked all the "I'll take anything!" boxes and explained that she was only looking for the real deal, a new batch of guys started writing to her immediately. They found it "refreshing" to come across a woman who knew what she wanted—which Lily finally admitted was a serious committed relationship and a family. And she felt like a big weight had lifted off her shoulders that guys now knew upfront what she was ready for. Mission "Real Relationship" was on!

Being ready for a mature relationship is normal, wholesome, and positively healthy. Be proud of yourself for reaching this point in your life, and tell the people around you (and reading your profile) just how ready you are.

IT'S *HOW* YOU SAY IT

Just as important as the words you're saying is using the right *tone*. Words alone are not enough. For the world to recognize what you are asking for, you essentially need to turn yourself into an optimistic magnet for the love you want.

And I say this because you may be used to using a different tone entirely when you talk about love, one I know all too well. For instance: You're not allowed to say "I want a relationship" with the exhausted, hopeless energy you'd use after sitting on an airport taxiway for two hours, grumbling, "I hate this damn waiting, I just want to take off." Yes, you may be feeling that want strongly in your soul, but if your soul is aggravated or desperate, your tone will come out that way.

To make sure you're telling yourself and the world what you want in the right tone, think about something you really want and *wouldn't* be embarrassed to talk about, and then mimic the positive tone with what you want in a relationship. For instance, "Mmmm, I want a cream puff!" or "Hell, yeah, I'll take a backstage pass to Madonna!" or "Two free tickets to Rome? I'm *in!*" Are you getting the feeling for this? Pinpoint that tone in your voice—the way you express those exclamation points—when you say them out loud. Then, say what you want in *love* with the same tone, the same optimism, and the same determination: "You know what, world? I'm ready for my big relationship!" The more you say it, the more you'll feel it—the stronger the positive feelings in your brain and body—and the sooner you'll attract it.

Have you ever tried to approach or thought about approaching the velvet rope of a party you're not technically invited to? You can a) walk up stammering about how you're not actually, um, on the guest list, or you can b) walk up to that bouncer with the confidence that you *definitely* belong ("Let me in, I'm supposed to be here"). And as those beefy doormen might admit, your attitude alone can sometimes get you through. So I'm here to tell you: You're *on* the guest list for love. You are expected and meant to be there. "Hi," you should be saying to the world, "I'm here for my big relationship!" With certainty like that, they'll lift the rope, and you'll be let right in.

Novelist Pam Houston asked for her big love out loud, and as she explained in her essay "The Cupped Hands" in O Magazine, she added that she'd be patient while the world worked out bringing it to her. As she stood on a breakwater in Provincetown Harbor Massachusetts, Houston broadcast what she wanted in the breeze. "'I think I am finally ready for you to send me a big, deep, generous love,'" she wrote of her speech into the sunset. "'But if you don't think I am ready for big love,' I continued, 'then maybe just a little romance to keep the conversation going . . . and if I'm not even ready for that, maybe just a sign that I'm on the right path.'" Two weeks later, Pam wrote, she met a poet in Taos, New Mexico, and two years after that, they were still together. "Though no relationship is made without effort," wrote Houston, "this one is proving to be that big love I prayed for on the Provincetown rocks."

Another woman who mastered her delivery is author Lisa Bonnice, who was a touring comedian and a divorced mother of two in Chicago when she announced she was ready for her big, true love. "I was ready to find Mr. Right," says Lisa. "I was in my bedroom in my crummy little Chicago apartment, and I was fed up with being single," she says. "So I stated, out loud to the universe, that I was done playing around and that I was open to attracting the man who would be my perfect match. One who would grow with me as I grew, one who would enjoy life the same way I do. I said, out loud, 'Okay, I'm done dating. I'm ready to settle down with the One. Bring him on!'"

Lisa said it only one time, but the *way* she said it—the tone she used—was filled with so much passion that her words went out with the right energy. Sure, she admits, she'd said similar things before, but her words never had the intention of her body and soul behind it. Never before was she saying it with both her mind *and* her heart, proclaiming that she was ready for it. "This time was different," says Lisa. "It was like a declaration, a statement of *fact*. I think the true power of the statement was that I deeply meant it, with every fiber of my being."

Shortly after her declaration, Lisa got a call from an owner of a club in Detroit, where she was scheduled to perform the following week. "He said my gig was canceled because the club had burned down! So I got on the phone and called every booking agent I knew, trying to fill the gap in my schedule." Finally, she landed a last-minute gig in a club in Virginia Beach; yet the day before Lisa was scheduled to leave, she got a call from the agent there as well. "He told me that Hurricane Hugo had wiped out the club, so my gig was canceled again!"

Lisa, panicking now, called the only place left on the list, where she'd started out years ago, in her hometown. "I begged the club owner to let me emcee the show—something, *anything!*—and said I'd stay with my parents for free instead of the club owner having to pay for my hotel room." The feature act that week at Lisa's home club was a fellow comedian named Jeff Sweeney. They fell for each other instantly, and they're now gloriously, perfectly, happily married. "I'm not taking responsibility for a fire or tidal wave!" she laughs, but she does feel the universe sure was doing what it could to steer her toward the right guy. And it's a good lesson: If you really want *that* guy to walk into your life, the guy you can have fun in line at the DMV with, then announce to the world that you're ready for it with a tone like Lisa Bonnice used: Pull it from the bottom of your gut and *say it like you mean it.*

There's another reason your tone matters: Speaking these things out loud with the right emotion works like an affirmation. Now, I've always felt like affirmations were kind of wacky ("I have a million dollars! I am special! Doggone it, people like me!") But I know more now. Here's how it works: Earlier, I mentioned the amygdala, those small almond-sized neuronal structures in your brain that store emotional information. In a way, it's like a computer hard drive of your emotions, because the amygdala stores details of feeling and thoughts whether you want them there or not. Remember the time you were cruelly rejected by a boy you liked? Or the time you were made fun of for the size of your nose, or the way you talked? Your amygdala remembers, too. And remember the heartbreak you felt when you found out the good-looking man you loved was cheating on you or in love with someone else? Well, your brain has that emotional memory stored and able to be called up as if it were yesterday; your body may even react as if you're "feeling" the memory all over again.

And now, every time you meet a good-looking guy, your brain routes that information through the hard drive of your amygdala to analyze the situation. Chances are, your brain will assess that new guy with doubt, self-protection and withdrawal or basic disbelief: "Yeah, right, as if *he's* going to be faithful."

It's no wonder your brain makes a beeline toward the bad. "We are always creating new neural structure, but negative experiences build neural structure *instantly*," explains Rick Hanson, Ph.D., founder with neurologist Rick Mendius, M.D. of the Wellspring Institute of Neuroscience and Contemplative Wisdom, and author of *Buddha's Brain*. "Positive experiences go through normal storage processes, but it's like we have a fast track for negative experiences," explains Hanson. "The brain looks for negative experiences, reacts to them intensely, stores them carefully, and retrieves them quickly. We're like Velcro for negative experiences, but Teflon for the positive ones!" He suggests people who get rejected in dating should actively look for good news, particularly the little stuff of daily dating life. What, for example, is your good news today? Perhaps the guy in the coffee shop was flirting with you this morning? Or you got a few winks online? "Over time," explains Hanson in his book, "the accumulating impact of this positive material will literally, synapse by synapse, change your own brain." What you're doing is using what we talked about earlier— neuroplasticity, the reshaping of the brain's neuronal pathways—to your optimistic advantage.

Affirmations and positive pronouncements don't erase those painful memories, but by programming new *positive* pathways in your emotional brain, you can outweigh the painful memories stored there, which will raise the bar on your self-image, your worth, and your self-esteem. Luckily, there's a formula for exactly how much positivity you need. "Our emotions obey a tipping point," says Barbara Fredrickson, Professor of Psychology at the University of North Carolina at Chapel Hill, and author of *Positivity*. "What seems to matter most is your ratio of positive emotions to your negative emotions. This is what I've called your 'positivity ratio.'" The tipping point, says Fredrickson, is three to one. "We need three positive emotions to lift us up for every negative emotion that drags us down."

So focus on some of that good news every day—at least three times more than you do the bad news—and imagine how it will feel to have joy in love. Because when it comes to the relationship you're hoping for, it's time to walk away from the past, feel better and stronger in the present, and positively hope for the very best in your future. Instead of saying, "I've never met a great guy," or "I'm never going to meet a great guy," shower the amygdala in your brain with all the hope and optimism you can. Say, "It's going to happen for me," and "I deserve to meet a great guy!" Because it will and you do.

And look, I get it that maybe you're not one to talk into mirrors, or announce what you're looking for in a morning meeting. But words have power—and words you choose to say out loud have even *more* power. The magic comes when you pull the words that matter most out of the many bobbing in your brain. See, inside your head, you're feeling a mix of it all— "I'm scared," "I want to meet someone," "I'm afraid I'll never have children," "I want a great love in my life." You have more thoughts swimming around in there than Kellogg's has cereals. I want you to leave behind the fears and the cynicism and negativity for a minute and fish out the positive thoughts to say out loud. Do what comedian Lisa Bonnice did: Say the words, out loud, *with every fiber of your being.* Say, "I'm ready for my big relationship. I'm ready for the real thing. Bring him on!" It's the official start to your getting the love you've always hoped to have.

PHASE THREE:

How to Choose Your Seed:
What Do You Want?

HOW TO CHOOSE YOUR ORANGE SEED

Have you ever made a list about what kind of guy you want? Through the years, you may have asked for things like: "Good sense of humor," "Taller than me," "Has dark hair, blue eyes, and dimples," "Intelligent," "Good with kids," "Successful," "Adventurous."

Well, here's what I want you to do with the love list as you've previously known it: Trash it. Crumple it up and throw it away. We'll be making you a new kind of specific list soon, but your current one may be holding you back and making the search for your half-orange even more difficult. **The fact is, what you want in a man is completely irrelevant! You don't even want a man. What you want is a *relationship*.** Let's go through a few things that might be on your list for what you *think* you want, and I'll explain.

Do you think you want a guy who's funny? *You don't*. What you want is a relationship full of laughter, in which he makes you laugh, and you make him laugh. It doesn't matter if other people think a guy has "a great sense of humor." That's beside the point. I dated a stand-up comedian once, and to be honest? It was pretty depressing.

Do you think you want a nice guy? *You don't.* What you want is a relationship in which your partner is nice to *you* and those around you; you want a relationship where you are treated as well and wonderfully as you deserve to be.

Do you think you want a guy who is "tall, dark, and handsome?" *You don't.* What you want is a relationship in which you're madly and wildly attracted to the man you're with. Again, whether or not other people think he's handsome is beside the point. He only needs to be attractive to one person: you. I've known plenty of women who set out seeking one physical type of man and ended up with another they found far more attractive.

Do you think you want a guy with tattoos or a motorcycle or a particular kind of badass car? *You don't.* What you want is a relationship in which you feel edgy and dangerous, with a lifestyle that feels like you're driving left of center from the rest of the world and you never know what excitement your life together might bring.

Do you think you want a guy who is fit and muscular? *You don't.* What you want is a relationship in which you live a healthy lifestyle with your partner. (Or perhaps you find men with muscles attractive, and, again, it's the *attraction* that's the point, not the muscles.)

The point is, it's time to start looking at what kind of *relationship* you want, instead of what kind of *man* you want. Because thinking about the relationship you want is something you can attach *feelings* to. And it's the feelings that are important.

I focused on a relationship where I felt I had a "partner in crime." I knew I wanted to laugh a lot, to be deeply loved, to feel inspired, to go on adventures together, to have a healthy sex life, and to be in a relationship in which I felt appreciated for the workings of my sometimes out-there thoughts. And that's what I got. And I got it because I focused on the feelings I wanted overall, not on any small details I'd sketched about how tall he was, or what kind of shoes he'd wear.

When you start looking at outside, physical indicators to choose the right guy (looks, job, suit, swagger), you get sidetracked. I used to walk in a room, seek out the tall, brown-haired guys, and ask if they were single. There could have been a dozen redheads, shaved heads, dirty blonds or mohawks in that room who wanted to love me, but they weren't on my radar, because I simply didn't know how to look for anything other than men with brown hair! Yes, I've heard stories of women who have asked for, say, a man with a pick-up truck or a ski season pass, who have gotten what they asked for—and I'm not saying it can't happen. In fact, some of the dating optimists in this book have done that. All I'm saying is that if you create a laundry list of tangible details you want in a certain type of guy, you don't even usher in the possibility of getting someone slightly different! It's not up to you to design your perfect man from head to toe. It's up to you to figure out how you'll feel your best self in a relationship—be it laughing or loved or hardworking or healthy or edgy or serious or silly—and then you just need to let the world bring you your big surprise.

By using dating optimism, you can eliminate your desire to describe your "type" to those who ask—and I'm guessing you think you have one. I had whittled myself down to a "type," too, and it's because, over the years, after dating numerous people, we finally discover patterns in what we want and don't want, which is healthy. However, we can also veer into judging physical indicators ("I don't like banker types" or "I'm not into blondes") so much that we're essentially typecasting our future. And typecasting is like funneling your vision. Picture it: Unlike the large end of a funnel you used to be open to, it's possible you've funneled your vision to such a small gap, it'd be nearly impossible to squeeze a guy through it with his skull intact! Do yourself the favor of opening back up to the idea that it's not the physical details of the man that matter, but about how the two of you will be together in a relationship. "I don't have a type," you can say. "I'll just recognize him when I see him."

Create a new tool for sizing up the men you met: the feelings you want in your ideal relationship. Consider it the half-orange version of a bat's sonar: *You will no longer be looking with your eyes, you will be seeing with your heart.* Using your sweet sonar will profoundly change how you look at a room full of strangers from this day forward.

Now let's figure out what feelings you *do* want in your ideal relationship, so you can start focusing on it.

BE SPECIFIC ABOUT THE ORANGE YOU WANT

After a decade or four of dating, it's easy to lose track of what the heck you want, so let's begin with the easiest first step: Look at other relationships you admire and pick the things you like about them, from the substantial to the seemingly inconsequential. Here, for example, are a few things I saw:

- I admired my parents' lifelong commitment—a marriage of forty-two years that not only withstood the test of time, but also seemed stronger because of it. I wanted that—a steady, committed, lifelong union.

- I admired how Jennifer and Sam called each other pet names like "Honey" all the time. And when they greeted or said good-bye to each other, they did so with a kiss. I wanted a relationship like that—one full of affection.

- I admired how Anna and Paul could talk intelligently about life and culture as equals. I wanted a relationship like that—in which we intellectually inspired one another.

- I admired how Andy and Carolyn checked in by phone a lot during the day; he would call her to pass along a quick message, and when she called him, he was happy to hear from her. I wanted a relationship like that—devoid of games and full of contact.

- I admired how Sophia and Ryan shared their social circle and were always together. Their lives became one, just like they said in the vows. I wanted a relationship like that—in which *we* were friends as well as lovers.
- I admired how Sara and Peter took their baby with them on their trips. I wanted a relationship like that—part of a family who traveled together as a team.

In these cases, you're looking at what kind of relationship you want as a whole. You're not just looking at how your partner would be with you, you're also looking at how you would be with your partner, which is equally important. In fact, thinking about what you would offer your partner is another way of pinpointing the relationship you want. "I think people often forget about what kind of partner you want to be in a relationship," says Ellyn Bader, Ph.D., co-founder of the Couples Institute. "When you idealize the perfect guy, the more you focus on how the other person would be, the less effort you have to do yourself. But it's important that you have some notion of how you want to be as well." Perhaps you want to be loving, low-key, trusting, in awe, respectful, supportive, or communicative. Add those feelings to the mix.

Finally, I want you to also consider that what you think you want might be different than what you need. Colleen Seifert, Ph.D., professor of psychology at the University of Michigan, says she experienced a revelation about what she thought she'd wanted once she met the man she was meant to be with. "I thought I wanted someone who was nuttier and more neurotic than me," says Seifert. "So I chased men who bordered on wild and unpredictable. But it turns out that I needed the opposite—someone unflappable, who is great in emergencies. That way, I can be the one to flip out and he's there to calm me down!" The fact that her husband Zeke makes her feel calmer is, she says, "a key ingredient to our relationship, and I never knew to look for that."

In fact, Seifert's experience is why those lists of what you specifically want in a guy may be holding you back. Because what we think we want and what we really need are often two different things. Instead, keep your focus on how you want to feel. If you keep your eye on the prize of being with a partner who makes you shine and feel like your best self, then it will be a lot easier to recognize him when you meet him—or when you don't. "I dated my gynecologist for a while," says Seifert, with a deadpan hint of humor. "I knew it would never work when he told me he'd never been inside a K-Mart and had never heard of Hamburger Helper. I couldn't live up to that! It was really a class thing. Eventually," she says, "he said he couldn't see us together for the long term, and I was relieved, because I couldn't either."

Based on those three factors, think about what you want your orange seed to contain for a minute:

1. What is it about the relationships you admire that gives you the warm fuzzies?
2. What kind of partner do you want to be to the one you love?
3. What might you need rather than think you want?

You can attract whatever relationship you ask for—as long as, at the essence of it all, is love. Nadine is a forty-one-year-old high-level editor at a magazine in New York. And two years ago, she told me one thing she was looking for in her ideal relationship: "I edited a story about a cool power couple, and I totally wanted to be them," said Nadine. "They were both doing big creative jobs, and mingled and networked in the same crowd. I always think about them when I meet a guy—how I want to be part of a power couple."

Now, that's definitely a start: Nadine is identifying what she sees in another couple that she wishes she had. When she first told me this, I remember relating. But what she was asking for—and what I and many single women have been guilty of asking for—weren't the feelings *she* wanted within the relationship, but rather how *other* people saw them. What, for instance, makes a so-called "power couple?" That they hug a lot, send witty texts to one another, and say "I love you" before they've dug out their eye crusties in the morning? Gosh, not that I've ever heard.

What makes a power couple is, instead, some combination of high-earning jobs or professionally recognized ones; a social calendar booked with events; their names in "Page Six"; their photos in a magazine. Sure, that's an exciting thing to want, but if you're going to focus on the feeling of being a respected part of a hardworking, networking team, where does your loving, inspiring bond fall in that equation? Perhaps you can squeeze it in, but it might have to move down the list a bit. And you know what happens when a desire for a loving relationship gets moved down the list? What you're saying is that you *really* want to be a powerful force of success and wealth and influence with your partner, and you also—eh, you know—want it to be full of love.

Anything you ask for that is *not* based on the adoring, compatible relationship you will have with each other should be a cherry on top. Money or power or success that you want in a relationship should be a gift-with-purchase—like the super sponge that comes free when you buy the twelve-piece magic mop set…that you ordered at two in the morning…because it seemed like a really good value at the time. Instead of asking for someone to sweep you off your feet with the intention of improving your station in life, make your life wonderful and be your *own* gift with purchase. Drew Barrymore said it best in an interview in *L.A. Weekly* when she explained what attracts her to stories about women who don't necessarily do what's expected of them, like *Ever After*. "What excited me most about that movie was that [it showed] the way I feel about life," said Barrymore. "Don't wait to be rescued. Rescue yourself."

Instead of asking to be part of a power couple or not-so-secretly wishing to be with a rich guy, think about what you want in your relationship that you'll get in the one-on-one moments *away* from public eyes: A feeling of trust and closeness? Lots of affection? Thoughtful gifts? Intellectually challenging conversation? A sense of support and security? Laughter? Or, think about the loving wants that may be entrenched within a relationship with a successful man, and work *that* into what you want in your dream relationship. For instance: "I want a relationship in which I admire what my partner does for a living and what he has chosen to devote his life to." Then, once again, just let the world bring you your big surprise.

"I realized," said Nadine, "that what I wanted in a partner is when you are completely secure with them and they *want* to be with you. I wanted security and love and affection and consistency—*that's* what a relationship is, over the years."

IT'S *YOUR* SEED, SO STOP IT WITH THE "SHOULDS"

As you hone the details of what you want in your dream relationship, remember one thing: It's *your* relationship. No one else's. If you had to get up and move to a cabin in Antarctica tomorrow—away from your job and his, away from your families and your social lives—what would you want in your relationship then? Think about what you'd want once you eliminate all the shoulds: who you think you *should* be wanting, *should* be dating, or *should* be marrying.

I'll never forget the day at *Glamour* magazine when my friend Kim walked into my office, slid the door shut, and said, "I'll tell you what you're doing wrong if you tell me what I'm doing wrong." I laughed out loud; I knew instantly what she was talking about—our dang love lives. We were both over thirty, agonizingly single, and our previous conversation involved the pros and cons of sperm donation and single parenting.

Well, I agreed. I gave her my best take on her "problem" (something

THE BABY FACTOR

When Nadine told me her story, she brought up something else I think those of you of child-bearing or child-raising age should address within yourself as well. Do you want children? Answer honestly, as if a magic genie will give you whatever you want, no questions asked. Do you want children?

I ask this because I've met a lot of single women who, just after they tell me, "I love being single!" they say something like this: "I mean, I thought I wanted kids, but I don't know. I mean, I have such a great life as is, so, yeah . . . who knows?" Well, if you don't know, find out! Get yourself the answer right now.

If your answer is no, great, you know where you stand. Not every woman needs to have children. The fact is, women who forgo the option to have kids are often stigmatized and spend more time than they should defending their decision. But parenting is a life-altering path and you have every right to choose an alternate route for yourself. If you want a kid-free life, you can tell those baby pushers to shove it.

If, on the other hand, you do want to be a mother, great, own it! You will attract what you think about, focus on, and feel. So if you want children, you're going to have to start saying so today, or the universe won't know to bring them to you. The next time someone asks if you want children, answer honestly, "Yes, definitely."

Before Nadine got honest with herself, she told people she didn't want kids: "I think I was repressing the desire because I was scared it wasn't going to happen," she says. "I just figured I wasn't going to have my own, so instead of being disappointed, I decided I just didn't want them." Eventually, she admitted her true desire to be a mother, and if you want the same thing, you have to say so, too. If you want a half-orange who makes you feel wonderful and wants to build a family with you, ask for that. Picture the image of you and your other half peeking over the railing of the crib at your sleeping baby or pushing your toddler on a swing. Invoke the images that make you feel like you're a family, and focus on that.

about how she was selling herself short by dating guys that weren't as cute or together as she was, and then resenting them for it later), and then she gave me hers.

"You," said Kim, "need to date more Khaki Tuckers."

"More what?"

"Khaki Tuckers. You know, guys who wear khaki slacks with their shirts tucked into them?" (Belt optional but encouraged.) "Those guys are more likely to be nice and reliable," she said, "and they're the ones looking for relationships." She had a point.

So I took her advice and I dated a few Khaki Tuckers.

One of those guys was Lance, a Matthew Modine lookalike who worked as a political writer for a news magazine. He was polite, clever, and a single dad living in Brooklyn. On our first date, he made me laugh and taught me quite a few things I didn't already know about some war that went on in the Balkans (as well as, um, where the Balkans were, exactly). I didn't feel much chemistry with him, but I knew I should give it time, because he had so many great qualities. At the end of the date, we kissed on the cheek and went our separate ways home. We had two or three more dates like this, with me trying to summon chemistry and trying to look forward to our dates, when really, I wasn't into this otherwise catch of a guy.

"I *should* like him," I kept saying. "So why don't I?" We eventually stopped making dates, and a few months later, Lance met a Swedish news reporter, fell madly in love, and they are now living together in Brooklyn. When I first heard that, I admit, I felt a tinge of regret: Oh no! Why did I let him go? What had I missed that the Swedish girl loved? Then I realized: nothing. Lance and I simply weren't meant for each other. And as soon as we both let ourselves off the hook, we opened ourselves back up for the *right* person to walk in.

Stop it with the *shoulds*. You either like him or you don't. You either feel it or you don't. You either want to go on another date with him or you don't. If you're trying to tell yourself for even one second that you *should* like him or feel it or want him, it's not right! Just because other girls might like the guy you're having dinner with, doesn't mean you have to. Even though I thought I should keep trying to make it work with Lance, he wasn't the guy for me. If you hear yourself saying, "Yeah, but I *should* like him," put him back on the shelf and step away.

Kim, incidentally, fell for her own smart, handsome, successful Khaki Tucker, a man she'd known for years, and they now have a three-year-old baby together. She found her half-orange and got exactly what she wanted. So declare a Do Not Resuscitate on dates that aren't working. Because forcing these dates is only holding the *both* of you back from finding the partners you both deserve to be with. That guy you think you *should* keep dating? He's better off with someone else, too. Give yourself and him the chance to find the right person.

AIM FOR THE PRIZE TREE—YOU DESERVE IT

Monk and author Thomas Merton once said, "The biggest human temptation is to settle for too little." I won't let you do it. You deserve more! And your future happiness depends on it. As psychologist and Harvard lecturer Tal Ben-Shahar explains in his book *Happier,* you must consider both your present experience and future one when making choices in life. Hedonists, he says, make choices that yield present benefit but future detriment (in love's case, choosing the sexy bad boy for a rush of excitement, only to discover later that he can't give you the enduring love you need). A person Ben-Shahar calls a "rat race" type makes choices based on present detriment but future benefit (perhaps choosing the dull man with a lot of dough, hoping that in the future, the money and security will make you happy enough to justify your choice). Nihilists, says Ben-Shahar, make choices that yield both present detriment and future detriment—without a lust for life, this is a type of person "who has given up on happiness," he writes. And happy people? They make choices that will yield them present benefit *and* future benefit. And that's what you owe to yourself in love.

I fear that if you settle for someone who's not right for you, sure, you may feel momentarily good that you're no longer alone. But once you send your wedding thank you notes and sink into the routine of daily life, you may find that without a zing of true love, respect, and affection at the heart of your relationship, settling won't seem so worth it after all. Instead, I want you to ask for a love that feels great for you now, and has great potential in the future—a relationship that goes light years beyond good enough and exceeds your expectations in every way! **I now grant you permission to want it all.**

Asking for it all was hard for me. Growing up Catholic, I was raised wearing navy uniforms and knee socks to school, and learning to be grateful for what I got—you know, don't look a gift horse in the mouth. (Though I was so certain as a kid that I wanted to be a nun, I sure didn't feel bad asking for more rosary beads and bibles.) It's a wonderful way to live, of course, but when it came to love, I mistook gratefulness for settling. After all, I had plenty of love around me: the love of family and close friends. And while a relationship was something I wanted, I didn't want to look that gift horse in the mouth by asking for yet *another* relationship. Thou shalt not covet thy neighbor's love life, right? So I thanked my family and friends and God for all the great people I had around me . . . and then I downed a bottle of wine by myself while watching You Tube videos of funny cats. When I began using dating optimism, however, I realized that I was using my gratefulness in the wrong way by shortchanging myself. You may be, too.

Mary is a thirty-nine-year-old news editor for a major network television station I met one night in Los Angeles. She was spunky, used big words like *monomaniacal,* and smelled like the most pleasantly faint gardenia musk. She was also single. She said she loved her life and worked hard at being actively grateful for it all—but that's where she got stuck. "I feel like I'm so lucky to have everything I have, that it's wrong of me to want more," Mary told me. "I have all the big things. My parents are still alive, I'm totally healthy, my bosses say I kick butt at work and have the best ideas, and I know I'm funny and people like me. Life has been good to me, so I feel like I can't ask for more. I feel selfish wanting even more on top of all that."

Here's the thing: Yes, you should be absolutely grateful and feel blessed for all you have. But don't let your gratefulness hold you back from asking for more—*especially* when it comes to love. **Wanting the greatest love in the world isn't a selfish act, because you want it for all the right reasons.** Asking to genuinely love and be loved by someone? That's the healthiest and most beautiful request there is!

You're a good person, right? And you know that with the right person, you will have *so* much affection to give. So if you settle for something average, that big heart of yours will be going to waste. Asking for more love is like giving a promise that you will *use* it. You know how good you feel when you give a gift to someone and you know they will appreciate every single second of it? Like, say, a massage for your stressed-out best friend, a wool shawl for your always-freezing grandmother, or a stroller donated to a new mom who can't afford one—it just doesn't get better than giving a gift to someone who will cherish it. Well, *that's* how the universe feels about handing out love to people who ask for it. If you ask for something based in love, you're actually starting a process of making the world a better place. Think about it: If you feel bountiful in love, you will be a happier, better person every single day, and more of a force for *good* in the world. If what you are asking for is coming from a place of love, then ask for more.

In fact, when it comes to asking for love, huge is the way to go. For once, it's healthier to supersize it! Why? Because it's easier to feel *more* passionate when you want *more* of something, right? If you want just a sip of lukewarm and slightly flat soda, you may not be so into it, but it's easy to get excited if you can imagine how it would feel to have a big, cold, glass of delicious, fizzling fountain Coke in front of you. The more passionate you are about what you want, the more strongly you'll *feel* about wanting it, and the more quickly and easily it will come to you.

Asking for a huge, fizzling supersized love that's perfectly right for you isn't a selfish act. It's a generous one! Meeting the love of your life will bring out the *best* in you. It will make you a stronger, better, more loving person, and it will make you want to accomplish even bigger, greater things with the gifts you've been given. You deserve that big love, and the world deserves you getting it. And whether you realize it or not, the world—and plenty of people you know—are gunning for you have it. That's a lot of loving energy going out on your behalf! Let it bolster your mission to bring your half-orange right to you, where he belongs.

BAN "JUST" FROM YOUR ORANGE DICTIONARY

As you pick your orange seed, I will not allow you to bargain yourself down to the lowest common denominator. And you *know* what I'm talking about.

Many times when I was single, I'd get so frustrated I'd say, "I just want a guy who has a real job," or "I just want a guy who actually likes me back," or, as you might imagine, "I just want a guy who isn't psycho!" Well, guess what? Along the way, I *got* those things. But the guy who had a real job? He was a total player. The guy who liked me back? He did so in a baby duck kind of way. And the guy who wasn't psycho? He was a partier who didn't know when to quit. You see where I'm going with this, right?

Using the word "just" is announcing to the world that you're looking to cut a deal. You think you can't have it all, or don't deserve it all, so you'll take just part of it. But that's *just* a sign you're giving up and taking less than you really want. And if you're asking for less than you want, you won't be able to create the buzz and focus necessary to bring it all to you. If you *want* it all, *say* you want it all, and then you'll *get* it all.

Just as I began my dating optimism experiment, I got sucked into a crush on a restaurant owner I'd met through friends. I wasn't attracted to him physically, but I enjoyed his company. He was smart and sweet, accommodating and kind, and with all the prominent people he socialized with, I couldn't help feeling fabulous around him. Granted, the first time I walked into his restaurant I was taken aback by the '80s paint-splatter pattern on his short-sleeve button-down shirt, but the gushing attention he gave me overrode it. Eventually, after a few visits, I started to like him—really like him. He got cuter every time I saw him, and I started seeing the potential of a relationship. He made it clear that he liked me, so I thought, *If I could find it in myself to like him back, we could make a perfect pair.* And so began my perilous journey down a road dotted with mixed signals.

The restaurant owner would invite me to pop by on Tuesday night so we could hang out. When I'd get there, we'd hug and flirt and talk about life outside the restaurant. He'd say things like, "We should check out this other restaurant," or "It might be fun to hit that concert." I'd tell him to call me, he'd say he would, and then . . . nothing. No call, no email, no text. Radio silence.

A week later, I'd "happen" to pop into his place with friends. "Where have you been?" he'd say, kissing my cheek. "I thought we were going to hang out! You said you'd call me!" Embarrassingly, I'd fall for the bait and switch: "But wait, I'd say, full of relief. I thought *you* were going to call *me.*" We'd wave off the misunderstanding and have a few drinks, but he'd never asked me out.

Here and there, though, I'd be buoyed by hope. One weekend the restaurant owner came to visit me at my beach house, and we spent a day eating lunch, checking out town, watching TV. Yet we never got past first base. Back in the city, his best friends would pull me aside and tell me with all the sincerity in the world that the restaurant owner liked me. "He talks about you all the time," they'd say. "And he needs someone like you—you're the perfect girl for him." Shame *he* didn't seem to think so, as the cycle would begin all over again. Did he like me or didn't he? Should I stick around or shouldn't I? Is this heading somewhere or isn't it?

Rather than recognizing that I wasn't getting what I wanted, I began *reassessing* what I wanted. By the nature of his job, for instance, he worked nearly every night until 4 a.m., and when he wasn't in the restaurant, he was out schmoozing on behalf of it. *Okay,* I'd think, *so maybe I don't need to spend lots of time with my partner. Maybe just having days with him would be enough. After all, I love being independent and having time on my own.* When the restaurant owner said he never wanted to get married, I said, "I don't need to get married. We could just have kids together instead." We high-fived. I thought we had a chance.

Finally (and embarrassingly), months into our flirtatiously chaste affair, I heard he'd begun seeing a recording artist and was going on actual dates with her. I was disappointed, but madder about one thing most of all: "Wait, this is so unfair," I told my friends. "I didn't even like him at first, remember? He *made* me like him!" Ah, there's nothing like the guy who "makes" you like him and then disses you in return. But the diss was a gift. It made me stop and look at what I'd been doing, saying, and considering settling for: *just* a phone call here and there, *just* days with him, *just* kids and no marriage. Basically, I thought I would be happy with "just" enough. But it hit me one afternoon: I wouldn't! I was on a quest to find my true other half, and I wanted *so* much more than "just" that. I wanted it all.

Create your Big Love List

Now that you know the specific elements of the orange seed you want, write them down, because the more senses you use to focus on what you want, the more easily you'll remember to want it. Start with a line at the top that says, "In my dream relationship, I want to feel . . . " and then fill in your own blanks. Create your Big Love List in whatever way feels comfortable for you: Type it on your computer, jot it in your journal, scribble it on a sticky note. No matter how you do it, you'll find that when you feel the *touch* of your pen on paper or your fingers on a keyboard, and you see what kind of orange seed you want written down in a Big Love List, it will seem even more possible. And the more often you look at it and focus on it, which we'll talk about later, the more energy you'll be creating to bring what's on that list your way.

Your Big Love List is similar to the one you bring a realtor. Have you ever had the feeling that searching for the home you were after seemed as futile as love does now? After all, it seems crazy that you'd be able to find a place with great light, hardwood floors, two-car parking, and old-world charm that happens to be ten minutes drive from your work. But when you hand that list to your realtor, more often than not, you find a place you love! Because it turns out many people only need room for one car, some like brand-new construction over old-world charm, and we all prefer different parts of town.

Seeing your list written down makes it evident that the dream home you have in your head *is* possible to find. And when you write down what kind of orange seed you want on a Big Love List and take it to the experts at the love nursery, you will find the same thing—that there *is* a seed just for you. The dream you have in your head isn't a dream at all. It's your blueprint for the perfect relationship and you can build from there. The relationship you want—your ideal orange—is within your grasp; you just need to plant your seed and bring it to life.

PHASE FOUR:

How to Plant the Seed:
Focus and Imagine Feeling It

We've all had moments when we've wanted to lose a few pounds. And I'll assume that you, like me, have learned the same thing I have: If you want to lose weight, sure, you can "think" yourself thin in a way, by mentally fighting your cravings and choosing the benefits of kale and lentils over fried chicken. But at some point, if you *really* want to see results, you're going to have to take it one step further: You have to get on that treadmill, hold those planks and do those reps. Because the more of your whole *body* you put into it, the more weight loss you get out of it, plain and simple. Well, focusing on love is similar. You'll definitely get somewhere if you only think about your half-orange, but you'll meet him faster if you put your whole body into it.

I physically changed my body when I thought about the orange I wanted, and there are two main parts to the process: how you smile and how you breathe. I'll tell you how to do both to create an orange buzz in your body that feels as good as when you're in love.

THE ORANGE SMILE

The smile you're going to learn is called the Duchenne smile, named for the nineteenth-century French neurologist Guillaume Duchenne, and it is considered the most "real" smile we make. Through a system called FACS (the Facial Action Coding System), the Duchenne smile has been found to have one major difference from the "real" smile and a "fake" one: While both smiles involve tugging at the zygomatic major muscle on either side of the mouth, which pulls the cheeks up, the "real" smile also contracts a second muscle, the lower half of the orbicularis oculi, up at the temples on either side of your eyes, which narrows the eyes in combination with the bulging of your cheeks.

Think about it: If you were asked to say "Cheese!" with the largest smile you could muster, you would most likely contract that first set of muscles around your mouth into a big cartoon grin. But your gut feels nothing. Now, try this: While you are doing that big fake grin, fake a laugh, exhaling while you do it, and see if you can activate the muscles tugging at your crow's feet. It should sort of make your ears wiggle. This smile, which activates both of those muscles, is the one that rings true to your brain as "real" and genuine, and the only one that will help create the orange buzz you want.

Make yourself laugh out loud if you have to, to get your smile going. This is the essence of Laughter Clubs, which were first formed in Mumbai, India, in the mid-'90s, but can now be found in other parts of the world. It's okay if you're forcing it at first, because it sets the wheels of emotion *in* motion. That's because the happiness/smile connection goes both ways: Research shows that not only does being happy make you smile, but the act of smiling *engages* the smile muscles, which sends signals to the brain of a person in a happy moment, thus *creating* happy feelings.

One study done by German researchers (Strack, F., Martin, L., and Stepper, S.) had participants view cartoons while holding a pen in three ways. One group clenched a pen between their teeth—inadvertently causing them to make facial movements similar to a smile. Another group pursed a pen in their lips, causing their facial muscles to mimic a pout. A third group held the pen in their hand. The participants who were already "smiling" with the pen in their teeth rated the cartoons they viewed to be much funnier than the other two groups did; though the participants didn't realize it, the muscles in their face were actually sending their brains a message that they were smiling and therefore happier, which made the cartoons seem funnier. Respected research psychologist Robert Zajonc, Ph.D., a former professor of psychology at Stanford, discovered that the effect of contracting facial muscles in a smile alters blood flow to the brain, which alters your mood. (He got his volunteers to "smile" by having them repeat the vowel sounds of a long "e.") Interestingly, Zajonc found that the act of forcing the facial muscles into a smile actually *reduces* blood flow to the nearby blood vessels, cooling the blood, which then reduces the temperature of the area of the brain that regulates emotion. I know that's an earful, but I want you to understand that smiling is no small gesture. Whether you're doing it naturally or forcing a smile onto your face, you are altering the state of your brain and inducing a positive emotional state when you really need one! Fake it 'til you make it. It can change your life.

Rebecca McCormick, a travel writer, celloist, and ordained minister from Hot Springs, Arkansas, hadn't had a date in six years when she decided she was ready for her big love. So she made her own version of a Big Love List on a piece of torn-out spiral notebook. She asked for a relationship full of integrity and compassion; for someone who treated children, waitresses, and taxi drivers with respect; and for someone who had the depth of a song-writer or poet. Every morning, Rebecca kept the same routine. "I would go into the bathroom, put on all my makeup, look into the mirror, and read the list out loud to myself. Then, still looking at myself in the mirror, I'd smile and say, 'I wonder if he's going to show up today!' she explains, with the warmest Arkansas accent. Her smile came naturally, Rebecca says, because she was just so excited about the prospect of meeting her other half. "It's like anything you want to do, like going on vacation—if you're looking forward to doing it, the anticipation is energizing!" Then she'd put the list away and go about her business. "I wasn't officially looking," says Rebecca. The plan was, like mine, to let her love land in her lap.

Six months later, on her way into a business meeting, Rebecca got stuck in the pouring rain with no umbrella. After shaking herself off in the office lobby, she ran into a man wearing a hard hat and jeans named Myron. He asked for her number and called two weeks later while she was panting in the middle of some crunches on her living room floor. Myron said, "I'm not sure whether you're dating anyone or not, but . . ."

"Are you kiddin'?" blurted Rebecca, "I haven't had a date in six years!"

Myron laughed along with her, and made a joke or two himself that led Rebecca to feel comfortable enough to add another item from the universal "Don't say it!" list: "My mother would *love* you," she told him, singing the word love.

Their first date one warm June evening went so well, Myron and Rebecca each admitted "feeling like teenagers," so the date lasted six hours longer than it should have. He proposed four months later, and the following March, they were married. That was eight years ago, and "it still feels as if we're honeymooning!" she says. And yes, she got what she asked for on her list. He's a warm, loving man who treats everyone he meets with great respect. But the most fun of all, says Rebecca, is that "he's a goofy poet who writes me love notes with toothpaste on the bathroom mirror"—the same mirror she used to smile into alone.

THE ORANGE BREATH

I don't know about you, but when I'm in the middle of an email triage—zipping off quick replies to the most time-sensitive queries before I hit the fun ones—I'll notice I haven't breathed in four messages. Sure, the air's coming in somehow, but it's like breathing through a cocktail straw compared to full, fresh lungs full of air. Well, the stress of life sometimes stops your breathing, too. The next time you're rushing to work or soldiering through your grocery list at the market, stop for a second and see if you've been breathing while you do it. In fact, check your breath right now: Were you breathing? And if so, how deeply? Sometimes you may notice you haven't inhaled deeply in hours. Well, you're going to work on that by doing an orange breath.

An orange breath is one of those healthy, deep breaths that takes seconds to complete as it fills up your lungs and expands your whole torso. Specially, it's like a diaphragmatic breath. Instead of the small, shallow breaths your body naturally takes on its own, this one feels like a two-part inhalation process: First, you fill your lungs up with air so that the area just beneath your lower rib cage expands; then, continue to inhale so that your chest rises up and out as well. When I took an orange breath, my stomach puffed out and my chest puffed up, which pulled my shoulders back and my chin up, and made me feel more open overall. It's the big, intentional breath you might take while raising your arms up above your head for a yoga mountain pose. If you find you have trouble taking a deep breath, "blow out all your air completely, which forces you to take a big inhalation," suggests psychologist Rick Hanson, Ph.D. Once you get good at this full orange breath, you can do it while you walk, while you drive, and while you sit in the waiting room at the dentist's office.

The orange breath pulls more oxygen into your body, and, because it is not the breath you take most naturally, focusing on it is beautifully calming. Inhale a round, bursting breath like an oversized orange, full of hope and positivity; then, slowly exhale all your stress, and all your dating doubts. Inhale that you are alive and vibrant and about to have a big, blossoming love in your life, then slowly exhale with satisfaction and relief that you *will*. For me, about two or three of these breaths in a row would completely change my state of mind in about fifteen seconds.

Like the smile/happiness continuum that goes both ways, so does the diaphragmatic breath/calmness continuum. If you are stressed out (i.e., a tiger is chasing you and you must run for your life), you're going to breathe quickly or hold your breath in panic; on the other hand, if you are breathing slowly and deeply, this signals to your brain that you are obviously *not* being chased by a tiger, which causes your body to calm down and relax. And that's the state of mind you want to be in when you focus on your orange seed: calm, relaxed, and happy.

COMBINE THEM TO CREATE THE ORANGE BUZZ

You're going to combine your orange smile and your orange breath to create a buzz within your body as you think about how great it's going to feel when you meet your half-orange. This gorgeous hum of positive energy is what I call the orange buzz.

I've heard this buzz you're aiming for explained in a few ways, and one I really like is how author Elizabeth Gilbert explains in *Eat, Pray, Love* what she learned from a Balinese medicine man: *Make your liver smile.* You want to feel like the very center of your body is smiling, from the core of your being. I find that if I actually picture trying to make my liver smile, I feel lighter and brighter—and wouldn't you know, a little smile sneaks up onto my face at the same time. If you can make your body and soul smile from the inside out, you're doing it right. And for those of you who are in tune with feeling surges of serotonin in your body, that's what you're aiming for: these small bursts of serotonin will communicate to your brain and connect to the positive thoughts, thus attracting exactly what you want. If you get the orange buzz going, you are effectively changing the activity in your brain, the response of your body, and the energy within and around you.

Neuroscientist Richard Davidson, Ph.D., professor of psychology and psychiatry at the University of Wisconsin-Madison famously discovered that one area of the brain—the left prefrontal cortex—increases in activity during meditation, especially when practiced by Tibetan monks, and this brain activity leads to an increase in optimism and feelings of well-being. In a sense, you will aim to approach this magical place of utter calmness, focused thought, and feeling of contentment.

For Rebecca, her smile in the mirror combined with her own voice reciting her Big Love List created a buzz in the heart of her belly. "When I hear myself say things," she says, "it's like programming my brain what to expect." She's right. Literally. We now know how the emotional brain works, and this *is* like programming your brain. "And once you tie the emotions and the heart in, that's how it comes!" says Rebecca. "It's a process. It's like a seed—you plant it, but you don't expect it to grow tomorrow. There's a waiting period. But instead of passively waiting, I said it out loud and started getting excited for it!" That excitement and that anticipation *is* the orange buzz. And your goal is to find your own way of calling it up. Smile and breathe. Breathe and smile. Look in a mirror or close your eyes. Find your own way to get your orange buzz going for a good fifteen seconds so it gives a good watering to your orange seed. "Don't let your attention skitter off to something else," writes psychologist Rick Hanson, Ph.D. of positive thoughts in *Buddha's Brain*. "Focus on your emotions and body sensations . . . focusing on these rewards increases dopamine release, which makes it easier to keep giving the experience your attention, and strengthens its neural associations in implicit memory."

Nadine, the editor in New York, found her buzz by doing a "water on the nightstand" trick. Here's how it works. "Every night before bed, fill a big glass with water," explains Nadine. "Just before you go to sleep, sip half the glass and feel what it would be like to have the relationship you want. While you drink the water, you live in the moment as if you are already in love."

Nadine advises: "Don't give the love you want a form: He's not white or Indian or black or a man or a woman, even. Just feel how you're going to feel when you're in a loving relationship. Drink it in." In the morning, reach back over to the nightstand and drink the other half of the glass of water while doing the same thing. For Nadine, the act of forcing herself to imagine her dream relationship every night and every morning had a profound effect on how she felt about herself. She had the orange buzz.

"Before the water trick," says Nadine, "I was focused on the fact that I was forty years old and thinking, *I'm never going to get married.* But suddenly, in the morning, I would go to work, and I'd be in a fantastic mood. I spent the morning being in love. I did this every day faithfully. I was in such a great place, I started getting picked up in the street! I got picked up in a cab once, too. And when I was in Watermill for the weekend, a dude picked me up on the beach. I mean, I was forty years old in a bathing suit, but because I'm putting out this vibe that I'm a friendly, nice person, he was into me." It doesn't compare to the best meeting of all: Nadine met her half-orange six months later.

The reason for the water trick success is two-fold. First, it's a scheduled moment of focus, a time to give your orange seed its fifteen seconds. Second, when you do it at night, you're taking advantage of being better able to absorb positive suggestions due to the hypnagogic effect of your coming sleep. "By holding something in your awareness for fifteen to thirty seconds, you are helping those brain neurons connect with each other and setting up your brain to review things while you sleep," says Hanson. "During sleep, your brain will consolidate what it's learned and create deep storage of the information." And you know how it works from there: the stronger those positive neuronal connections, the easier it will be for you to create your orange buzz, the more optimistic you will feel, and the more positive energy you will send out.

Some women have taken this "buzz" to an—*ahem*—whole new level with something else you can pull out of the nightstand. I should warn you:

Those with virgin ears might want to skip this part, but the brave should carry on, because it can enhance your whole state of being. A woman I'll call Gwen has been scouring the singles scene and getting depressed for quite some time because she desperately wants a guy to "get" her. She admitted that one evening, while she was feeling a little randy and had no partner to get busy with, she thought about what she wanted in a man while she pleasured herself (yep, she means *really* pleasure yourself, until you create an orgasm), and she recommends trying it. As you lay there in complete peace, do what Gwen did: Focus on the waves and warm feelings that are washing over your body, and think about how being with the right guy will make you feel just as wonderful. Though she hasn't met her right guy yet, her ritual makes her feel more content than she's *ever* felt about finding love. The wants–meets–pleasure trick does work: I know another woman (she wishes to remain anonymous, too . . . I guess I can see why) who performed her own variation on this, and she met her husband *two weeks later.*

While this technique might be a bit much for some women, it makes perfect sense to me. These women were taking their happiness into their own, well, hands. And while they were focused on their dream relationships, they created an orange buzz of pure joy within their bodies. It's like Pavlov: Your mind and body learn to connect thoughts of your dream relationship with happy feelings within your body. Physiologically, there's another reason this works: Dr. Daniel Amen has found in his SPECT brain scans that orgasm significantly decreases deep limbic system activity—basically, cooling off the emotional brain and calming you down. Sex with a partner, found Dr. Amen, also creates a bonding effect for women, due to the neurochemical changes set off within your emotional brain (there again, the proof that "casual" sex really isn't). So the way I see it, sex with yourself while thinking about the partner you *want* can create a bonding effect with your dream relationship. Once the two of you are intertwined, it will be hard to settle for anything less!

CREATE A LOVE-VISUALIZATION

You've heard about positive visualization: the practice of creating an image in your mind's eye of a positive result you would like to see happen, and then visually walking yourself straight toward it. It's a therapeutic tool practiced by executives, athletes, performers, and plenty more working to achieve their dream—and visualization *works*. What do they call Bill Gates and Steve Jobs? They were *visionaries*, people who saw a future in which everyone had a personal computer, even though that world didn't yet exist. Albert Einstein, Christopher Columbus, and Martin Luther King, Jr., also saw a future that didn't yet exist. Yet they still did everything they could to make their visions a reality, and they succeeded. It's the *vision* they all had that made a difference, so we're going to take a page from the successful person's book of secrets.

Laura Wilkinson is an Olympic gold medalist in the ten-meter platform dive, and she credits the mental practice of visualization (in times she wasn't physically practicing) for her success. "I've had such a great experience with visualization," Laura told *Women's Health* magazine in 2008. "It helps you know your dives, so when you get up to do them it's as though you've done them that many more times. Everybody at the Olympic level is in great shape and has great dives. But it's all about who can do them when it counts. Visualization, at least for me, gets me to that point. When I first tried to visualize diving, I couldn't make myself go into the water straight. I couldn't do it all. It takes practice, just like diving does. I just had to be patient enough to practice it."

Don't you want to do the same for love? You can. Here's why it works: The brain and nervous system cannot distinguish the *thinking* about an action from the *doing* of that action. The same way your motor skills can create new neuronal pathways in the brain that make you better and better (with, say, a tennis swing), simply imagining yourself doing those very same things will, in essence, have a similar effect.

In the early '90s, Alvaro Pascual-Leone, Professor of Neurology at Harvard Medical School, conducted a number of experiments mapping how the brain learns a new skill. One involved two groups of people who had never studied piano. He taught both how to play a sequence of notes, showing them which fingers to move and letting them hear which notes were played. Then, he had them practice for two hours a day for five days. One group practiced physically by playing the music with their fingers. The second group practiced "mentally" by imagining themselves playing the sequence and imagining the notes that would result. The result? By the end of the five days, the students who practiced mentally were as accurate as the ones who used their fingers, and the scans of their brains showed similar changes in the brain maps for both groups! More recently, researchers at Texas A&M's College of Medicine conducted a 2007 study about the benefits of mental rehearsal for medical students learning venipuncture (the act of drawing blood from a vein). After a demonstration of the skills and thirty minutes of physical practice, one group of students were allowed thirty more minutes of physical practice, while another group of students received a thirty-minute session of guided imagery. (A third group had no practice at all.) The result of this study was similar to Pascual-Leone's: Those who practiced mentally did as well as those who practiced physically—and both did better than the group who didn't practice at all.

Once again, it's that neuroplasticity at work when you practice mental visualization on a regular basis, using the power of your mind to change your brain. "Learning physically alters the brain," writes Jeffrey Shwartz, M.D., in *The Mind and the Brain*. He says, citing work by psychologist William James, "As neuronal pathways are repeatedly engaged . . . those pathways become deeper, wider, stronger, like ruts in a well-traveled country road." And that's what dating optimism can do with your brain when you think about the relationship you want. By visualizing and feeling a future that is full of all the positive emotions you *want* to experience in your dream relationship, you will be strengthening the positive neuronal connections you already have when you think about love, creating new connections, and maybe even unmasking buried pathways of positive associations you've had about love in the past.

If, for example, some of the Spanish you learned in high school starts coming back to you the minute you pass through customs in Mexico, that's an example of unmasking buried pathways—and you can do the same with your dating optimism. Your neuronal pathways can be connected again with the hopeful feelings you used to have about love so that a life of warmth and happiness and affection seems to roll out of your body every single day. Remember, you want the synapses of those old thoughts you have about relationships—that you'll never get one, that love may pass you by, that you'll descend into old age all alone—weaken and wither like frayed string. And when you think about love from now on, bring positive feelings with it, and allow this new view of your future change your mind and your brain for good.

Like Laura Wilkinson said, it takes practice to get good at visualization. But the more you use your love-visualization, the better you'll get at imagining yourself as a loved, hugged, appreciated, and adored woman. The feeling of being loved will become so second nature to you, your connection with your half-orange will come naturally, because you've been practicing for your relationship all along!

Now, it might seem easier to visualize yourself doing something concrete like Laura Wilkinson did—diving into the water at the perfect angle. It's a purely mechanical, physical act that you have seen others do with your own eyes in the Olympics. But finding your half-orange is something you *haven't* done, so how in the world can visualize *that*, right?

Baloney. Have you seen a young couple pawing at each other on the subway platform? An elderly couple holding hands in the park? Or even good friends of yours who gaze into their boyfriend's eyes in a way that made you want to crawl into a ball and cry with jealousy? Well, I've seen it. And so have you. Which means you *can* visualize it. All you need to do is replace those images of other women in love with images of yourself, and picture winning in love: Visualize smiling together on a park bench or cooking a sexy dessert together in the kitchen while sharing a bottle of red wine.

You can also use love-visualizations to quell possible dating pitfalls. If you get anxious or tongue-tied when you meet cute guys, create a visualization to prepare yourself next time. Picture what usually goes wrong (say, using self-deprecating remarks when a man inquires who you are: "Oh, I'm nobody, I'm just Julia's friend."). Then, have the imaginary man ask again, and this time, picture yourself relaxing, smiling, waiting a beat, and then looking that cute guy in the eyes and speaking from your confident heart. ("I'm Julia's friend. Nice to meet you. How do you know her?") The more you can practice your love-visualizations, the stronger and more well-tread those neuronal pathways will get, turning your love-visualization into second nature in your brain, your body, and your heart. Of *course* you'll be confident the next time you talk to a cute guy. And of *course* you'll be sitting on a park bench smiling at your half-orange. Because you're mentally training yourself to become the woman now who you want to be in your great relationship later. Once again, your thoughts are changing your brain, which is changing your body, which is altering how you see the world and what you attract. It *works.*

Numerous doctors, psychologists, and neuroscientists are using the powerful role of thoughts to heal the body. Back in the early '90s, journalist Bill Moyers investigated the field of psychoneuroimmunology in his PBS series and book *Healing and the Mind*. In it, he interviewed doctors, scientists, and neurobiologists who have helped patients manipulate vital energy with their minds to improve, and in some cases eliminate, chronic neurologic and muscular diseases. Using visualization to imagine a healthy body can *turn* the body into a healthy one. And using visualization to imagine yourself as a happy, confident, gorgeous, loving woman will turn you into that woman right now. Once again, you will be dressing from the inside out. You will *become* one half of the orange you want to find.

Now that you know how it works, let's create a love-visualization of your dream relationship. Pull some ideas from your Big Love List about what you want to feel in your dream relationship in the future. Then, the next time you're stuck in line at the drugstore, pull up an image, focus on it for fifteen seconds or more, and feel stronger and brighter about it the rest of the day. The more vivid and detailed the better, because the more you "see" it, the more powerfully you'll feel it.

Let's start with the image of a Saturday ten years from now. Follow along by filling in your own ideal responses to the options I provide so you can imagine your relationship alive and well in a particular surrounding.

It's a random Saturday, ten years from now. You have *met* your half-orange, and at this point, he's in your life, by your side, loving you like you've never been loved.

Where are you? Take a minute to picture your surroundings. Do you live in a little house with a green lawn in the backyard? A modern apartment? Some other home of your dreams? Where is your half-orange right now? Is he on his way home with takeout for dinner, or working on the gutter on the side of the house? Or maybe he's outdoors playing with your two kids?

What are doing tonight for fun? Staying in to snuggle while you watch a movie? Playing Jenga? Going out for burgers with another couple?

What will you do when you wake up tomorrow? Go for a run together? Or sleep in and have sex all day because even now, ten years later, you still can't get enough of each other?

Live in the image for a moment and fill in new details each time you do it. Having an image like this is like fertilizer for your dream relationship, which is why I call it "feeding the orange seed." When you truly feel those warm, happy, positive, optimistic feelings about your other half, you give your seed a better chance to grow.

From here on out, I'll give you some reminders to concentrate on the orange you want. You can do it for fifteen seconds at a stoplight, or while riding the elevator up to your office, but definitely do it. Because the key to making dating optimism work is that your desire *must* be something you focus on regularly: every day, or even every few hours if you're up for it. This way, over time, you will change the neuronal pathways in your brain related to your search for love. More and more, instead of seeing marriage and kids as a futile goal that brings you down emotionally, you will equate love with the amazing one you're about to find, and you'll emanate with positive feelings. Your dating optimism will become like a cartoon fresh-baked-pie scent, one that wafts out windows and into the noses of people passing by. The stronger it is, the more easily your half-orange will be able to trace it right back to you.

I know it can be hard to make it a part of your daily life. These "Feed the Seed" reminders will help you practice focusing on your orange, so that by the end of this book, it will have become second nature to you. And that is precisely what will make it work.

MAKE A DREAM ORANGE BOARD

Let's take your visualization to the next level by providing you with a literal picture you can look at every day that represents what you're looking for in a relationship. For me, that involved making a relationship "Dream Board"— a poster full of images I cut out from magazines that represented what I wanted in my orange.

Here's why it works: It turns out, our subconscious minds respond most to *visual* cues, which is what's behind the "subliminal perception" research used by advertisers and marketers who plaster billboards with subliminal emotional cues that affect our choices ("Why, yes, I am a courageous being who might value the opportunity to 'Do the Dew.'") Create your own visual reminder of emotional cues about what you want.

I admit, I was wary of making a Dream Board at first. My friend Todd had told me about a friend of his who'd made one years earlier to great success. I said I'd be open to it, but I really had no plans to do it on my own. Then, one rainy weekend, Todd walked into our beach house balancing three oversized pieces of fluorescent Oak tag from the stationery store, along with glue sticks, an extra pair of scissors, and a bag full of magazines for himself, Yvonne, and me. It all felt a bit *Blues Clues* looking at the preschool supplies sitting on the table. But once we put some music on the iPod, opened a bottle of wine, and gave ourselves up to the task, it ended up being a rewarding, fun project that reaped rewards far exceeding the skills needed to do it.

So what do you clip out for your Dream Board?

First, cut out images of couples interacting in ways that you'd like to: curling up in bed, holding hands, relaxing side-by-side on the beach, riding bikes, jumping in the air, paddling a kayak, kissing, hugging, toasting glasses, or cradling a baby together.

Next, look for photos that represent experiences you want to have *with* your half-orange: maybe you cut out a sailboat, a hiking path, a lobster meal, a mouth singing, an airplane, two tennis racquets, a bottle of champagne, running shoes, or a museum.

Also, you might find images that represent how you want your half-orange to treat you. Maybe you find an image of a man handing a woman tea. Or a man cooking at home. Or a man's eyes appearing soft and sensitive, like he's really listening to you. Or a man holding a wrapped gift (say, a little blue box?). Seeing images like this might help remind you that the guys you've been texting who can't seem to find free time for you before midnight . . . well, they probably won't be making you tea or listening intently as you talk about your family anytime soon.

When it comes to cutting out images of guys, try to avoid cutting out men solely because they *physically* look like the man you think you should be with—i.e., don't cut out four dudes with Patrick Dempsey hair because you want to date a dark-haired man, or a guy in an expensive suit because you want someone with a certain style. Remember, you're no longer using those physical descriptions to recognize your other half. From now on, you're using your heart as your eyes and focusing on how you want to *feel* with the right guy. But you can certainly cut out images that represent how the right guy might make you feel: a man in cycling gear who reminds you of health, a guy in a private jet who reminds you of travel and adventure. The goal is to give yourself a visual image of how you want to feel, but not to confine yourself with his physical likeness.

You can also cut out scenes that symbolize how you want to feel beside your partner in your life together. For instance, a field with a breeze bending over the wildflowers might represent how open and free you want to feel with your half-orange. Maybe you cut out a bright green herb garden, for how healthy you want to be. Maybe a shot of the rushing Colorado river can be a symbol of how energized you want to feel, or a view of a calm blue sea can symbolize how relaxed you want to be by your partner's side.

Aside from all the visual cues on your board, cut out words or advertising taglines you like, such as "love," "healthy," "travel," "satisfied," "affection," and "The real thing." On my board, for example, I glued on terms that read, "lucky girl," "together forever," "There's no one you'd rather be with," "life," "mom," and "family."

Finally, cut out plans you have for the future. These images don't need to include a couple or a partner, but might just represent what you want in your life once you're sharing it with your other half. Maybe you cut out some cute babies that look a little like you, a Cape Cod–style house, a Jeep, and a fireplace.

I understand that maybe you're not the crafty type and, quite frankly, would rather not be. Fair enough—I hear you. Cut outs and glue sticks aren't for everyone. If you feel at all like Sarah, twenty-seven and single from Long Island—"It's not that I'm a big cynic or anything, but a 'Dream Board' is just not me"—then maybe a less-involved variation will work for you. I still want you to retain the benefit of having something on your wall that reminds you in a *visual* way of the relationship you want.

For example, you don't need to fill an entire piece of poster board. Instead, consider cutting out just a few pictures or words and sticking them on the cover of a notebook or journal, or on the cardboard that comes in some packages of photo paper. One artist I know glued pictures onto an old particle-board painting palette and leaned it on a bookshelf against the wall.

For those "No, really, you're not hearing me—I'm *not* into Dream Boards" types, maybe you would take an even smaller step: Tear out one image that speaks to you from a magazine or newspaper. Tear out a page of a J.Crew catalog of a couple lying by a pool or a shot in *Star* magazine of a pair out shopping at Target together. Just find an image that reminds you in *some* way of the feeling in your belly and soul of how you want to be in your dream relationship and post it up. That way, when you see it staring back at you from your desk or fridge, it will provide a reminder ("Oh, that's right!") to think about and focus on how you want to feel with your half-orange. Which is the point. However you follow through, do yourself a favor: Do it! Visual cues like this can have a huge benefit.

Christine Duckett, a nurse in Atlanta, Georgia, built a visual Dream Board of what she wanted. On it was a sexy cowboy, a horse, a red Mercedes, and a family. It's not that she wanted to marry a cowboy with a horse literally, she said, but she wanted a relationship with someone who had old-fashioned values and a love of the great outdoors. As for the car and the family? Yeah, she wanted those. About a year later, she was working as a bartender when a man came onto her at the bar.

"Baby, you're my next wife," the man told her in the thickest Southern accent. "He looked like a cross between Tim McGraw and Toby Keith," explains Christine, "but I had no intention of being anyone's 'next' wife!" Still, she was stunned when she heard that Sammy designed auto parts for her dream car: Mercedes Benz.

Christine found him funny, but in a friends-only, *so* not for her kind of way. But Sammy wouldn't be discouraged. A few weeks later, he stood up on a karaoke stage singing "Lookin' for Love" from *Urban Cowboy*, then announced to the room that he was in love with her. But Christine still didn't see him as romantic material. Finally, remembers Christine, Sammy offered her a deal: He said, "How about you go on a date with me, and if you don't love me in the end, I'm gone forever." She laughed: 'Pick me up at six.'"

During dinner, Christine felt strangely moved by how genuine and honest he was. And when he asked to kiss her goodnight, she let him. "He did the whole grabbing-my-face thing and it felt like on *The Brady Bunch*, with the fireworks?" says Christine. "Afterward, I ran into my apartment, started crying, and told my roommate, 'I'm getting married!'" She and Sammy were engaged four weeks later and got married within the year.

For their first wedding anniversary, Sammy bought her—what else—a red Mercedes. And two years after that, a man walked into his car dealership and offered to sell him a horse farm, which Sammy bought. As for that family, Christine and Sammy also have two kids, ages 6 and 7, which doubting doctors had said was close to impossible, even after reversing Sammy's vasectomy. Doctors gave them a 2 percent chance of conceiving, and said it could take years; thirty-one year old Christine was pregnant three months later. "I don't listen to doubt," says Christine. "I refuse to speak about anything that's not an intention of what I want. I'll find you twenty reasons why the things I want can happen!" Well, everything Christine put on her Dream Board certainly did, and with that kind of certainty and visuals to help back it up, the same can happen for you.

Oh, and Anne Violette, the writer and wedding photographer who grew up in Maine, *drew* her ideal man on a 30 x 40 inch canvas that she put up in her living room. "He had no face, because I was open to the possibilities of what he might look like," says Anne, "but he had big muscles and a Superman shirt, holding up flowers—to represent a strong yet sensitive guy." Four months later, Anne, now living in Delray Beach, Florida, went home to photograph a wedding in her home state. Out for drinks after the wedding, she struck up a conversation with a man she met who also lived in Florida. They became friends for months until finally, on their first official date, "we got lost thirty miles out of the way because he was staring at my legs!" That was a year ago, and Anne moved in with her muscular, sexy guy six months later. He dotes on her regularly and makes her gourmet dinners nearly every night— and, yes, he also brings her flowers. They are now talking about starting a family together and Anne gives credit to finding him to the optimism in her heart and the vision she laid out on that canvas. "Because of my positive outlook and what I put on my board, I met my soul mate. I wasn't in a hurry or desperate. I just drew it on the poster and then kept on with my life."

Dream Boards can even bring you things in ways you didn't expect. Mary Cornell was dating a man in her home state of Colorado when she decided to make a Dream Board about all the things she wanted out of the relationship. After a trip to Seattle, Mary and her boyfriend discussed moving there, so she cut out the Seattle Space needle and glued it on her board. She also cut out a diamond engagement ring and a cartoon of an old-fashioned maid because she hated doing housework. "I put the board in my office where I looked at it eight hours a day," she said. Sadly, though, her relationship didn't work out. "He didn't want to commit," she says. After the breakup, Mary embraced her single life and signed up for online dating. Well, one of the first people to contact her happened to be a man from Seattle. "I thought, 'Oooh, this is weird!'" she says. Even weirder: They hit it off so well, she moved up to Seattle a year later—to a home where her boyfriend already had a regular housekeeper doing the cleaning up. Two months after that, he gave her an engagement ring, and she couldn't be happier. "I found the love of my life," says Mary, "because I believed it was possible."

Building that Dream Board worked for me, too. Although I was living in a New York City pre-war walk-up apartment in the Village, I made a Dream Board full of palm trees, wide swathes of ocean, and walls covered in pink flowers. I also glued on photos of airplanes, a pregnant woman, and some cute little babies. I ended up marrying my half-orange in Mexico, on the ocean, and now live in a neighborhood full of hot pink bougainvillea flower vines. As I write this, I'm looking at two palm trees outside my office window. I don't know exactly when the pregnant woman and little babies on that board will reveal themselves, but I have all the confidence in the world—the same hope and certainty I had about love—that this will be a part of my life, too.

GIVE YOUR SEED ITS FIFTEEN MINUTES OF FAME

Now that you've planted your orange seed, you need to give your seed its fifteen minutes of fame, because like anything you're nurturing, it needs attention to grow. You don't necessarily have to do it all in one burst. It also works in little bits, like the small meals they say you should eat throughout the day. Each time you focus on your seed (in the shower, blow-drying your hair, driving to work, waiting for a meeting to start) invite fifteen seconds of your orange buzz into your body, and then, with that orange smile on your face and that orange breath awakening your body, turn to your love-visualization image for a few minutes. You can feed your orange seed anywhere, and you should.

Here's why: In this MTV, multi-tasking, CNN-news-scrolling era, we are used to having multiple thoughts piled on one another. No thought weighs that much more than another because there are too damn many of them in our minds at one moment. Our thoughts become diffused into one, flat line.

If you want love—really want it—you have to tip the scale. You have to give what you want more thought and more focus than *anything* else. You need to create a visual blip of intense thought in that one particular area of your life so the universe picks up on the fact that you want it. Remember, the world only picks up on your most intense, passionate thoughts, right? It gives you the things you give *most* of your attention to. So if you're spending five minutes a day thinking you want love, but spend six *hours* focused intently on creating a mind-blowing ad campaign for work, well, guess what the world will bring you first?

I'm not saying you should slack off your job. In fact, being good at your job will only make you feel better about yourself, which will make it easier to get your positive emotions flowing. But if you're passionately thinking about work six hours a day, you're going to have to put a hell of a lot more passion and intense thought into the love you're hoping to get, too. Psychologists have a term for this struggle, called "resource conflict." When you have two or more goals and you're pulling from the same tub of resources to reach them—in this case, asking your brain to focus on work and love—you end up with resource conflict. Trying to focus on two things at once with the same intense passion is not going to bring either goal to you any sooner. So if you want love, you need to create a salient spike in your thoughts—like a pointy blip on a hospital heart rate monitor. The universe needs to feel the tip of the scale.

Remember my friend Lily, the writer who was always able to make her career happen? I knew that part of the reason she wasn't finding her half-orange was that she was so wrapped up in publishing her novel, she didn't have an ounce of room left in her mind to focus on anything else. I assured her, "As soon as your mind is no longer in a daily laser focus on your book, you will have an endless amount of room to focus on your other half, and your half-orange will feel the sign he can waltz in any time!"

Tipping the scale is what attracted the right guy for chiropractor and workshop leader Lara Fernandez. At age twenty-eight, Lara felt she was pulling in a lot of the same guys in different bodies, "men who weren't ready for a commitment," says Lara. "There was a lot of game-playing." Not up for the games, she went on what she called "A Dating Diet." "I didn't do *any* dating," she says. "I dated myself!" Some nights, she loved her life. And on others, she admits, "I was really lonely. I'd think, *I'm such a loser, I'm home by myself on a Saturday night.*" To help in her process, she decided to make a list of what kind of relationship she wanted. Lara, for her part, wanted a best friend, someone she could communicate with about everything. Slowly, after adding items like this over time, her Big Love List grew to twelve long pages.

But the most important thing about her list wasn't how long it was. It's that she didn't put it away in a drawer and forget about it. Instead, Lara tipped the scales. "It was right next to my bed, and I looked at it every day," she says. "Every few weeks, I'd add things. And sometimes I'd repeat the important things. If it's important, I think it has to rise in priority like that." Lara felt that to really get what she wanted, she had to focus every day on finding love. "If you're like, 'Whenever he comes, whatever, no big deal,' it doesn't work. You have to say, 'This is important!' I was an athlete preparing for a triathlon. *That* kind of important, that kind of commitment."

And the more she focused on her list, the more she felt like she was going to get what she wanted. "It started feeling inevitable," says Lara. Turns out, it was. Two years later, she and Johnny met on Match.com. "Within three weeks, we knew. And within three months, we were pregnant and thrilled." They are now nine years into their marriage, with an eight-year-old daughter, Isabelle, and Johnny is the most communicative man Lara has ever known—so much that they are now doing workshops in the San Francisco Bay Area, helping other couples find love. And if you want love badly enough, do what Lara did and make it important enough to give your orange seed its fifteen minutes.

GET YOUR MOMENTUM GOING

Your goal is to feed your orange seed and get in a great place as often as possible—where you feel a momentum going, where the future looks gorgeous, and where your optimism is going full throttle. If you have a hard time manifesting those feelings out of thin air, use what you already know gets you in a great mood. The idea is like popping the clutch in a stalled car. Now, I know most of us drive automatics these days, but you may have heard how this works in an emergency with a standard one: If you can't start the car from a still position, you get some momentum going first and pop the clutch while you're already moving. Well, you can get your dating optimism started like this your own way.

One fallback that always puts me in a great mood is music (Daft Punk's "One More Time" and Beyoncé's "Crazy in Love" both got my positivity pumping at the time). I'd play those and be in an *instant* good mood, ripe for thinking and focusing on something I wanted. Another fallback? Calling my

> ### FEED THE SEED!
>
> ### The Thinking-of-You Image
>
> You see something that reminds you of your half-orange, and you want to let him know you're thinking of him. Do you text him, "Just thinking of you, xoxo" and get a cute message back? Do you call him and say, "I love you?" Do you leave him a funny or sexy message on his voicemail? And what about him? Will he call you or email you a funny video when he thinks about you during the day? Feel how wonderful it is that however you contact one another, you can do it straight from your heart without second-guessing a thing. He *wants* to hear from you, whether he's in a meeting or waiting for you in the other room. And you want to hear from him. Your love is in perfect balance.

best friend and hairdresser Todd and telling him I needed some compliments. "You're the prettiest girl in the whole world!" he'd say. "What man *wouldn't* want a woman with hair as slammin' as yours?" Soon, I'd be laughing so hard (and feeling so darn pretty) I was ready to pop the clutch and keep my momentum going by thinking about the love I wanted. Try it: Find something that puts you in a great mood first, and then use the buzz you have going to feed your orange seed. Maybe it's doing yoga or eating a peach. Maybe it's taking a drive up a winding road with the windows down and the heat on. Or maybe it's hitting a comedy club that gets you laughing, cools down your emotional brain, and reminds you how happy you deserve to feel with your other half.

GET IN A GRATEFUL PLACE

When I was still single and searching for love, I had a ritual every time I started to feel bad about it. I would ask myself, "Woman, what would your twelve-year-old self think of the life you have now?" Go ahead, ask yourself the same thing: Would your younger self be proud of you? Hell yeah she would! Now list your own reasons why. Have you found something you're good at and enjoy doing—whether it's a paying job or a rewarding hobby? Do you offer your time to help people who have less than you? Have you overcome a difficult period in your life? Are you stronger or braver or wiser than you were as a child?

For me, I spent so much time walking from place to place in New York, I used that as an opportunity to focus on all I was grateful for: I was grateful that I lived in a city I loved. That I was healthy enough to walk on my two legs. That I was on my way to meet friends who really cared about me. That the sun was shining. That I had enough money to live on my own.

Then I would smile and breathe in my gratefulness until I felt my liver smiling—until my gut was buzzing with happy, positive feelings. That moment—just when my body was doing its orange buzz—I would feed my orange seed: *Soon, I'll have someone walking beside me on days like this. I know I'm going to meet a guy who will be as happy and grateful as I am to have such a wonderful life.*

Sometimes it takes looking at things from a new angle, which is what Tal Ben-Shahar, Ph.D., taught as a Harvard professor in his Positive Psychology lectures. In one lecture, he showed students a picture of geometric shapes and asked them to count how many shapes there were. Then, after joking that he doesn't actually know the answer, he asks them what *time* it was on the clock in the picture. Gee, well they weren't looking for the time. "I focused you on something entirely different," Ben-Shahar said to his students, "another part of reality." The fact is, there are different ways to look at your life. Lately, you may have been focusing on the hole of what you don't have in your life: a romantic partner. But that's all you've seen: the *lack* of it— the glass half-empty. But there is another part of reality in your very same story, and that's what is *in* that half-glass. Happiness is relative. There must be some things in your life you're grateful for, thankful for, and thrilled about, whether it be in work, in friendships, in your free time, your hobbies, or your health. Focusing on those things will help you feel positive about your life again, which will create positive energy in your body, which will, once again, attract positive things.

GO, DOROTHY, TO YOUR HAPPIEST PLACE

Here's a trick I used every weekend that generated immense benefits: I would go to my favorite place, the place that made me feel my happiest and calmest and most in love with my life. The way I saw it, if I was searching for my partner in crime—my other half in love—he would love my favorite place as much as I did.

If you live for skiing, can you imagine your other half absolutely hating the snow? And if you love the beach, can you imagine your other half despising the sunshine? My mother, a therapist, pointed out that, sure, you could give up your favorite place in the world for the right person, "but that's a lot to give up. That means leaving a part of yourself behind." You could make it work. But it doesn't sound like a *dream* relationship, does it?

For me, my favorite place is Ditch Plains Beach in Montauk, where I've rented a little beach bungalow for a decade known as Captain Dusty's. The house is a run-down, one-level shack with wood-paneled '70s walls, bright orange living room curtains, fisherman lamps on every table, and a washing machine that floats in a foot of basement water when it rains . . . but I adore it. About four months into my love experiment, I started heading to Ditch early in the morning for coffee, with my dating optimism in mind. I'd stand barefoot on the beach, watching the water sparkle in the sun like diamond facets. Then I'd take in the sea air with a full orange breath, and listen to the waves crashing onto the shore. I was happiest looking out at the water, feeling free, where the possibilities of life seem as endless as the horizon. It was in that moment that I would feed my orange seed: I'd picture my life partner standing there beside me, feeling our toes get buried in waves of tidal sand, loving the beach as much as I did.

Of course, your dream might look and feel and smell entirely different, so think about your favorite place in the world. Is it a picnic table at your favorite Texas barbecue joint? A botanical garden? A baseball game? On a bench overlooking a canyon that takes your breath away? At your parents' house? A dive bar? A five-star restaurant with a champagne cocktail in your hand? Wherever that place is, *go* there. Literally. Sit or stand in your favorite place and begin to work up a good dose of your orange buzz: Breathe in and smile a deep, true smile as you imagine how lucky you are to have found a person so miraculously, perfectly right for you that he loves this place as much as you do.

For Erin, thirty-two, a high school teacher in Michigan, the place she loved most was Spain. Yep, the whole big fat country. After a brief trip there with her high school Spanish class, Erin went to Granada for seven months during college. Spain brightened her, she says. It made her feel alive.

It was a stark contrast to how she sometimes felt at home, years into a relationship with a man she'd begun dating at age fifteen. "He was a wonderful person, but we had nothing in common but our community, and we didn't share the same views or goals in life," says Erin. First and most important, her husband wanted children, and Erin didn't. And second, her husband didn't share her love of travel. "When I made extra money or worked overtime, I wanted to use the money to travel. He preferred to stay home. I know people told me that marriage is about sacrifice, but how much sacrifice is okay? How much is okay until you're not being yourselves?"

After Erin's husband had proposed when she was twenty-three, she went back to Spain to visit friends; there, she met a man named Ignacio, who made her stomach flip and her mind whir. "It is so incredibly corny, but I felt like the earth moved. I wondered, 'Why am I feeling this way about someone I don't know when I'm about to get married?'" She chalked it up to cold feet—nerves building into butterflies over her approaching wedding. And then she went home and got married. Four years later, Erin and her husband divorced. Despite the inevitably difficult ordeal of separation, they were able to remain amiable. "He even said to me, 'If you're still living here in town in five years, I'll kick you out!'" she remembers. Erin had a few relationships with some great guys over the next few years, "but I told everyone that I wouldn't get married again unless a guy really knocked my socks off."

So rather than focusing on dating, Erin focused on figuring out who she was. And one way she did this was by going back to her favorite place in the world. "I traveled throughout different parts of Spain a half-dozen times while I was single." Spain gave her the orange buzz without her even trying. And every trip only cemented in her that living and teaching in her small Michigan town wasn't enough for her anymore. "I recently looked back in my journal and saw that I had written, 'I'm going to stick it out one more year here. I know I'm supposed to do something else, and I know it's coming soon.'"

Hmmm, now that sounds a lot like a woman who is positively focusing her energy on bringing something new into her life, doesn't it? Like someone who is so optimistic about her future, and so open to opportunity, that it couldn't help but come to her? It's like my sister asking for the opportunity to travel. And my story of asking for love. In fact, another part of Erin's story resonates as well—the fact that she *told* everyone what her plan entailed.

"A year earlier, I'd told all my colleagues that I would let my teaching certificate run out at the end of its two years as a way to force myself to try something new," says Erin, laughing at the memory of their reactions. "They thought I was crazy! But I kept saying, 'I just know the universe has something else out there, and I don't know what it is.' I couldn't explain it. I just felt really positive about it and figured I'd sit and wait to see what presented itself."

Erin, if you'll notice, didn't know *how* she was going to bring about something new. She just knew that she wanted a change more than anything, and she was determined to make her dreams happen. It occurred to her at one point to pack up and move to Spain for good, but the logistics—quitting her job, getting a visa, starting a new life—seemed too daunting.

Almost four years into her single life, Erin was teaching a book to her Spanish students. The story featured a character named Nacho. One of the students commented that surely no one *really* called themselves Nacho, did they? "I told my students, 'Actually, I knew an Ignacio once, and he liked being called Nacho.'" She went home thinking about him. Wow, Ignacio. She hadn't seen him in seven long years.

Then, less than twenty-four hours later, Erin got an email from who else? *Ignacio.* "My heart dropped into my stomach!" she says, as she read his email that simply said, *"I doubt you still use this email address, but I just thought I would check."*

Things from there went quickly for Erin and Ignacio, who talked on the phone for four to five hours a day. "We reconnected when we were focused on our lives and ourselves, and—*bam!*—along comes a person you desperately want to be with." They had endless amounts in common, from their love of travel to their relationship histories to their political and religious views. And after a knee-knocking conversation in which Erin admitted she didn't want children, Ignacio exhaled with relief; No, he said, he didn't want them either. Four months later in Northern Spain, Ignacio proposed. A year later, Erin moved to Logrono, La Rioja, where she is now marketing herself as a private English tutor and teacher and finalizing the details of their wedding. "He's *mi media naranja*," Erin says in the most natural-sounding Spanish. He's her half-orange.

"If someone had told me a year ago that I was going to move for a man, I would have laughed," Erin says, hearing her story through her own ears now. "I never thought I'd do anything for a man. Though, really," she adds, "I'm not doing this for a man, I'm doing this for me. I feel like my whole life has been preparing me to be his wife. I know it sounds like a cheesy love song, but that's how I feel. Trust me, I used to roll my eyes at that romantic movie crap, but now I know exactly what they mean. I feel like I have finally stopped seeking and am simply living."

Before she left for Spain, Erin emailed her ex-husband to tell him it was just shy of that five-year-mark he said he'd hold her to. Just another example of the coincidences piling up, of Erin getting everything she asked for. It was so surely meant to be.

GO WHERE YOU ARE LOVED

When you're not going to a place that you do love, here's another great trick: Go to the place where you *feel* loved. This is what I started doing a few weeks into my experiment, and here's why: More and more, when I'd go to a club or a bar, the people around me in those crowded rooms weren't in harmony with the happy, positive buzz I was feeling in my gut. So, instead, I hung out with my best friends, my sister, and my parents, who made me feel the most loved of all—their love *did* match the warmth in my heart. Just like getting a car rolling so you can pop the clutch, go where you are loved and whirl around in it.

There's something deeper going on here, and it has to do with the emotional memories you're storing in your brain. When we're kids, we may think only sticks and stones can break our bones, but the fact is, whether we realize it consciously or not, words and actions are sticking to us all the time, ultimately affecting what we think of ourselves. If you grow up being told you're overweight and lazy again and again, guess what you'll start believing? And if

BEWARE OF THE RISING MAN

There are plenty of guys out there who aren't necessarily good for you, of course. But when you're on the path of dating optimism and asking for big things on your Big Love List, one specific type of man is likely to pop up, so I want you to keep your eyes peeled. This type seems to rise above the rest in looks, power or prestige—all the things that seem great on paper. The problem is that this type of man feels his star is shining so bright, he believes his own value is higher than yours and still rising. Thus, he's what I call a Rising Man.

The Rising Man has expensive clothes on his back and fierce determination in his eyes as he rises up the ladder to career domination, feeling more confident with every step up that he deserves a gorgeous, wealthy or well-known babe on his arm to join him at the top. If you're not beautiful or rich or well-connected enough to feed into his long-term plan to ascend to an above-average existence, you need not apply. Sure, he's happy to charm you and bask in the adoration you give him that he feels he deserves, but as soon as he gets what he needs from you—succeeding in the challenge of getting you, or a night of booty, or maybe an introduction to someone who can help his career—he'll move on to the next best thing.

To be honest, it's hard to resist guys like this at first. After all, they're successful, they're confident, and the way they make us work for their attention is enticing. But once you learn to tune into your the guys you meet say you're not girlfriend material each and every time, guess what you'll start to agree with? You have the amygdala to thank for that, of course, that little part of your brain we talked about that holds onto emotional memories for you. Before I began using my dating optimism, I just thought it was important to be out there—out on dates, out at parties with potentially new people, out meeting friends who might have single friends. But when I didn't succeed in snaring someone's attention, it worked against me. If I approached a cute guy at a party and got blown off, I'd feel worse about myself than I did *before* I went out.

I remember one night I went to a trendy bar for an event and ran into a former colleague. He was standing with a handsome television newscaster he knew, and when I walked over to greet my friend, he introduced us.

new tools to recognize your half-orange—seeing with your heart, not your eyes—you'll be able to filter out men like this more quickly. Because if a Rising Man isn't making you feel special and loved and worthy, he's not worth pursuing! And if a Rising Man is so concerned with pursuing his own career instead of making sure you're happy as a team, he's not right for you! With a Rising Man, all those feelings you've been focusing on—feeling loved, feeling appreciated, feeling gorgeous, feeling smart—tend to be pushed to the side while he makes himself feel all those things.

My wise mom Katherine says she and fellow therapists might refer to guys like this as narcissistic. "And he's probably very insecure, by the way," she says. "Despite his good looks, his narcissism makes him want to be sure he is surrounded with what he thinks will make him look good . . . a blonde, or someone famous, because he needs to look good or people won't be impressed by him." I wish I knew that at the time. But I did know one thing for sure: When I was around men who overlooked me and made me feel small, I didn't feel the orange buzz or an uplifting zing of hope. I felt like a loser. We attract what we think about, focus on and feel, right? So I realized that if I wasn't feeling positive about myself, then I wasn't helping my single situation one bit! And if you ever find yourself in situations like this, you're not doing yourself any favors, either.

"Hi," I said, putting out my hand. "I'm Amy."

The newscaster nodded at me with a "Hey," but *ignored* my hand.

My male friend generously tried to break the ice. "Amy's a writer," he said, "we used to work together."

"Really?" the newscaster asked, looking sideways.

"Yeah," I said. "It was about, what, five years ago? We used to work on—"

"Heyyyy!" The newscaster was hooting at another guy walking past, then clutched his hand and yanked him in for a hug. The newscaster turned back around and smiled at us. "Yeah. Sorry?" he said, looking just over my shoulder to see who else he could find to talk to.

"Oh, no . . . it's okay," I said, "I was just, you know, saying how we used to—"

"Well, hi, beautiful!" the newscaster then shouted to an approaching blonde. He kissed her boldly, gazed in her eyes, and took her hand.

I gave up trying to talk to him after that, but I felt like a dope. I had walked into that party feeling good about myself, and I was giddy to see the friendly face of my old colleague—but I ended up crushed by his friend's rude behavior, which I couldn't help but take personally. Of course I knew, deep down, that the diss wasn't about me—I mean, the guy didn't even take five seconds to try to get to know me. But I was still rejected, and it made me feel like crap. And if you put yourself in situations like that enough, the thoughts reflecting back at you—"You're not worth paying attention to you," "You're boring," "You're not cute enough," "You don't seem very interesting," and "I'd rather talk to all of these other women instead of you"—start to stick.

Use the sticking factor in your favor. Go to where you are loved and appreciated, and let those feelings flow over you. Being loved is the best drug in the world, and after you roll around in it for a while, you'll realize you're becoming more and more a person to be loved. You're putting on the costume, zipping it up, and becoming that woman more and more every day—once again, you're dressing the part from the inside out. Don't wait to love and be loved by your half-orange—bask in that love now.

It's the same principle at work with some women who are struggling with infertility. I'm sure you've heard stories about women who can't get pregnant, yet the minute they adopt a child, a positive line shows up on the pee stick. Similar things happen, I've learned, when you adopt a dog. My friend Carrie was with her husband for four years when they decided to start trying to have kids. Aside from her age (she was in her mid-thirties) and the fact that this was their first child, there was an even bigger barrier in their path: They were focusing all their thoughts on negative things like miscarriages and failure and how "it's too late," and how "we should have done this sooner," and how "now we'll probably never have a baby."

Obviously there was plenty going on in their bodies physiologically that they'll never be able to know for sure. But emotionally, what I witnessed was the concept of pessimistic magnetism in full form. They were

FEED THE SEED

The Family-and-Friends Image

You and your half-orange are gathered with the people who mean the most to you. Are you at a family gathering at your Aunt's house, sitting Indian-style on the floor? Or are you with your very best friends, dunking pita chips into spinach dip and laughing about the old times? Where is your half-orange? Is he sitting right next to you with his arm around your shoulder? Is he in the kitchen pouring you a drink with an extra lime, just the way you like it? How is he interacting with these people you love? Is he gabbing along? Telling his own stories? Engaging quietly with the relative or friend beside him? How amazing is it that the partner you've found fits so well into a group that means so much to you? They love him, he loves them, and seeing it all makes you love him that much more.

getting what they gave all their attention to: failure. I know the experience was heartbreaking because they wanted a child with all the energy in their souls, but as they started doing hormone injections every night, they still couldn't help saying with every prick how much they worried they would "fail." They made two attempts at IVF; both failed.

During their efforts, friends encouraged the pair to get a dog, and when the second IVF attempt didn't work, they agreed: At least they could have something to love and take their minds off the struggle. Well, from the minute they brought home little Major, their entire demeanor changed. Suddenly they were cuddling their puppy saying, "I love you, munchkin!" and "We'll take care of you, little one!" It wasn't five months later that Carrie got pregnant on her own, and I'm convinced it was because by getting a dog to love, they created the feelings they wanted to feel in the future with a child. They were dressing the part as parents from the inside out. While acting as parents to this little puppy, they became the positive, calm, happy future parents they aspired to be.

So become the person you want to become by going where you are loved. I know you may have doubts about stepping off the trail of the husband hunt. I sure did. I thought, "Maybe this is crazy" more than a few times when my mother and I would be picking plants from the nursery. "I mean, am I really going to meet the love of my life while I'm hanging out with my mom?" I'd wonder aloud. The fact is, your job is to want that great relationship, that's all; it's not your job to figure out how to make it happen. Just go where you are loved and bask in the feelings.

Added bonus? The more you surround yourself with the feeling of being loved, the more your lovability quotient will go up. (Yep, it's a real thing!) According to psychologist Suzanne Segerstrom, Ph.D., the lovability quotient officially measures your own expectation that you will be found lovable within a romantic relationship; but as far as I'm concerned, *any* kind of healthy love or relationship can add to your lovability quotient. And when that goes up, people (dates, guys, your half-orange) will begin to see you in just that way—as a totally, incredibly lovable woman.

SMELL AND TASTE YOUR ORANGE

We learn faster the more senses we use, and since you're training your emotional brain to learn what it feels like to be in a healthy relationship, the more senses you use, the better. Smell in particular goes a very long way, as smell goes directly to the emotional center of the brain—that deep limbic system—where it is processed along with your emotions. No wonder smells and feelings seem so strongly connected. (I still can't smell Drakkar Noir without thinking fondly of boys from high school.) So now, use scents to your advantage to link the emotions you want to feel in your dream orange with what makes you feel positive and happy now.

When you're walking outdoors, inhale the smell of fresh cut grass or the warm scent of pine trees while you imagine how wonderful it will be to explore the outdoors together. When you're standing in line at Starbucks, inhale, smile, and use the scent of coffee to imagine sitting in bed next to your partner drinking a hot cup on a Saturday morning. When you're out eating spicy food with your friends, imagine how great it will be to find someone who'll try new things with you, bite for bite. Or maybe you're calmed by a particular aroma of incense; in that case, take in the comforting scent while you focus on the relationship you want.

I used to spend time in cafés with my laptop, and while I sipped my latte, I would smile, inhale, and love-visualize what it was going to be like when my other half walked into the café to meet me after a writing session. I'd look out the window and imagine hearing him order a latte for himself. Then, I'd think about what details I might tell him about my day—and because this was a man who loved me to bits for who I *really* was, I'd think about all the minor details that other men I'd dated would just groan about.

You know, like, "So, honey, I think I might have to bite the bullet and get those cute flats at J. Crew after all," I'd tell him. "I mean, I've wanted them since I first saw them in the catalog, and I didn't buy them for three months, but they *just* went on sale and my size is selling out, and I think I'd regret it if I didn't get them, because I just know I'll wear them all the time . . . "

And then I really *would* smile in that café because I knew the man who loved me would say, "Well, then stop all that yammerin', baby, let's go get 'em!"

MAKE ROOM IN YOUR HOME AND HEART

One day, while researching a story on Feng Shui, I read about how single women who want a relationship should have couple art in their home. Huh?

I glanced around my apartment to see what I had hanging, and, though I'd never thought twice about it, my own art surprised me: I had framed black and white photographs of the dancer Martha Graham, and the opera singer Maria Callas in the hallway. A full-page photograph of Brigitte Bardot from *Paris Match* magazine that I'd bought at an antique market in Nice was hanging in my bedroom. And in the living room I'd hung a painting my sister did of a nude female reading in bed. I'd put these women up because I was motivated by their strong faces and their enticing lives. But still: four pieces of solo women! And in the kitchen I had one gorgeous wine glass I'd splurged on. There it was again, *el numero uno*. Inspiring? Hell, yeah. Putting me in the twosome frame of mind? Not so much.

So I thought about some of my favorite couples in art, and went to work. At a poster store, I bought a movie image from *A Man and a Woman*, a French film I'd liked with a title I loved, and I placed it right next to my couch; there, I'd look at that couple kissing as a reminder that I wanted someone to kiss me that way. Just like a couple you might paste on your Dream Board, the art or knick-knacks in your house send similar subliminal emotional messages to you. Whether it's an image of two animals in the

African desert, or two lovers kissing in Times Square, perhaps it's worth adding something to your home that sings *duo*. If it doesn't look or feel like there's room for your other half to squeeze into your life, *make* room.

SEE THE SWEETNESS IN OTHER COUPLES

From now on, I'd like you to see other couples in love with pleasurable thoughts instead of jealous ones. Trust me, I know this is a toughie! When my single self saw couples cuddling, instead of being happy for them, I'd feel sad, a little jealous, and would sometimes verge on bitter: What did those people have that I didn't? Why would that guy be dating her instead of me? It seemed so unfair. The whole world seemed to be coupled up but me. What was I doing wrong?

If you're wondering the same thing, you're not doing anything wrong. But you are focusing on the wrong *thing*. If positive energy attracts positive things, then it's time you started looking at those couples in a positive way. Instead of seeing those couples as Superman's Kryptonite, see them as Popeye's spinach. Let couples *feed* you. Instead of feeling sad or jealous when you see a happy pair doing what *you* want to do with your half-orange, see it as proof that the love you want exists. It is possible.

If you see a couple cuddling on a park bench outside of the museum, look at them and engage your dream orange: Close your eyes, breathe deeply, smile, and imagine yourself on that same bench, next to your half-orange.

If you see a couple at an airport rolling matching luggage wearing Panama hats and big grins, engage your dream orange: Picture yourself with your other half, buying iced teas before you board a plane together.

If you see a photograph of a cute celebrity couple in *Us Weekly*, typing on their Blackberries and kissing—a busy couple who still make it work side by side—look at them and engage your dream: This can be you.

If you see a couple playing on a blanket with a little baby, nuzzling each other, engage the vision of your dream orange: Smile as you picture yourself on that same blanket, on that same grass, with a cute, happy baby.

When Laura Rubinstein, a life and business coach from San Diego, embarked on a journey to meet her other half, she fed her soft side with the sweetness she saw in other couples. "I started seeking out couples to hang out with, to have them rub off on me. It was nurturing for me. I'd look at couples on the street and they were an affirmation to me that if I'm seeing them, the possibility of having a deeply rewarding relationship was inevitable. I knew in my bones that if they had it, I would have it, too." Laura also spent time with like-minded women who were pro-relationship, rather than toxic single women who were trying to keep her that way.

Another thing Laura did was take the "dress the part" angle of her life seriously. Since she wanted to be romantic in a relationship, Laura says, "I said, I'm going to live a romantic life right now. I bought myself flowers, and cooked nice dinners for myself and my friends." Her feeling was, "If you want to be cuddled, nurtured, and romantically involved, let go of the struggle. Put nurture back to the top of the list and watch how the world shifts around you."

A year later, Laura met a handsome friend of a friend at lunch, though she got the vibe that he wasn't looking for a relationship; it turns out, he had just signed divorce papers that day. Eight months later, however, he joined her yoga class. Laura felt he was into her, but was confident that if it was supposed to happen with him, it would naturally. She was through "pining for men," says Laura. "It's wasteful energy. We're the egg and they're the sperm, so they come after us, right? The egg is supposed to take care of itself, be comfortable in its environment and then pick the right one when he comes!" So Laura dated other men and "trusted that if it was going to happen with him, it would." Nine months later, he finally asked her for coffee. They dated for two years and have now been married for seven—and they have the most nurturing, romantic, loving relationship Laura's ever had. In fact, she and her husband may *be* one of those couples you see being affectionate in public from which you may take strength. Use what you see in others to affirm that want you want does exist. If they can have it, you can too!

WISH FOR IT, EVERY TIME

The best way to feed your seed regularly is to remind yourself to think about it and feel what you want as often as possible. One great way to do that? I used all those chances at "wishes" to feed my orange seed by closing my eyes, smiling, breathing in a big breath, and thinking, "I wish for my half-orange to come find me soon."

For example, when you see a shooting star, this is your wish. When you lose an eyelash and someone tells you to blow, this is your wish. When you blow out candles, this is your wish. For me, when the clock said 11:11, this was my wish. I even changed my online banking password to . . . well, let's just say it was relationship-related. The point is this: If you are living, wishing, walking, breathing, and smiling with an orange buzz, you will feel better than ever. Those around you will be astounded at how happy, calm, and content you've become. And your half-orange? He'll love you for it most of all.

SCREW PROTECTING YOUR HEART— GET YOUR HOPES UP!

A few months into my experiment, I met a guy who worked at an events production company who was cute and insanely driven. We went for drinks, and within a half-hour, I was picturing our future together, full of nights out socializing with artists and designers and weekend jaunts to Miami and L.A. But when my friends asked me about him, instead of building him up, I built him *down*.

"He's great," I said, "but I mean, he works so much, he's probably a workaholic. But whatever, I don't care, he seems like kind of a player anyway. And from certain angles, he's not even that cute . . . "

My game was, if I told my friends that I didn't care if he called me back, well, then if he *didn't* call me back, I could pretend I didn't care. I was just so used to self-protecting that I never dared put myself out there in the first place. And I did it with the guys themselves, too: I would say I wasn't looking for something serious so that in case the guy said *he* wasn't looking for something serious, I could save face and avoid appearing hurt. In reality, I'll never know who was or wasn't looking for something more back then, because I was usually the first to jump the gun.

The truth was, I *did* care if the event producer did or didn't call me back, and I did care if he was or wasn't looking for something serious with me. But I figured, what good would it do to tell the world that my hopes had been crushed again and that I was feeling more and more unwanted? I preferred my pretending to their pity. In short, I worked very hard to keep my hopes down. It was a ridiculous backwards system—and it didn't work!

In the end, the events producer did turn out to be a bit of a player and was too busy planning events to make time to see or call me anyway. (Funny, though, he found plenty of time to text me late at night.) In essence, he was a case of the Rising Man.

"See?" I told my friends. "He was just what I thought, no big deal, I expected it."

But the truth was, I was disappointed. I wanted to be the one girl who turned him around, who made monogamy worth it for him. And when I realized how I really felt, I flipped it once and for all. What was I *doing*? I was a dating optimist now; I had to be positive and hopeful about my future. I had to build my hopes up, not build them down!

From then on, I was honest about what I wanted, and I told my friends how much I *hoped* things would work out with my dates. Sure, I still got the Heisman here and there (what my friends and I call it when a guy is running away from you with his palm out to block you—just like the football trophy pose), and it was embarrassing because my friends now *knew* I was disappointed. But I was being my authentic self, and with every failure I turned the dial up on my hopes even higher.

You need to stop protecting yourself, guarding your heart and preparing for the worst so you won't be let down. It doesn't work! If you want love, you can't just reveal the little peephole in your heart to people. You have to open the whole door. And if you get hurt, so be it. But let's be honest: you'll be hurt if you get turned down at the peephole, too. You'll be hurt a little less, sure, but you'll still be hurt.

You know what that self-protection is really all about? The emotional brain. "The pain of rejection creates an automatic self-protective reflex that's driven by the emotional brain or limbic system," says Peter Pearson, Ph.D. "It's not a conscious choice, it's an automatic reflex. When you've been disappointed repeatedly, you stop wanting, in an attempt to spare yourself the pain of getting your hopes up and being disappointed again. It's a reflex to stop wanting. It's not sabotage, it's self-protection." Pearson says it's in our blood. "We're hard-wired to connect, but we're also hard-wired to be self-protective when we feel threatened. That is *not* a problem to solve," he says. "It's a condition to live with and dance with. We will never ever resolve that once and for all. Honor both parts."

I'm sure there was a time in childhood when you had high hopes for a big relationship or a wedding. Yet over the years, after being let down by one bad apple of a man or one bad string of dates, you've decided it's easier to expect less than to go through the pain of not getting more. Lowering our hopes is our effort to avoid being hurt, but you know what else it is? It's *lying* to yourself. You're pretending that you don't want something you really, truly want. And that's crazy!

You deserve it all. And to get it all, you have to gamble it all. You need to reclaim the sense of hope you had in childhood. Get your hopes up. Get 'em way, way up. **You have to rediscover the scary world of hope if you want true love.** You want it all and you deserve it all, remember? So start hoping in a huge way. It's the only way the universe knows how big a box to put your gift in.

Here's an example that might seem odd, but you know who I admire? The women who go on *The Bachelor* and *The Bachelorette*. No, it's not the sanest or easiest way to meet a man, what with television cameras hovering over your dates, microphones clipped under your shirt, and, perhaps, a harem of women mackin' on your man. But the women who end up on air have something positively special going for them: All of them are saying—not just to themselves, but to the bachelor they want and to millions of viewers— "I want a relationship. I want to find true love." To that I say, good for them!

What they also learn as they carry on is that in order to go full throttle with the plan, they have to throw all caution to the wind, drop the protective "I'm so tough" armor, and show their vulnerable sides. Of course the minute many of them do that, they end up in that dang limo crying their way home, but I have yet to see a woman on the reunion show saying she regrets giving love a shot. Opening your heart up is good for you. Sure, when you have big hopes and it doesn't work out, you feel big, awful, achey disappointment. But if you're looking for a big love, go big or go home.

I used to say I wasn't the diamond ring kind of girl—or a wedding kind of girl, for that matter. In fact, just before I began using dating optimism to bring me my true love, I remember walking into a jewelry store as a favor for a friend to price a diamond ring she and her husband wanted. I'll never forget standing in that store, surveying the diamonds under the glass counter. I felt so out of place because I couldn't see myself in there . . . ever. I really, truly, couldn't even *imagine* it.

A year later, when Todd, Yvonne, and I were making our Dream Boards, Yvonne started gluing oodles of diamond photographs on hers. When she asked why I didn't have diamonds on my board, I gave my usual speech that went something like this: "Yeah, I'm not the diamond ring kind of girl. I don't really care about having a wedding and all that stuff. I just want to be with someone I love, no bells and whistles. I'd be happy wearing a paper clip around my finger if a man gave it to me."

She rolled her eyes. "It's a *Dream* Board," said Yvonne, reminding me what I had been telling her. "Isn't that what you said? It's not what you *think* you'll get, but everything you could *imagine* getting in your wildest dreams. That's the point." She was right. I wasn't taking my own advice. I wasn't supposed to settle for "just" enough. I was supposed to dream big and hope for the best.

Suddenly the diamonds I saw in those magazine ads started looking pretty good. *All right, sure, I'll put some on here,* I thought. And the more pages I turned, and the more I let myself go with the "dream" idea, the more I realized that, despite the cliché of it all, yeah, I kind of did want a diamond ring. Or, more honestly, I wanted someone to *want* me to *have* a diamond ring. I wanted someone to love me and adore me enough to want to give me beautiful things, whether I thought they were practical or stupid or materially unimportant or not. I wanted someone who loved me so much, he didn't care about the clichés—he wanted to give me the fairytale.

I realize *not* everyone wants that. In fact, my friend Maryellen would probably laughingly gag if she read this and then give me a wholehearted razzing about falling for those cloying diamond advertisements—not to mention the idea that a piece of jewelry is needed to display a commitment! But the fact is, no matter what opinions other people have, we need to be true to ourselves and to what we want.

I'm not saying that every woman who says, "Diamonds aren't me" is fooling herself. We're all different. I'm just admitting I realized *I* was fooling *my*self. I *did* want diamonds, but once again, I was intent on protecting myself. I wanted to make sure that just in case I never got them, no one would look at me with pity. Instead, they would look at me and think, "She doesn't have a diamond ring, but that's only because she's not the diamond kind of girl! She's so cool. I wish I cared as little for all that material stuff as she does."

Let yourself hope for your dreams. Stop letting little things like life and practicality get in your way. After Yvonne's speech, I put all sorts of over-the-top things on that dream board: a trip to Africa, a convertible car, a sub-Zero fridge, and plenty more. I also found three beautiful engagement and wedding rings I thought were just gorgeous: One was a solitaire flanked by two slightly smaller stones. The second was a plain band. The third was a band of teeny diamonds all the way around. Yvonne was right: I had to want it all and hope for the best!

A few short months later, I met my half-orange and got up the nerve to show him my Dream Board. He studied it with a seriousness that surprised me, and he even pointed out a few things he wanted, too. (Machu Picchu, make room for us.) Eight months after that, he proposed to me with a band of teeny tiny diamonds, with plans to design a solitaire flanked by two smaller stones with my great-grandmother's stone. I was stunned at the moment, of course, but I was also blown away by the choice of the ring itself. "Did you ask my sister about this? My friends? How did you know I wanted a band of teeny diamonds?"

He answered with all the obviousness in the world. "It was on your Dream Board," he replied. Hope, I'm saying, is a powerful tool.

PHASE FIVE:

Nurture Your Sapling to Bloom: Live a Happy Life

DON'T MAKE DATING A PRIORITY

B elieve it or not, as a dating optimist, dating is actually not the priority.

"Wait . . . what? It isn't?"

No, it isn't. Remember how I told you your job isn't to figure out how to get what you want? Your job is just to want it. And the problem with dating is it can sometimes become such a chore that you lose track of the big picture: You forget to feed your orange seed. I'm not saying you shouldn't date. Just that you should only date if it's fun. If you're having a blast meeting new people, if you love the surprise factor built into blind dates and your body is buzzing with positive energy as you do it, date away!

However, if going out to singles events, creating an online dating profile, or agreeing to go on a blind date makes you bristle with negative emotions, stop doing it. Dragging yourself out to date is like forcing yourself to eat a piece of stale molasses fruitcake because you've decided you're going to enjoy life by ordering more desserts.

"See how much I'm living it up? I'm eating a huge piece of cake," you'd say

"This is—gulp—just awesome." All those calories, all that effort, you're not even enjoying. You probably can't even conceive of g this ludicrous, right? If you're not enjoying it, don't do it!

I remember being out with my girlfriends one night and feeling less relaxed than they looked. Then I was smacked with the truth: Of course they were sitting back relaxed—they were already attached! If I wanted love, I thought, anxiously, I need to be out there, on the singles scene, doing something toward my goal.

As Suzanne Segerstrom, Ph.D., has discovered in her research, optimists are "doers." They're the ones persisting at tasks because they're confident their hard work will result in a positive outcome if they stick with it. But I want to lift the weight off your shoulders that you're not "doing" enough if you're not dating. I assure you: **By following the half-orange plan, you are doing something. Changing your thoughts is the biggest thing you can "do."** What's the most important item on your Thanksgiving turkey-day shopping list you have? The turkey. That's how important your optimism is. Changing the way you think is number one—the protein on the plate.

Remember, you want and need that orange buzz going as often as possible. Think of it like a cat's purr: The more you're purring with positive energy every single day, the more positive things you will attract, and the easier it will be for the world to respond with positive results. So if dating is making you tense, frustrated, or stressed, then it's doing the very opposite for your love life than you intend! Yes, you're out there, you're taking chances, and you're making dates, but what kind of energy are you putting out in the world? "This sucks." "I'm tired." "I don't feel like it." "I knew this wasn't going to work out." "It's hopeless." "I feel worse than I did yesterday." "This just proves there aren't any good guys out there." So what are all those thoughts going to bring you? Sucky, tired, antagonistic, hopeless love situations that are going to make you feel worse than you did yesterday. So if you start feeling dread or drearinesss about it all—or worse, you feel hopelessness or despondency coming on—abort mission!

When I got to the point where all I wanted was a relationship, I began to forsake fun with friends or family or loved ones if I felt it would take away from essential but-I-might-meet-a-guy time. I had that little beach house in Montauk I've mentioned, and I *loved* it there. The problem? My only friends out there were some gay men and a married couple. Which meant that every weekend, I had to make a choice: I could either have fun with my friends at the beach or I could stay in New York and meet a man I could marry. On the weekends that I chose Montauk, friends would say in a judging tone, "Oh, but aren't you trying to meet a man? How are you going to meet a man out *there*?" They were right, I thought. I *wasn't* meeting men out there.

One weekend, when I had to choose between a good friend's birthday clambake on the beach or a big party in Brooklyn full of single guys, I heard those voices in my head: *Aren't you trying to meet a man? How are you going to meet a man out there?* I had to look out for myself, right? I had to try to meet someone. So I skipped the clambake and hit Brooklyn. . . . where I soon assessed I had made a very wrong choice. The few single guys there weren't

> ### FEED THE SEED
>
> ## The End-of-Day Image
>
> You've just finished your work for the day. Picture how you'll meet up with your half-orange: Will he arrive home with groceries to cook dinner? Will he suggest the two of you get out of the house? How will you greet each other? Will you give each other a big kiss and say, "Hi sweetie," or will he grab you in a bear hug and say, "Aw, baby, I *missed* you." Will you talk about your day with one another over food or wine? Will you cuddle on the couch over the low hum of the television? Will you climb into bed and read? Feel how comfortable you are with one another, wanting the same thing: to decompress and relax with the one person who feels most like home.

doing it for me at all. Great, just great. That's when I learned my own golden rule: Dating *isn't* the goal. Doing what makes you happy *is.* Here's why:

Why do you date? To meet someone.

Why do you want to meet someone? To have a relationship and maybe start a family with someone.

Why do you want a relationship and a family with someone? To be happy.

Well, instead of *waiting* to become the happiest person by dating and meeting someone, start being the happiest person you can be now.

MAKE A BEELINE FOR THE HAPPY

Don't aim for just any happiness. Aim for what will make your soul sing and your body buzz with warm feelings, which will send your desire for love into the universe like a bright, beautiful beacon. To get there, do what makes you deeply happy and get to a place where your heart and soul are satisfied, gratified, and full, where you feel like you're truly the best version of yourself. This type of happiness has a name: *eudaimonia.* In essence, eudaimonia (a term that dates back to Plato and Aristotle) is a state of happiness in which you feel like your most authentic and satiated self. And positive psychologist Martin Seligman, Ph.D., in his book *Authentic Happiness,* identifies two ways to approach it: through "pleasures" or "gratifications."

Pleasures have strong sensory elements to them, and can be considered "raw" thrills: ecstasy, orgasm, comfort. That may mean going out for one big wild night of tequila shots or ordering a pile of smothered chicken, mac 'n' cheese, and cornbread from your favorite soul food restaurant. It can mean trawling through Twitter for an hour, catching up on your favorite celebrities' Tweets, or for some women, picking up a hot guy for one night of "I've still got it" sex. In seeking ways to take your mind off your singleness, "pleasures" are often the go-to moves because they bring results quickly. And when you need a short-term momentary pick me up, by all means, dive in. But you may find that when the pleasure is over, you feel nearly as empty as you did before.

The latter and more satisfying way to reach eudaimonia is through "gratifications." Rather than aiming for a burst of immediate pleasure, you can immerse yourself in "gratifications" over time, and they stick with you afterward, for hours, days—maybe longer. These are activities like reading a good book, embarking on a four-hour Martha Stewart recipe, writing poetry, knitting, editing a family video on your computer, going for a long bike ride, or gardening. But you don't have to go gratification alone. It could also mean playing a game of tennis, delving into a deep conversation with one of your best friends, or volunteering at a cancer walk. Social scientist Mihaly Csikszentmihalyi refers to activities like this as moments you feel "flow," when you find yourself in a zone of complete absorption, doing exactly what you want and never wanting it to end—a feeling, again, that you are feeding the best part of yourself.

For the most part, gratifications are activities attached to a goal, and numerous studies have found that goals are actually what make us most happy. Richard Davidson from the University of Wisconsin has found patterns of brain activity indicating that we achieve our most positive states of mind when we are reaching toward a goal. You're single, right? So instead of using the time to wallow in depression about it, use the time to learn Photoshop or train for a marathon—something that takes advantage of your full potential and gives you a purpose with a destination in mind. (And no, the goal of finishing the *America's Next Top Model* marathon doesn't count.) If you're feeding your best, most authentic self and reaching goals large and small, the positive energy you'll create within yourself is *exactly* what will draw him to you.

Stephanie is a thirty-nine-year-old events producer raised in Chicago who spent years working in human resources for big business companies, including Disney, who brought her out to Los Angles, and Oxygen, who hired her to head up their HR department. It was a high-stress job with hours to match, and the hard line she applied to her work filtered down to her dating life.

"I became the three-date girl," says Stephanie. She didn't like going on dates with guys she knew weren't going to work out. Instead, she used her free time (the time *not* spent dragging out efforts to create chemistry) to make herself happy. The way Stephanie put it, instead of trying to find a relationship to make her happy, she made a beeline straight *for* the happy, knowing the relationship would come later. What she didn't realize was that she was making gratifying choices, building her eudaimonia.

Stephanie's biggest step toward happiness was adopting a dog, Lulu, which changed her the same way it changed my friend Carrie and her husband (who'd been failing at IVF). Pets do this: They tap into the softer part of you and make you appreciate the loving and adorable parts of life more than the difficult, dramatic ones. Sounds like just what you want in love, too, right?

Well, Stephanie got lost in watching her dog leap through the dog park, roll around on the rug at home, and learn how to sit and shake and heel. Taking Lulu for walks was like going on small getaways for Stephanie, where she met all her neighbors and realized, more and more, she would be happy whether she met someone or not. Life was good! And it was during those nights walking the dog that Stephanie realized that's how she wanted to feel *all* the time. In fact, she became so addicted to her change in her attitude, she made a literal change in her life.

Oxygen announced it was closing down its Los Angeles offices, and Stephanie was told she'd have to come to New York to keep her job. But as exciting as New York can be, it was the exact opposite of what Stephanie wanted at the time. So she quit her big cushy job and applied for a job as a waitress in a hotel restaurant.

Six months later, Stephanie approached a cute coworker she'd noticed months before, and she and Jason spent the day together as friends. Though she didn't see romance in the air, she accepted a date with him a week later. A few hours into the night, says Stephanie, "I got a weird feeling in my stomach. I just knew he was The One. I just knew." They began dating immediately, got married, and Stephanie is now a senior event manager for the very hotel she started working for. Two and a half years into their marriage, Stephanie just gave birth to their first child, Olivia, and couldn't imagine starting her family with a better man.

Your eudaimonia may come in different ways. For Parker, our resident dating pessimist, it comes in challenging herself to do interesting things in life. "Every week, I try to do one thing that makes me uncomfortable," she says. Whether it's taking a writing class or hitting a new music event, Parker is determined to keep at it. She feels that not only does she benefit, but so do the people with whom she interacts. "Worst case scenario," says an accomplished Parker, "doing new stuff is what makes you attractive to other people, right? If you're not reading things and going places, what's making *you* interesting? If you're looking for someone who has a sense of adventure, well, what are *you* doing that shows *you* have a sense of adventure? Guys are looking for something too, and if you're not bringing something to the table, why would they like you? Even if you don't cook, telling people you meet about your cooking disaster is a lot more interesting than saying you don't try at all."

CARPE DATE 'EM

In the movie *Something's Gotta Give*, Harry (Jack Nicholson) asks Erica (Diane Keaton) if she wants to go for a walk along the beach. She stammers and wavers until finally he says, "It's just a walk, Erica, not a marriage proposal." Try to think of your dates the same way. It's not a long-term commitment . . . it's a latte. So take it one step at a time. You know that saying *carpe diem*—in Latin it means seize the day? Instead of carpe diem, carpe date 'em. Look at your nights out like a dater's approach to the 12 Steps: Take it one *date* at a time. I know I struggled with it.

It was about this time when I went on a date with a guy I met online. His picture was draped in shadows, but it was artsy and cool, which I found super attractive. Walking toward the restaurant to meet him, I thought, *Ooh, maybe we can have this cool, creative life together, where he can make art and I write.* When I was a block away, I started getting excited. *Oh, I hope this one is it! I hope I feel instant sparks!* Then I saw him sitting there outside the restaurant. My heart sank. He was skinny, pale and had the fuzzy chin beard of a ninth-grader. I was so disappointed I wanted to turn around and go home.

Then it hit me: I believed that I was drawing the love of my life closer to me through optimistic magnetism, and I was certain I would meet my match. If that was true, then I had to trust there was a good reason for this date. *I know my dream relationship is coming,* I said to myself, *and the world works in mysterious ways. Everything is leading me there, including this date.* Then I sat down and started to enjoy the date for what it was: a step on the journey toward meeting my half-orange. It wasn't a marriage proposal, it was a glass of wine on warm night. *Smile and relax,* I told myself. *Enjoy the ride.*

KEEP THINGS LOOKING UP ... LITERALLY

Here's something else that will help you keep your optimism up, along with your mood: Take a walk and look up. I know it may sound rudimentary, but the key here is the *physicality* of it. Once again, instead of just engaging your mind, you are bringing your whole body into it, because how you hold your body will actually affect your mind and energy. So tilt your chin back so your line of sight is either looking ahead boldly or up toward the sky when you're outside. Chuck, a successful commercial and film editor, pointed this out to me, saying, "You can't be depressed when you walk, especially if you look up. Because when you're looking up, you're engaged with the world."

Chuck says he learned this years ago from acting coach George Morrison (Morrison is famous for teaching Gene Hackman, Stanley Tucci and Edie Falco, among others). And he's right, because looking up is about striving for better, for brighter, for more. We look up to people we admire. We look up for inspiration. And when life seems to be laying down Aces, we think, "things are really looking up!" Like the smile that goes both ways (when you're happy you smile, and if you smile, you feel happy), looking up will do the same thing: If you want things to be looking up, you yourself should be! Think about it, says Chuck. What is the stance of someone who is feeling down on themselves and depressed? Their posture is hunched, their chin is hung, and they're looking down. And what you see there is more of the same: dirt, grease, bugs, mud, cracks in the concrete. But think of the things you see when you're looking up: Birds flying free. Tree branches reaching toward the sky. The way the sun lights up the clouds in watercolor shades. Airplanes soaring at thirty-odd-thousand feet flying people home to their families or off to dream destinations.

Australian Aborigines used to do spiritual wanderings called "walkabouts," which now refer to walks on a journey of self-discovery that make you feel more connected with the earth. You can still do that today, whatever your landscape. Whether you're walking down a tree-lined suburban street, a telephone pole–lined city block, or a quiet path near your house, walking is good for your soul—as long as you're looking up while you do it. Not to mention, when you're looking up, that's a pretty good way to let cute guys see how pretty your eyes are.

Actress Becki Newton from *Ugly Betty* (she plays the wickedly hilarious receptionist) told me the story of how she met her husband when I interviewed her for *Page Six Magazine*. As a young girl she always dreamed of being on Broadway, so Becki was thrilled when she finally moved to New York City and got a job in Times Square . . . as a waitress in the Times

Square Brewery. But she was always looking up at the bright lights and theater marquees, dreaming of the day she'd make it big. One day, in the subway, she was looking up and around at the crowd when she made eye contact with a cute guy walking past her. They both smiled, and he eventually walked up to her to say hello. It turns out he was an actor starring in *The Full Monty* on Broadway, and he invited her to come see his show. She went (she, uh, liked what she saw) and the two began dating immediately. Becki believes—and so do I—that she fully attracted all of it. Not only did she get her man, Chris Diamantopoulos, but she got even closer to her Broadway dream at the same time. Soon after, she married her dream man, and got her own name in lights on TV.

Learn from Becki and look up when you go out. "The only thing you'll miss by not looking down is money on the ground," says Chuck. "But," he grins, "probably not enough to make a difference."

Don't put off doing couple-y stuff— do it now!

For a long time, I put off buying myself nice dishes for my kitchen. Why? Because I kept thinking that when I got married, I'd register for some nice ones, so why bother getting any now? I'll tell you why: Because putting off things that will bring pleasure into your daily life is doing yourself a disservice.

Look at the list you're waiting to begin, and start checking it off now: Buy yourself a queen-size mattress. Learn to surf. Or, like Stephanie did, get a pet. Because guess what? Putting off things means you're taking potential joy away from yourself. And isn't that just ridiculous? Really. You deserve to be happy right *now*—not just beginning on some vague day in the future when your true love comes along.

Parker's friends gave her a Jet Blue gift card that, for a long time, she was waiting to be part of a couple to cash. "I kept putting off using it, because I was hoping to use it with a guy," she says. But with three months left, a use-it-or-lose-it policy, and no potential date on the horizon, Parker got brave and booked a trip to Mexico, all by herself. "My biggest worry was eating alone, just having to say, 'Table for one.' But every time I got uncomfortable, I thought of my fearless friend Kim, who I wish I were more like. She traveled around the world by herself for a year, so I figured I could survive a week on the beach!" In the end, Parker relaxed, read, swam in the sea, ate *chilaquiles* in the morning, and drank Coronas with vacation pals she'd met at night. "I was really proud of myself," says Parker. "It reminded me what's out there in life, that I could be doing so much more."

Besides, someday—maybe sooner than later—your life may be very different. You may have the husband of your dreams, and the baby you desire, and you won't be able to fly off at a whim. One friend of mine jokes that when the man she married first invited her to his parents' house in Boca Raton, Florida, she rolled her eyes. "No offense," she told him, "but hanging out with your parents in Boca isn't much of a vacation." Now, with a two-year-old, they spend *every* vacation at his parents' house in Boca because it's easy and free! Some things you should do while you can. Do you want to while away your time as a single woman on the stand-by line of life, or do you want spend your time *living* it?

DO WHAT *YOU* WANT . . . NOT WHAT YOU THINK GUYS WILL BE DOING

Dating optimism is about you. *It's not about the guys.* I know it's easy to *say* you're doing something for you, while deep down, you're doing it because you think you'll meet a cute guy. Trust me, I know that trick! And that's pressure you don't need to put on yourself.

During my love experiment, I was assigned a story to spend a week trying to pick up men. One of my assignments was to take a cooking class at a kitchen store, and it had classic romantic comedy written all over it: With the "excuse" that I was working on a story, I just knew I'd end up partnered with a cute guy as we took turns stirring the sauce and catching each others' eye. Instead, I walked into the event to find three rows of plastic folding chairs facing one stove. The chairs, meanwhile, were full of a dozen middle-aged women, and one twenty-year-old engaged girl who giggled that she was trying to learn a few recipes so she could be a good wife—*not* what I wanted to hear.

Your intentions are not as secret as you think, remember. They are actual impulses of energy activating your emotional brain that affect every cell of your body. So what makes you think that if you're wandering into a tango class to try to meet someone you can get away with pretending you didn't? Do things that make *you* happy, that make your heart sing, whether or not guys have anything to do with it.

Take it from Margie, a publicist in Toronto, who had more than a few setbacks in her search for love, including one failed marriage. Well into her single days and living in New York at the time, Margie and her friend decided to enroll in an eight-week wine tasting class taught by a famous sommelier. Sure, it was partly because they thought it would be fun; but more honestly, they were thinking, "Ooh, maybe we'll meet some cute guys!" Instead, says Margie, "at the very first session, we ran into my ex-boyfriend taking the class with his new girlfriend, the woman he ended up marrying."

A few months later, Margie was drowning in work and told her boss, "I'm dying inside, I have to do something for me." So she planned a trip to France for a month to learn the language. And, again, it was for her, but she had romantic dreams in her heart. "In France, I admit, I thought I would meet my match, or at a minimum, a handsome Frenchman," says Margie. Then she laughs. "But I spent most of my time in a class full of characters like a pregnant nurse from Oslo, a Japanese man who spoke very little English, and a woman who had to learn French for a job. We all had a hilarious time, but there were definitely no suitors there for me!"

Margie doesn't regret her trip for a second, because aside from her secret quest to meet a man, she also felt empowered. "I remember being in the airport without my computer for once, and the smile on my face was ear-to-ear. It turned out to be the most delicious, wonderful experience ever." It also taught Margie a big lesson: She was going to make her choices based on what would make *her* shine—man or not. "The more I did things that made me happy, like taking trips with girlfriends, the better I felt." So when she got the idea to rent a beach house for the summer of 2005 with her girlfriends, she dove in and made it happen.

One July afternoon, between taking a walk outside and cooking dinner with her girlfriends, Daniel walked in. He was visiting from Toronto, as a guest of one of her roommates. Margie didn't pay much attention to him at first—she felt he seemed nice, but a bit plain. "He didn't look like every other guy I'd dated," she says, "the same high-powered, intellectual, commitment-phobes I went out with over and over again." But by the end of the night, Margie couldn't help but notice Daniel. "And it's a good thing I did because I totally could have missed out on the love of my life."

Daniel asked her out, and a week and a half later, he flew back into New York to take her to dinner. "As we were sitting across from each other at dinner, I thought, 'Wow, maybe we'll get married.'" They began dating immediately thereafter, flying back and forth from New York to Toronto. "It was unlike any relationship I ever had," says Margie. "Every ounce of me knew it was the real deal." By February, he proposed. By April, Margie had moved to Toronto. They set their wedding date for July, and a month before the wedding, she found out she was already pregnant! Margie and Daniel have now been married for over three years, and have a three-year-old daughter, Abigail.

"I totally believe my love story had to do with being comfortable in my own skin, and hopeful and optimistic about meeting someone," says Margie. "You have to follow your bliss."

Your goal is to be your happy, content, calm self, doing something just for you, and not with the intention of trying to snag a guy out of it. Which is exactly the same psychology at work behind the phenomenon of the Grubby Glow.

THE GRUBBY GLOW

There are two kinds of nights out on the town:

   a) The nights you plan a big night out, when you shower, you shave, you wax, you pluck, you blow out your hair, slip into your sexiest heels, and suck in your stomach so you can squeeze into your cleavage-baring, skin-hugging, make-a-guy-melt top.

   b) Those lazy nights when you haven't shaved your legs, you're still wearing the T-shirt you woke up in paired with jeans you haven't washed in weeks, and your hair is pulled into a low ponytail so people can't tell how greasy it is.

Now here's the quiz: Which night are you going to end up kissing a hot guy in a dark corner who wants to take you home to rip off your clothes and ravage you?

Annnnnnd . . . the answer is b. Like the gravitational pull of the moon that causes the tides to ebb and flow, there is a strong and as-yet-unmeasured power that pulls men toward you when you're *really* not ready for it. This, my friends, is the mysterious appeal of the Grubby Glow.

At some point in every single woman's life, you awaken to its power. As one friend of mine used to say, "I have nothing to wear to this party, but I know if I go out and blow money on something cute, I'm guaranteed not to meet anyone." And before I started using dating optimism, I would seriously debate shaving my armpits for fear of ruining my mojo—of being, as Parker calls the opposite, "groomed for doom."

The magnetizing power of the Grubby Glow is no accident. See, the nights you're over-prepped and super-primped and urgently scanning the room for a guy to appreciate it are the nights you're not believing in the certainty that your half-orange will find you no matter what. On those nights, you may be thinking, *Come on, guys, notice me! Look how hot/cute/sexy I am tonight! Don't you want to date me . . . and love me . . . then marry me?* And those thoughts are coming from a place of fearing you won't get it if you don't flaunt it. In essence, you're sending out "I need to get some tonight!" pheromones reeking of desperation and anxiety, which emanate from you like the garlic in shrimp scampi a day later. It makes your loneliness seem larger and your biological clock tick louder. And you know what happens when your biological clock ticks too loud? Men mistake it for a bomb and go running for cover.

So what about the nights you don't prep yourself, when you go out looking like your most natural self? Those are the nights you shine with confidence. On those nights, you're probably thinking, *Since I'm obviously not going to meet a guy tonight looking like this, I'll just enjoy my friends and appreciate the music.* Well, guess what energy that sends from your body? A message that you like your life. Your positive thoughts put out a positive feeling to the universe that you feel calm, content, and happy; without even realizing it, *those* are the nights that your true smile creeps up all on its own. That's the version of yourself you want to be when you're in a relationship, right? Where you feel beautiful in your skin, no matter how little makeup you're wearing? Then that's the version of yourself you should aim for. Dress from the inside out.

Erica, twenty-seven, was a teacher in Fort Lauderdale who had just gone through a breakup of a five-and-a-half-year relationship—a relationship that had involved a lot of changing who she was to keep him happy. She was just getting back into the dating game when one evening, a neighbor flagged her down. "Oh, Erica, I heard you were single," she said. "I have the perfect man for you!" She told Erica about Adam, a handsome firefighter nine years her senior, and insisted Erica let him buy her a coffee.

Adam called her soon after and they made plans to meet on a Friday afternoon. "I figured, 'If I like him and he likes me, great,'" she says, "but I was through pretending to be something different. I knew the right guy had to like me for *me*." Erica didn't wear anything special for her date, nor did she do her makeup or her hair—but she *was* wrapped in the fabric of her authentic self when she snatched her purse from her desk and headed to Starbucks as if it were any other afternoon. "I wasn't looking my best, I was just being who I am." Little did she know, the Grubby Glow was working its magic.

The minute Erica spotted Adam outside Starbucks, she felt an instant attraction, and their quick coffee lasted over two hours. One year later, on Valentine's Day, Erica moved out of her condo and into a house with Adam. "We're going to start looking for a new house together soon," she says, smiling at this part. "He says he wants to find one we can *grow* into. I like that."

I'm not suggesting that you stop showering, shaving, and waxing if you feel better about yourself when you do. What I am suggesting is you make sure you're doing those things for yourself, not for the purpose of hunting and landing a guy. *Your intentions matter.* Look and feel beautiful from within, and you'll be more attractive than anything you can wear on the outside.

Remember: If you're focusing on your dream relationship and *really* feeling what it will be like when your half-orange comes along, he'll come! He'll come whether you're showered and shaved or not. He'll come if you're dolled up at a dinner party or stuck in line for a port-a-potty. He'll show up whether you're wearing a little black dress and sexy heels, or a sweatshirt and jeans on the way to the post office. And he'll find you beautiful because he won't be drawn to you by your primping—he'll be drawn by the gorgeous energy you're sending out. Trust me, he'll barely notice the expensive dress or cheap gym outfit because he'll be so busy looking at how happy you are, thinking, *Now, that's a woman I want to come home to every night.*

SQUASH THE OLD
"UM, WHO'S GOING TO BE THERE?" LINE

Every single woman knows *exactly* the line I'm talking about. Personally, I should have been wearing a pin that said so when I was single, just to make it easier, because I was guilty of doing it so many times. The dialogue goes like this:

Friend: "Hey, I'm having some people over on Friday night. Wanna come?"

Single Girl: "Uh, maybe, I'm not sure if I can. (This is most often a lie to stall the decision. A Single Girl will always become free if a potential prospect is mentioned.)

Friend: "Okay, just let me know."

Single Girl: "Alright. Um, who's going to be there, anyway?" (This is tossed out in a casual tone that implies it doesn't matter who's going, but is actually translated as: "Are there any single guys I haven't met yet going? If not, it's a lot of hours spent doing an activity with you that, albeit fun, will waste some valuable meeting-a-guy time.")

One weekend, I got an email from an acquaintance named Rae saying she was organizing a game of touch football in the park on Sunday. Rae was single as well, so my heart soared for a minute: *Ooh, maybe she'll get some single guys there.* But I didn't want to embarrass myself and ask her who was going. Fate stepped in: An Evite arrived for the football game with fifty names on the list. Thirty of them were guys.

"Are you going to come?" Rae asked a week before.

"Um, maybe, not sure yet," I said. "I'll let you know!"

The Plan-a-Vacation Image

You and your half-orange decide that it's time to get away for a vacation, just the two of you. Where will you go? Do you already have a place in mind, like a sunny beach resort where you can lie side by side and slurp frozen drinks? Does he want to whisk you away to a city he's always wanted you to see? Or are you a couple who gets away often, in short affordable weekend trips to go camping or mountain biking for a few days? How lucky you are that the two of you are on the same page, anticipating a vacation you're both eager to take. It's just you and he traveling together, lost somewhere in the world.

See, I wasn't sure because I was busy checking the Evite to tally the guys' responses. I was waiting to see what guys like MarkB and TedH and FunnyBen would say. Eventually, the responses rolled in. MarkB said, "Trish and I are definitely there!" TedH said "The GF's away, so I'll join you!" and FunnyBen said "Add two more— Mr. and Mrs. Smith would love to come!"

Suffice it to say, I turned out to be "busy" that day and didn't go to the touch football game. And I felt like a fool for doing that. I still do. Your new modus operandi is to do what's fun, do what makes you happy, and *don't* let the guest list affect your decision. Remember, you're *going* to meet your half-orange. It doesn't matter if you spend your time shopping or playing touch football, as long as it's making you completely, totally eudaimonically happy.

THERE'S A REASON YOUR LOVE IS NOT HERE YET

The world wants you to have your half-orange. But ordering love works a bit like ordering a couch from Crate & Barrel: You can have the blue couch with the aluminum legs today; or, you can have the beige couch with the wooden legs next week; but if you want the beige couch with the aluminum legs, well, that's going to take at least 6 to 8 more weeks. That's just how it is. And unfortunately, there's no customer service department in the sky to ask when to expect your great love. But since you're thinking about what you want with all the positivity in the world, believing you will get it, and expecting it to come your way, it will. The energy you have created within and around your determination has made it certain. It just might take a minute to align those stars for you. So let go of the reins and let the world steer you and your half-orange toward each other.

Psychologist David Myers, author of *The Pursuit of Happiness*, explains that optimists feel a great sense of control about their destinies, but control alone will not make them happy nor bring them what they need. "The recipe for well being," says Myers, "is a mix of ample optimism to provide hope, a dash of pessimism to prevent complacency, and enough realism to discriminate those things we can control from those we cannot." The fact that you cannot control every detail of how and when you will meet your half-orange and who he'll be isn't just how it works, it's part of the fun! Revel in the idea that the world *will* bring your half-orange to you as soon as you're both good and ready. Remember, novelist Pam Houston wrote about how she let go of controlling what would come and agreed to have patience—and she met her big love two weeks later.

In the meantime, note the benefits of being on your own. For me, when my sister got her dream job traveling around the world with a rock band, she invited me along for visits on the ride. I snuggled up in her big free bed in places I'd never been to, like Amsterdam, the south of France, and Hawaii, and—as two single sisters with no ties at home—we spent two weeks on a road trip through New Zealand. Had I been in a committed relationship, I might not have done all that. (Three in a bed is just plain awkward … well, unless you're Samantha on *Sex and the City*.) Plus, all that traveling only cemented for me the idea that I wanted travel to be a big part of my life in my dream relationship. I wanted someone who, like me, wanted to take off on life's adventures.

Pinpoint what you've been doing as a single woman that is actually making you a better, happier, smarter, cooler, or more well-rounded woman—one even better-suited for the day your half-orange comes your way. Your single life is not time wasted and your bumpy path through bad dates and relationships is experience gained. In fact, the awful down moments are ultimately good for you—and I say this as someone who has been there, who has felt the lowest of the lows. You name the style of self-pity, I've wallowed in it. But the fact is, it's *important* to feel all that junk. Laughing and crying are just opposite sides of the same emotional coin, and to fully experience one, you have to lie in bed with the other. Like addicts who have to hit bottom to be ready to climb back out, I think the tough stuff in dating makes us stronger and wiser and gives us empathy and understanding for a partnership, as well as the ability to appreciate the love you get. You will be a better partner to your half-orange having been through the hell of dating depression. And what you're doing *right now* could simply be a part of the universe's magical plan to bring you what you want.

That's what Serena, thirty-two, learned the hard way. After three years in a relationship with her boyfriend in New York, she finally broke up with him when she realized he couldn't give her the love, attention and communication she wanted from him. On her own and unhappy in her career choice in non-profit, she moved back to her hometown, Chicago, and in with her sister, while she figured out the next step in her life. Being home reenergized her. And one day, during lunch at the Cajun place where she waited tables a couple of summers during college, she and her former coworker there had a good laugh about how funny it would be if Serena donned her apron again a decade later. "Then I realized," said Serena, "'Wait, maybe I *should* get a job here again so I can put some cash in my pocket while I figure out what to do.'"

Three days later, in between wiping down bottles of hot sauce on the lunch shift, she was questioning everything: She was having no luck with other job interviews, had no money in the bank, and most depressing at the time, had no love life. "All the guys I was meeting were players or commitment-phobes, just like my ex," says Serena. "I told my sister that I was officially *done* dating guys who weren't relationship material. I remember it clear as day. I said to her, 'I don't necessarily need to meet the love of my life, but I want to meet a *nice* guy. I want to meet someone who will remind me that great guys with good hearts are out there. For now, that's all I ask.'"

Six weeks after that, Serena was put on a night shift she'd never worked. And as she was walking across the floor, she noticed Joe, who used work at the restaurant with her a decade earlier. "Joe was the nicest guy, and it turns out, he had *also* taken up *his* old job to help pay for the photography career he was building." The coincidence was astounding, and a flicker of attraction for him shot through her. Serena and Joe went out one night, ended up on a trip to Italy for their former coworker's wedding a few weeks later, and two months after that, moved in together in Los Angeles. That was four years ago and Serena, who now works in advertising, knows that she has that crooked path to thank for leading her to the love of her live. Yes, it escorted her through a painful breakup and a humbling return to her Chicago roots, but it's exactly what she needed to appreciate Joe. "I would never have known to look for a guy like him if I hadn't gone through the other stuff," says Serena. "I had to be in that place in my life to realize that I really, truly *wanted* a nice guy—enough that I deliberately asked the world to bring me one."

Ask and you shall receive as soon as you—and your half-orange—are ready to meet. I assure you, it'll be well worth the wait.

DON'T STALK RELATIONSHIPS!

To stalk or not to stalk? And by stalk, I mean showing up at a party where you know he's going to be, wearing your sexiest shirt and your highest heels, then pretending when you see the guy who isn't calling you that—oh my God, that's *riiiiight*—you forgot was going to be there. A dating optimist never stalks a relationship. If it's going to happen, it will. If it's supposed to be this person, it will be. If it's supposed to happen today, it will. And if it's supposed to happen next week instead, well, you're going to have to let go and roll with it.

But that doesn't mean you can't have a hell of a good time as a single woman. So let's find you a gauge for your future actions: The next time you wonder if you should pursue something, push it, or stalk a potential relationship, check in with your orange seed and ask yourself this: *In your dream relationship, do you want to feel the way you do right now?*

If you feel happy, secure, confident, and maybe a little daring, then smile and go for it! Make a move. Give him a call. Write your phone number on a napkin and drop it on a table. Because maybe, as my friend Todd and I always say, "You won't regret doing it, but you might regret *not* doing it." After all, you're going to need *some* wild stories to look back on someday, right?

But if you're staring nervously at the face of your cell phone, making yourself crazy as you debate whether or not the voicemail you just left was the right mix of coy, sass, and a laid-back dash of "whatever" to get him to call you back (because, quite frankly, it's been two hours since you left it, and the night is now on its last legs) well, is *that* how you want to feel in your dream relationship? Doubting yourself? Wondering if you're as great a catch as you thought you might be? Feeling like you being "you" is just not enough?

The next time you find yourself wondering if you should pursue something or push it one step further, check in with your orange seed. It will tell you what to do.

BE YOUR FABULOUS, QUIRKY, IMPERFECT SELF

We all deserve to be loved by a partner for the same reasons our best friends love us: for being every absolute, authentic bit of ourselves. Think about it: When you're with your best friend, you're not primping in mirrors before you sit down with her or watching what you say. If you order enough Chinese food to feed five people with your best friend, you're going to want a guy who finds Chinese chow-downs just as appetizing. And if you curse like a sailor with your best friend, you certainly want a guy who finds it funny. I don't mean that you should belch your soda if that's what you do with your best friend (I mean, there's still something to be said for manners and making good impressions), but it's time to own your unique personality so your half-orange can see and love you for it.

When I finally brought my half-orange around to my best friends, you know what one of my favorite compliments was? "It's really cool," they said, "you're exactly the same around *him* as you are with us." Ah, finally. You deserve the same thing: to be your total, complete, unedited, imperfect self with your half-orange. Because really, if you already feel you're holding back or hiding parts of yourself when you're first dating, can you imagine how much effort it will be to play someone different for five more decades?

I once went to the movies on a date, and after I finished all my popcorn, my date shook his head and joked, "We should have just tied that popcorn like a feedbag around your neck!" I laughed along (and, honestly, if you saw the way I scarf popcorn, you would have laughed, too). But thinking about it later dampened me like a squirt of fake butter. I was so embarrassed, I didn't order popcorn on a date again for years, even though I go to the movies more for the popcorn than the movie itself. And so began my trend of going to movies alone so I could chow down on the extra-large popcorn combo without worrying that I was turning off my date. Once I became a dating optimist, however, I marched proudly up to the counter once again. And the man I'm with now loves me for it. The other day, when my half-orange and I were at the movies, he said, "I think I want some popcorn tonight. Do you mind sharing yours or . . . wait, never mind, I'll get my own." We laughed and then munched side by side like I'd always dreamed of doing with my other half. Make it easy on yourself: **Play the part of *you*—you're the only one who can do it so effortlessly.**

That's what Julie Dow had always done, and she gives her bold confidence credit for meeting her half-orange at a funeral. (Yes, a funeral.) Julie is a thirty-something with a deep raspy voice and a throaty laugh who describes herself as sarcastic within thirty seconds of talking with her. She's a TV editor in Stamford, Connecticut, who says she doesn't know where she gets her sass, since her Florida family is a little bit sweeter. But the guys she was meeting on the panhandle sure weren't sweet: "I dated a lot of cocky SOBs," says Julie. "They were very boring, and a lot like Fred Flintstone—they were like cavemen. They wanted to take care of me, and they didn't want me working. They had issues taking me seriously, like I was a pretty thing on their arm. I was like, 'Hey, I have brains!'" Julie's problem in dating was that the guys she met never "got" her humor. In fact, after dating one guy for eight months, he broke up in a letter he left on her windshield that read, "You're a strong woman. You're very sarcastic, and I'm intimidated by you." When Julie told me this, I thought for a second about my own bucklings in the past. Whenever men said something like that to me, I'd think, *Hmmm, maybe I do come off a little strong . . . maybe I should let the guy do the chasing . . . maybe I should back off and let him make the jokes . . .* But Julie? She kicked her Fred to the curb without a second thought. "He was a wuss, so I told him, 'I'm sorry if you can't hack it.'"

Despite the fact that Julie heard this from more than a few men before and after, she was never tempted to change for anyone. She knew who she was and what she wanted, and she vowed that, man or no man, she was going to live it up in life—and try doing so in Boston by the time she turned thirty, "because I loved it there so much."

A year later, Julie attended the funeral of a so-close-she-called-him-uncle family friend in Miami. There, she spied Stephen, who, with his slender frame and balding head, looked nothing like the guys she usually dated. During a family gathering afterward, she overheard him telling a few ninety-year-old women that he liked to give noogies to manatees in the ocean—"and they believed him!" laughs Julie. "That was it. I fell in love with him that second." But the true kicker was that when the two first talked, Julie was her loud, sarcastic, strong self, and Stephen ate it up. "I dished it out, and he dished it right back. He was so sarcastic." Oh, and there was a cherry on top: He was from Boston.

The next night, Julie and Stephen had their first kiss on a moonlit boat ride ("I know," she cackles, "don't you just want to puke?") and he called the next day. "There was no stress," she remembers. "We didn't put on an act. It felt like I'd found my best friend. My friends say, 'He's *you*.'" Their first official date was at Jazz Fest in Louisiana, after which they spent the next two years getting to know each other by phone and through weekend visits. Everything about him fit what she wanted. "He was patient, funny, and he treats me like a princess, but at the same time, he keeps me in line and doesn't let me get away with crap. He also understood that I was very independent, that I didn't want to date a Fred Flintstone." They dated for almost two years in different cities, and Julie eventually moved to her dream city of Boston one year before she turned thirty. Since then, they've gotten married, moved to Connecticut, and still reel about how they met. "We like to think my uncle set us up," says Julie.

But Julie teaches us all something about holding onto who you are—and that goes for flaws, too. Maybe you butt in to other people's stories too much, or you're always late, or you tend to be critical or too uptight or too shy. The time has come not to hide your flaws, but to embrace them. Start looking at your imperfections as the entertaining dowry that comes with being you! Because, let's be honest, that's true love. You don't want to be loved for the ways you're just like everyone else; you want to be loved for what makes you stand out.

Give yourself that gift: Keep chugging along as your authentic self so your half-orange can recognize and appreciate you for it, wherever you two shall meet. "My friend is going to a funeral next week," says Julie. "I told her to keep her eyes open."

CAPTURE YOUR TRUE SELF WHEN YOU SAY "CHEESE"

If you have a dating profile up online, do your fabulous self a favor and take a shot that reveals you—the real, true, happy you—on the outside. No more faking. If you've posted a photo of you holding a dog just so guys will think you like them, delete it. If you're only showing a blurry shot from the neck up because you feel you're carrying more pounds than you want, change it. If you're forty-five and saying you're twenty-nine, come on, stop it. Do you want to be loved for some character you create, or do you want to be loved for gorgeous, unique, wonderful *you*?

Karen is a thirty-nine-year-old entrepreneur from Los Angeles who was living in London for two years and liked using meals to make love connections. "I had so many dates over lunch and dinner, my friends joked I should write a book." She already had a title picked out: "A Girl's Gotta Eat!" But when Karen (who still, somehow, manages to stay slim) was finally ready to find the real thing, she read an early version of how to meet her half-orange and spread the word online that she was looking for love. There, she was straightforward and "one hundred percent honest" on her profile, "because I was sick of trying to fit a square peg into a round hole." She posted her income, her height, her shape; she specifically listed her favorite restaurants;

and she wrote that "Yes, definitely," she wanted kids. "I don't understand why anyone would *ever* lie in their profile," she adds. "There is someone for *everyone*. If you don't want people to like you for who you are, why are you doing this?" Then Karen, who knew of the importance of putting all your hope in every basket, posted the happiest photo she could find of herself to represent the positivity she was feeling. "I was the most positive I've ever been about dating because I just *knew* that it was going to happen for me no matter what, so I sat back a little and enjoyed watching how it would."

Follow Karen's lead and give your dating self the best online gift you can: a flattering photo. Here's how: Go to a place that makes you happy with a camera and either a friend, tripod or flat surface close by. Maybe it's your sunny living room, your back yard, or in front of your favorite tree. Then, before the camera comes out, love-visualize what you want in your dream relationship as you work up an orange buzz. Smile and inhale a deep breath as you think about how exciting it will be to meet this magical partner you're meant to be with; slowly exhale the stress of mismatches you've had before. Inhale the anticipation and excitement that you don't know where you'll find him; then, slowly exhale those old fears that you thought you never would.

Then—and this is important—I want you to look into the camera as if, on the other side of that lens, the love of your life is peeking through the viewfinder. He already loves you, and he's looking at you with adoring eyes, because he can't believe he found you. Look into that lens and say with your eyes, your smile, and your heart, "Hi honey! Hurry up and come get me!" Do you feel it? Can you make your liver smile and your body tingle with thoughts of how great you're going to feel when you meet him? *That's* the photo you want your future half-orange to see. That is the shot that he will fall for if he happens to be looking—the one that shows the *true* you—with your true height and your true age and your true desire to be in a serious, committed relationship. No apologies, no masks, no faking it. You deserve the real thing, and the only way you'll get it is by putting the real thing out there.

And guess what? Someday, somehow, someway, your half-orange will see that photo. Maybe he'll see it before he meets you, or maybe he'll see it on your fridge after he's already fallen hard. But he'll surely look at it and say, "That's one of the most beautiful photos of you," and you'll know why.

"That's because," you can tell him, "I was looking at *you* when I took it."

ACCEPT WHAT THE UNIVERSE THROWS YOUR WAY

While you're busy living your authentic, gorgeous, happy life the way you want to live it, I'd like you to keep one thing in mind: Pay attention to what is being sent your way. Because if you're working hard at feeding your orange seed, then the world around you will be trying to help it grow. So let it!

This reminds me of the joke about the guy who gets stuck in a flood and has faith that God will save him. Have you heard this one? Here's how I know it:

A man is stuck in his house when a flood breaks through. As he climbs out the window, a guy in military jeep drives by and shouts, "Get in!" The man replies, "No, that's okay, I have faith in God. He will save me."

As the water rises, the man climbs into a tree. A guy in a boat floats by and tells him to climb in. "That's okay," he tells the boater below, "God will save me."

The man then climbs onto the roof, where another boat offers him a ride. Again, he turns down the offer because he knows God will grant him a miracle.

Finally, when the water is chin-high, a guy in a helicopter throws down a ladder and shouts for the man to climb on. He waves it away, mumbling, "God will save me." Well, the next thing the man knows, he's standing in heaven with the other people who have drowned in the flood. "What happened?" he asked God. "I thought you would save me."

"Sheesh, man," said God, "I sent you a car, two boats, and a helicopter, what more did you want?!"

If you are buzzing with positive energy and focusing on your orange, the world will send you all sorts of things to lead to it: surprising party invitations, last-minute trips, new opportunities at work, and a sudden desire to eat a certain food or try a particular gym class. Or, in my case, an invite to a touch football game I should have accepted.

In fact, science shows that the more "prepared" you are to experience chance encounters, the more likely it is that you will. This is based on a premise called "predictive encoding," studied by psychologist Colleen Seifert, Ph.D., the woman who knew she'd personally feel most comfortable with a man who'd actually heard of Hamburger Helper. In short, "predictive encoding is like mental rehearsal, preparing what you want to do in advance, so when a particular situation comes up, you'll recognize it," says Seifert. I'll explain by telling you how Seifert used it to find her other half.

Over a decade ago, Seifert was an assistant professor of psychology at the University of Michigan working to earn tenure. It involved sixty-hour work-weeks for six years—which meant that Seifert, thirty-four years old at the time and shy by nature, didn't have time for a social life. But the morning after she successfully earned her tenure, she felt a distinct feeling of emptiness in her life; her work goal had been achieved . . . so now what? As she celebrated her good news with one sole coworker, she wondered: Why didn't she have more people around her? Who would she celebrate successes like this with in her future? She certainly never pictured celebrating with a husband.

"I've been overweight my whole life and have always struggled with rejection," says Seifert. When it came to men, she says, "I was always really conservative about likelihoods. I don't think I hoped enough. But I had a need to be connected to people, and it was enough to make me want to change." So Seifert made a conscious decision to make good things happen in her life from here on out—to make connections with people, so she could be surrounded by relationships and love. So she "encoded" a predictor for a new behavior she wanted—and it would be set off every time she met someone new. "I decided that when I started to talk to someone, or reached out for a handshake with a new person, I was going to take a breath, listen to what they were saying, look them in the eye, slow it down, and just try to be present in that moment of meeting them."

Later that day, Seifert stopped at the dry cleaner a few blocks from her home to pick up her clothes. The man behind the counter, Zeke, smiled at her and made some friendly and slightly flirtatious conversation. "Here was this cute guy, and I couldn't believe he would go out with someone like me," says Seifert. But thanks to the more outgoing behavior she had planned to use, when the man asked for her number—to put on the dry cleaning ticket—Seifert got bold and asked, "Are you going to call me?" Zeke said he would, and he called that same night to ask her to the movies.

After dating for a few months, Seifert remembers the moment that sealed the deal for her. "The clincher was when we went to a vision clinic because he had a problem with his eye," she recalls. "He had me laughing in the waiting room for *four* hours. I just thought, 'Most of your life is spent waiting, right? At doctor's offices, car repair shops, stoplights . . . well, *this* is the guy to wait with.'" Zeke proposed on Christmas Eve, they got married a month later, and they've just celebrated their ten-year anniversary.

"When I tell the story I get chills again," says Seifert. "I can't believe this happened to me, it's so wonderful. It's like the feeling of love and acceptance you have in your original family, but I never thought I would get to have that with an adult male." And it came about because Seifert made the conscious decision that something like it *would*.

"That morning, I wasn't telling myself I have to go find someone to marry," she says. "But I *did* believe that good things would happen and that I could have a richer life if I just looked up into people's eyes and said something. The fact that you are talking to people you normally wouldn't means that other opportunities will be open to you that wouldn't be there otherwise. You cut off the possibility of all the things that could happen by talking to them if you *don't* talk to them at all."

Take advantage of the fact that you, too, can create your own opportunities, and lay the groundwork for your own positive encounters. Some call the magic moments *serendipity*. The Chinese might call it luck or fate. Carl Jung referred to a theory of synchronicity, a theory of meaningful coincidences—a crossing paths within the collective unconscious. Seifert says the basis of her study is all about opportunistic planning, and it's exactly what dating optimism is all about. If you *plan* for the opportunity of love landing on your doorstep—or sidewalk, or grocery store line, or vacation tour bus, or restaurant table next to yours—it will actually increase the chance that you will *notice* it when it does. It's like telling your TiVo to record all the movies with Paul Rudd in it (and really, why wouldn't you?) and finding more films recorded than you knew existed. Once you know specifically what you're looking for, you'll find it just falls in your path.

So how do you do it with dating specifically? As Seifert's study explains, once a pending goal has been associated with a specific cue, the presence of that cue later will automatically bring the goal to mind. Well, your goal is to notice the signs that lead you in the direction of your other half, right? So create your own cue that will remind you to tune in and do this. For example, one cue could be that as soon as your foot hits a certain mark on the sidewalk, you remind yourself to look up and take in the world. Or you might decide to accept all invitations for a while. To help you, encode your new response into memory: Think about hearing, "Would you like to . . ." and practice answering, "Why not?" Then, when invitations come along, you'll remember to say "Yes" first.

Or perhaps you do exactly what Seifert did: From now on, you will use a cue of saying "Hello," to engage in conversations with each person you meet. "My friend and I go to the same horrible cocktail parties and while I end up with the boring academic in the corner, he somehow finds the fascinating person who used to work for the CIA," says Seifert. "His motto is, 'I think you can get an interesting story out of everybody, and it's our job to bring out the story.'" Think of your dating life the same way: The world will put people in your path, and it's your job to create your own opportunities with each one of them. "That's what optimism is," says Seifert. "If you give up, it's never going to happen. So by being optimistic, you at least open a path where it *could* happen."

KEEP EVERY PATH OPEN

Our proud pessimist Parker likes to say that while she doesn't know where she *will* meet her other half, she's convinced of where she *won't:* online. "Have you seen the screen names people pick?" she whimpers. To be fair, I saw some of her wooers: One had the username "drgnlord" and another joked in his profile that "Hoffa is buried in my basement floor"; the most unsettling was a 58-year-old man who sent a photo of himself cropped from the neck down wearing a red Speedo. "He said he couldn't show his face because he worked for the government," sighs Parker. There were plenty more normal-seeming and nice-looking guys in the mix, too, but Parker isn't buying the process. "The person I'm going to be with is *not* going to be on there," she says. I had to talk her off the precipice of such pronouncements, because making a declaration of where you *won't* meet someone is like closing off an entire highway that might lead you to your destination! Don't discount anything. Don't decide what he'll look like, where he'll live, or how you'll meet him. The more open you are to possibility, the sooner he can come into your life.

Closing off paths that could bring the two of you together is like saying you want to take a trip around the world . . . but you refuse to travel by plane. Sure, you can get where you want by boat and train and car, but cutting out the option of airplanes is closing off a significant portion of your possibilities. That's not to say it can't be done, but why do it? Why take away that option for speedy travel and surprise joy? What happens if you end up in Australia with an offer from a hot man for a free ride in a seaplane? What a shame to knock that option off the board before your trip even begins.

The point is, with dating optimism, you have to be open to all the channels, and to creating your own opportunities. Open your eyes, your ears, your heart, your soul, and those persnickety assumptions you have locked inside about how you're going to get what you want. Remember: It's only your job to want it, it's not your job to figure out how you'll get it. The world *will* bring you what you want, but you have to be open to letting it. Take some chances, try some new things, and travel down paths where you *don't* know what will happen for once. Then, see how much closer you feel to your half-orange when you reach your destination. My guess? Much.

Lara Fernandez, the woman who made a twelve-page Big Love List and ended up meeting the most communicative man she could have imagined, had to open her eyes to the push the world was giving her before she met him. It began one Sunday when she was still single and her friend suggested she put a profile up on Match.com. "That's so cheesy," Lara said at first, "I'm not desperate!" The next day at work, someone brought up the dating site in a conversation. And the day after that, someone *else* told a story about three couples who met the very same way. "I had to acknowledge the signs," said Lara. "I was clearly being nudged, so I joined up and made a profile on a lark." A month later, she met up with her first date, and felt no sparks. "See?" she told her friends at first, but she gave it another shot. Her next date was with Johnny, the man she married.

Your love *will* come to you. From now on, allow yourself to respond to the surprising moments that might lead you there. If you're staying positive and feeding your orange seed, the universe can't help but deliver what you're asking for. Let it!

GIVE YOURSELF THE "YNK" SPEECH

With the energy you're sending out, the universe will bring your dream relationship to you, however crazy the route. This is so important to remember, I cannot say it enough: It's not your job to find love. It's your job to want it and believe it will come. I hate to bring up a goofy movie, but yeah, Kevin Costner said it best in *Field of Dreams*: "If you build it, he will come." Maybe he won't come right away, but bit by bit, day by day, date by date, people and circumstances will come that bring you even closer to your half-orange.

Trust in the world to follow the energy you're putting out to take you step by step toward the place you need to be. Because YNK: You Never Know. You never know what you'll learn each time. You never know when you'll meet a cool new friend, be offered a new job, or be asked to join an organization that can change your path, who you meet, or what you become. You never know what surprises lie around the corner for you.

Atlanta, Georgia, resident Jodi Rosenberg went on thirty blind dates in less than two years. Why? "I was in a good place personally with a great job and

> ## FEED THE SEED!
>
> ### The Birthday Image
> It's your birthday five years from now. You are with your half-orange, squinching your eyes closed because he's asked you to. Where are you? Outdoors? Indoors? What do you hear around you? Friends? Kids? Beautiful silence? When you open your eyes, your half-orange is giving you the gift of your dreams. What is it? You look at him and smile—you can't believe how well he knows you! It's true: You've met a man who adores you so much, knows you so well, and loves you for every crazy habit you have—and he's proving it to you now. How lucky are you?

friends and family," says Jodi, "and the dates kept my social calendar very full. I never turned down an offer for a set-up because I figured you just never know who you will meet!" She also saw all that dating as good experience getting her out of her shell. "I'm actually quite shy, so I never thought I would be comfortable on a blind date, but I got a lot of practice." Through it all, she says, "I kept my girlfriends very entertained with the stories—like the guy who showed up in sweatpants." Eventually, a girl on Jodi's tennis team arranged a set-up with her husband's friend, and when the friend and Jodi first spoke on the phone, "There was something about his voice that I really liked and then we had a great first date." And, she says, it was those blind dates that preceded it that cleared the path for something brilliant. "I learned from all of those other dates about what I didn't want in a relationship or a partner, so it made it even more clear that my now-husband was worth hanging on to for as long as I could," says Jodie. "I think if I'd met him earlier, I may not have known what it was I was looking for or may not have been happy enough with myself to be able to share my life with him." Jodi's now been sharing her life with her husband for eight years and it's feeling pretty happily ever after.

Do those romantic comedy plots come from promptly planned and arduously executed dates? No, they come from letting life happen in the most natural, unplanned, crazy, awkward ways, because you never know. Surely, for example, there have been people you've been surprised to like. I, for one, remember how fourteen years ago I ran into a guy I went to grade school with, formerly a goofy kid two years younger than me with a spiky haircut cut who sang "Jailhouse Rock" in the fourth grade play. But when I saw him at a bar in our hometown the year I graduated college? My, my . . . he had grown up. I never would have *imagined* I'd be attracted to him when I was in grade school, but as a college kid, he was mature, sexy, intelligent, and entertaining. We dated for a summer and spent nights talking on the phone for hours at a time. I was too caught up in our age difference to be able to run with it, but we had a great two months before we went back to school and lost touch. The point is, *you never know* who you might meet, or who his friends may be, or who you might be attracted to. Enjoy the surprises. That's what's so fun about the ride!

Nadine, the New York editor, was just as surprised as anyone when she stumbled upon love. She'd been using the "water on the nightstand" trick for nearly six months when her friend Dani sent an email out to her friends asking if they knew any single men Nadine might like. (Notice once again: If you tell your close friends that you're ready and looking for that big love, the message hits the network of the universe—and maybe even someone's email group list—and it grows.) Dani got word of a great guy who'd just moved to New York from Nantucket, so she invited him to her New Year's Eve party. "There's a guy I want you to meet," she told Nadine. "He lives upstate, has dogs, he likes to garden and cook . . . and he's straight."

At the time, Nadine had plans to spend New Year's Eve at a club in the city, so at first, she resisted the invite. But then again, she thought, her quest to meet guys in the city hadn't been successful so far, so maybe it was time to do the *opposite* of what she'd been doing and hightail it out of there. This led Nadine to a New Year's Eve party in upstate New York.

Nadine brought a cute dress to wear, but by the time people started arriving, she was too tired from setting up to change into it. "I was wearing jeans, a brown cardigan, and Blundstone work boots." But she was so content, her Grubby Glow was surfacing. Then she glanced at the food spread and noticed The Brownies—and she says it that way, that seriously: *The* Brownies. "I'm very picky and skeptical about other people's brownies," says Nadine. "But I saw this pan of brownies on the table, and I took a piece. It was rich and fudge-y but just the perfect amount of cakey and crumbly, so I looked at Dani and said, 'These are the most *delicious* brownies I've ever had. Who made them?' She pointed her finger across the room at this guy, and it was the guy I'd gone up there to meet. And I swear to God, a voice in my head said, 'This is the guy you're going to marry.'"

Nadine laughs at herself even saying so, assuring me she doesn't usually fall for little voices. But when Nadine and Hubert started talking, they found they had heaps in common. They started seeing each other, kissed one February evening, and Nadine was hooked.

She was also, however, having a crisis of expectation. How could she make it work with a guy who lived two hours away in the country? She was looking for a guy who was her professional peer, who worked in her industry in some way, who lived in the city . . . wasn't she? So she and Hubert split up so she could find out. But everywhere she looked, the signs pointed back to him. "I thought I wanted someone who was intellectual and in New York society, but I went out with a professor and it was awful," she scoffs. A few months later, she went to the Caribbean on her own and spent the whole trip thinking of how much better it would have been if Hubert were there. Finally, one afternoon, Nadine says, "I was shopping at Nicole Farhi and tried on a dress, and I remember thinking, 'I bet Hubert would like this dress.' At that moment, I was like 'Nadine, what are you *doing*?'" She called him, and they began dating again. Three months later, on a trip to Paris, he proposed on the balcony facing the Arc de Triomphe. They just got married and are now splitting their time between her place in New York City and his place upstate, for which they're researching how to get bees for a beehive.

"Women tend to reinforce the whole cliché romantic comedy ending to each other," says Nadine, "but every great love story I read is the one where he's *not* the guy she thought she would marry and she's incredibly happy." Well, I hate to break it to Nadine, but meeting a man on New Year's Eve and being proposed to on a balcony in Paris is about as romantic as it gets! But I get her point just the same. It's not about finding the man you *think* you're supposed to have, it's about discovering the one you're meant to be with. And it benefits you to keep this in mind as you make your choices of who to spend time with. Choose the people who are interesting, who make you laugh, who make you feel great about yourself. From there, *you never know* what could happen. Nadine learned it, too: You never know who you'll end up with. You never know what one group email, or one New Year's Eve invite, or one bite of a brownie might bring. And you never know when a guy you never pictured being with can turn out to be the one man you can't live without.

FIGHT OFF THE "I'M STILL SINGLE" PANIC!

Just because you are becoming a dating optimist does not mean there won't be times that you freak out, and life starts looking like one straight path to dying crotchety, wrinkled, barren and alone. I want to give you some tools to stave off these bouts of worry. Why? Because worry is a wasteful emotion.

In the wonderful book called *The Gift of Fear*, Gavin de Becker, a specialist in security issues, talks about how fear—*real* fear—is different from the nervous, panicky anxiety we call fear. In fact, he writes, "The very fact that you fear something is solid evidence that it is not happening." If you're afraid a burglar might break into your house, it's evidence the burglar isn't already breaking a window. If you're afraid your plane might crash, it's evidence you're not already nose-diving toward the ocean. Do you get that? The fact that you're *fearing* it means it's not happening. And panicky worry is the same thing. If you're worrying, like I used to, that you might end up alone at eighty-nine, in a nursing home, never having found true love, well that's proof right there it's not happening.

And your worrying isn't getting you any closer to the goal, because the panic you feel is causing changes in your brain and body that aren't helping your cause. Mark George, M.D., from the National Institute of Mental Health, did a study of women using PET scans of their brains, that found that when the women focused on "sad" thoughts, the deep limbic system in their brains heated up and became overactive. In Dr. George's studies, when the female participants were focused on happy thoughts, their deep limbic system actually cooled down. The dynamic also works in reverse: If your limbic system is overactive, then you're likely to interpret or read situations from a more negative point of view; and when it is cooled off and less active, you will more likely see them from a positive one. This is big stuff, because your body is affected by the warming and cooling of your emotional brain as well.

When your emotional brain heats up, your body tenses up: your heart rate increases, your muscles tense, your brow furrows, your gaze drops, your face falls. You won't feel relaxed, you won't *look* relaxed, and you won't attract what you're looking for—which is someone who makes you feel the opposite of these things! And if you let your emotions get the better of you, they can lead to real anxiety and even, in some cases, that fight-or-flight response of pure panic.

Believe me, I know what that's like. One night, just before I began my dating optimism experiment, I spent an evening with two couple friends while watching my single wing-woman for the night hook up with a cute guy. I walked home alone, and, on my way up the stairs to my empty apartment, started to have my very first, full-blown panic attack. I didn't know what it was as I paced dizzily in my twelve-by-twelve foot living room, but it flashed me back to the visits I made to a cardiologist in high school, fearing I had a damaged heart. *I must have been right*, I figured. I looked at my cat Minnie who was peering up at me, and I just thought, *I'm going to pass out and have a heart attack and die, and Minnie will sit on me for five days before my friends and family freak out enough to break down the door.* After debating whether I should call an ambulance or wake up my sleeping friends, I finally walked my wobbly legs down my stairs and onto the street, where I felt better knowing that if I had a heart attack on the street, a human would find me, instead of my cat. But after fifteen minutes of walking in the fresh air and my pulse still pounding, I became so convinced I was having a heart attack, I waved down a taxi and asked him to take me to the hospital. I told the driver my fears of dying in case I passed out in the back seat, and I remember him replying, "Are you sure you need to go? It really doesn't, you know, seem like you're dying."

God, how embarrassing. It's hilarious now, of course, because he was right. I wasn't dying at all. But for any of you who have experienced an anxiety or panic attack—when you really do think you're taking your last breaths and you'd prefer not to expire in a taxi with a stranger—it's not quite as funny at the time. I had a few more episodes after that, which all came on when I was alone, and I eventually learned how to quell an attack before it happens (by talking myself down from impending panic and breathing deeply and slowly to bring my heart rate back down), so I haven't had a panic attack in years. But for months after that night, walking up those stairs to my empty apartment was troubling. All I kept thinking as I took each step up was, *I'm alone, I'm alone, I'm alone, I'm alone.* And as I'd close the door to my apartment, locking myself in with Minnie, my heart would start to pound, my breathing would quicken, and my mind would spin with wild fear. It took a concerted effort to break free from the dooming cycle of panic.

Aside from learning how to

FEED THE SEED!

The Valentine's Day Image

This year, you *have* a Valentine, and it's someone you feel your complete self with. So, how do you celebrate? Will he take you out for a romantic dinner? Will you take him out? Or will you order takeout and curl up on floor cushions to eat it? Do you write him a card or make him one? Or do you both wave away Valentine's Day as a Hallmark holiday and vow, as you take a bite of cold leftover pizza, to be kind to one another every other day instead? Smile and inhale the warm feeling as the two of you thank the world for bringing both of you together, because now *every* day feels special.

quell my physiological reactions, I also found a way to get the word "alone" out of my head. Why? Because you get what you think about and focus on. And if all I was thinking about was how alone I was, well, what do you think I was attracting? Any time the word "alone" came into my mind, I flipped it and focused on the word I did want: "together."

To cement the idea, I also proved to myself that I *wasn't* alone—not for one dizzying minute. I had a family who loved me, best friends who called me daily, and my friend Todd who called me hourly. I learned to stop fearing the idea of being alone, because, although I lived by myself, I wasn't *alone*. This didn't sink in immediately, and admittedly, I kept falling into the same depressing gutter of thought: *Who cares if my friends and family love me— I want a guy to love me.* But I talked myself out of it again and again. *Oh, come on.* I told myself. *Could you be any more ungrateful?* There are, after all, people on this Earth who don't have family, who don't have friends, who don't have coworkers who care, or a feeling of community around them at all. So I made myself go through the list of people who would care a hell of a lot if I dropped dead on my apartment floor. (A cell phone contact list is a good place to start.) I had plenty of love around me that I was overlooking *entirely*. Yes, I lived by myself, but I was not alone. I simply wasn't. And neither are you. So wipe the worry lines off your face and forge ahead without the fear.

CHANGE YOUR "EXPLANATORY STYLE"

At this part of the half-orange process, you know what's on your Big Love List and you should be taking time to create your orange buzz as you imagine getting it. But in your daily life, as you meet new guys and dabble in dating, it's also important to watch your self-talk to be sure you're not overly judging the situation or making blanket negative statements about yourself. **What's important in dating optimism is not necessarily what *happens* in your love life, but how you *explain* it.**

One of the most important steps in becoming a dating optimist is to change what positive psychologist Martin Seligman, Ph.D., calls your "explanatory style," which is basically how you explain your setbacks. Once you begin to explain what has already happened to you in an optimistic way, you will get better at looking at what's coming in the future more optimistically as well. Let me set up an example and see how you think you'd react:

At a party, your friend points out her husband's friend, Gabe, who is single, cute, and standing alone by the guac and chips. After she introduces you both, you talk for a while and you feel like you hit it off and have a lot in common. Gabe then excuses himself to go the bathroom and says he'll catch up with you in a bit. You grab your friend and tell her how adorable he is, how great it seems to be going, and, by the way, how hot is it that his name is Gabe! Thirty minutes later, however, you see Gabe with another (younger, hotter) single girl at the party. This time, his arm is around her waist, he's gazing into her eyes, and she's giggling back.

Now, what is the thought going through your head?

- "Why don't guys ever *like* me?
- "That's it, it's proof. I'm never going to find anybody."
- "I'm obviously not pretty enough to get the guys I like."
- "He just doesn't like me that way."
- "They have a better connection tonight than he and I did."
- "If this guy doesn't like me right now, maybe he just isn't the one for me."

By the time you got through to the second half of those answers, you may have realized what I'm getting at: The first three answers have a pessimistic explanatory style, while the last three have an optimistic one. And here's why: According to Seligman's research, pessimistic explanations for setbacks have distinctive qualities about them: They are *pervasive, permanent,* and sometimes *personal.* For instance:

- A dating pessimist sees a setback as pervasive, as something that covers all categories across the board ("Why don't guys—all guys—ever like me?")

- A dating pessimist also sees a setback as permanent ("I'm never going to find anybody.")

- A dating pessimist may also look at a setback as personal ("I'm not pretty enough.")

When you find yourself saying the words "always," "never," or "ever," this is a pretty good sign that you're treading in a puddle of pessimism. And we know what happens when you focus on negative thoughts: You attract negative things. So your job is to change your past setbacks in love so you will get better at changing how you see your *future* in love. Think of fighting your own negative thoughts as role-playing with yourself. Instead of pep talking your sobbing friend out of the gutter, talk *yourself* out of it! And you will do so by seeing your dating setbacks as *temporary,* as *specific* to the situation, and as something that's *not personal.* Because as long as you see your situation as a temporary one that will pass, you give yourself hope for the future! So from now on, when a guy doesn't cling to you at a party or ask you out when you want him to, this is the new way you'll explain your still-single status:

- Your dating setback isn't with *all* guys, it's only with the one who's disappointing you right now. ("He doesn't like me that way. Oh well. The right guy will!")

- Your dating setback isn't going to last forever—it's going to last as long as this drink, and then you get a clean slate tomorrow. ("If this guy doesn't like me right now, maybe he just isn't the one for me.")

- And the fact that you haven't yet met your dream guy isn't personal—it's not because you aren't good enough or kind enough or smart enough or pretty enough! It's simply because the world hasn't yet brought you and your half-orange to the same place at the same time.

And, by the way, if you keep *thinking* you're not good enough or kind enough or smart enough or pretty enough, guess what you're attracting? Men who *don't* think you're enough of those things. Remember, you're looking for your perfect match, right? Well, so is everyone else! So if a guy isn't feeling it with you, it's not because of a flaw in you. It's because he wants a better connection with someone else ("They have a better connection tonight than he and I did.") and so should *you*.

See dating as a match game

If you need some more help to keep your explanatory style temporary and specific, think of your dating life like the match game Concentration. On your first turn, you uncover a monkey. In looking for its match, you turn over . . . an elephant. Oh well. It's not a match. So what do you do? You flip the elephant back over, shrug, and wait for your next turn. That's what your dating life can be like. When you turn over your next date and notice he's not a match for you, look at it from a temporary, specific, and impersonal point of view: You're just not a match, it's that simple.

In Concentration, when the monkey card doesn't find its match, it doesn't start crying, or beating itself up for being too much of a monkey when clearly if it had been more like an elephant, things might work out. The monkey doesn't think, "Well, maybe if I change the elephant and teach him how to swing from trees, I think we could really have something, you know?" Because then, of course, the pair would find that after months of torturing themselves by trying to change each other, it's just not going to work.

Love is a match game. If you turn over someone who isn't your match, shrug and wait for the guy who is. That's all there is too it. In Concentration, the monkeys eventually find each other and the elephants eventually find each other. And when you find your match, so will you.

The same rules go for those negative things you're saying about yourself. If you find yourself saying you're "too" this or "always" that and "the most" of something else, I can tell you right away what those things are: Not true. When you use extremes to describe yourself, it doesn't mean you're the most of anything—it means you're exaggerating. From now on, dump the drama and get real. Do the same thing with the negative thoughts you have about yourself that you would do with setbacks in dating: Pep talk yourself out of the gutter.

BE GRATEFUL FOR ALL THE GOOD GUYS

When I first started focusing on my dream relationship, I was on a constant high. But at some point, after a few guys blew me off, bored me, ignored me, dumped me, icked me out, or just never called me back, I started doubting if I'd ever find a good man. That's when I found myself saying what all we single women say at one point: "There are just no good guys out there." I hear it all the time, and the fact is this: There *are* good guys out there, and it's time you noticed it.

Karen, the entrepreneur who dined her dating way through Los Angeles before trying her hand in the U.K. said that noticing those good guys is what tipped her hope over the top—especially because she was starting to worry she would never find the right guy. "I have always been an upbeat, optimistic person, but after a lot of mediocre dates, I started to think maybe my 'half-orange' had met with an early life accident and would never find me," laughs Karen, "because he was dead!" But mid last-year, she says, "I started to do some of the things you said, like clipping what I wanted in love out of magazines, and working up those warm and fuzzy feelings." Despite the fact that the economic depression led to some big changes in her life, she still kept up her dating optimism. "My business I was consulting for hit a financial hiccup, so I took a holiday job at Banana Republic on Regent Street," explained Karen. "Like you suggested, I would purposely observe couples and how they interacted and I was shocked at how many guys were really enjoying shopping with their girl-friends! I'd never dated anyone who would go shopping with me. So I would talk to the men when their girlfriends were in the fitting room and I could not believe how many great guys I met—guys who were really happy and doing extraordinary things for the women they loved. It really started to give me hope. Basically, when I opened my eyes, I found love all around me."

A few months after becoming grateful for those good guys—and just six months into the half-orange plan—Karen met Mark, a fellow Californian and a business chairman on a stint in London who responded to her per-fectly honest profile online. They didn't date long before she realized, "he was *one* of those really great guys I was noticing all around me," she says. "He is so smart and sweet and really loves me for *me*." So much that when Mark recently joked with Karen, "You seem perfect to me, so what's *wrong* with you?" Karen explained it was the precision of their fit. "I said, 'The things that most people think are 'wrong' with me and scare other guys away are the things that you *love*. My confidence, my drive, the fact that I talk about sex all the time, that I'm loud, opinionated, and laugh way too much. And of course my huge appetite.' He said, 'But those are your great qualities, that's what makes you Karen!' And I said, 'I know. You love me precisely *for* all the things the other guys I dated *didn't*.'" To prove how much he loved her, Mark just proposed. They're now moving back to Los Angeles together and planning their wedding, which will fall fourteen months after Karen offi-cially became a dating optimist. Hey, "a girl's gotta eat" wedding cake, too.

So look for the good guys *you* see out there. You must have a guy friend you care for, who deserves to have a big ol' love of his own. And surely, among all of your friends, there must be some boyfriend, *some* husband who treats your friend so well, it makes you want one just like him. Maybe the good guys you know are already taken or not the guys for you, but it's important you remind yourself that good men *do* exist. Because if you focus on them, you are more likely to attract them and *notice* them when they cross your path. Remember how we talked about the minute you start wanting a Toyota Prius, you suddenly see them *everywhere* on the road? *It's the same with men.*

Of course my friend Parker loves ix-naying this idea from every angle.

"The guys out there don't like strong women," she said recently.

"Sure they do," I said.

"None that I've ever seen," she replied. (Notice Parker's use of the extreme words "none" and "ever.") Because if, like Parker, you convince yourself that good men who like strong women don't exist, then—duh—why would you even bother looking? Instead, keep your heart open and your eyes peeled, and before you know it, good men *will* reveal themselves to you.

At about month seven in my experiment, I reviewed all the men I knew who were really great guys: My dad, for one, is a great photographer, a mad scientist, and most important, a sensitive soul. But there were more great men in my life: My uncles. My cousins. My best guy friends. My friend's husband. My former coworker. My buddy from college who was always so kind it made me cry. If it helps to think of more well-known good guys, do that. Will Smith seems like a super nice guy, right? Actor Justin Long couldn't be sweeter in real life—or more appreciative of strong, smart women. And what about Bono? I've hung out with him some, and it turns out he really *is* as warm and inspiring and real and funny as you'd hope he'd be. The point is, the more great men I reflected on, the more great men started revealing themselves to me. Try it, you'll see.

While you're at it, review the good boyfriends you've had as a reminder that sometimes you actually *do* have good taste and are capable of liking men with admirable qualities. For instance, I never forgot the guy I dated one summer who asked me out for lunch on our first date—which was a far cry from most guys, who tried to get me drunk over dinner. Another night, that same guy drove me to a private beach, then pulled out a bottle of wine and a picnic blanket from his trunk, showing me romance wasn't dead. If you're grateful for the men you've known then and see now, you will bring more of them to you.

Carolyn Curtis, Ph.D., the executive director of The Healthy Marriage Project in California, has a motto that worked for her and can work for you. "If you can find one good guy, you can find two," she says. When she was a single woman, she looked at the evidence of great guys as proof that they existed, and that, surely, she could find one for herself. "Even if he's married, it's a step in the right direction if you can actually see what a good guy looks like. What does it feel like when you're around someone like this? If you can find one good guy, you can find another for yourself."

If you're one of those women who can't even find *one* right guy you might have what Curtis calls a "broken picker." People with broken pickers misunderstand what a good guy is—say, confusing danger or excitement or lust for love. "If you have a broken picker you can't see a good guy if your life depended on it," says Curtis, "because you're not accustomed to looking in that direction!" Lucky for you, as a dating optimist, you have been focusing on all the right, good, healthy things you deserve in a relationship, so you'll be better at recognizing them than you've ever been.

Curtis met her good guy at a work conference, and she reaps the rewards to this day. "When you tell good men what you want, they go out of their way to accommodate your needs," says Curtis. "When you tell these men how you feel, they put effort into understanding and accepting it." Isn't this the kind of guy you want, with a healthy dash of sex appeal thrown in? Seek out guys good enough to deserve you, and you'll bring yours even closer.

KICK THE RUMINATING OUT OF THE ROOM

I was in a taxi on a 30-degree night, stuck in street repair traffic, and late for a party at some posh place uptown Yvonne had invited me to. I hadn't really felt like going, but as a dating optimist, I decided that instead of going to my usual downtown spots, I was going to do the opposite. *I need some "new" in my life,* I thought. *It would do me good to go to a new part of town and meet some new people.* Unfortunately, I was dropped off at the wrong address, eight blocks away, in high heels and all I wanted was my old couch, my old remote control, and my day-old leftovers.

I was about to walk into the party with a huge frown on my face so everyone could pity how crappy my trip was, when I realized…*What will I gain by being the whining, miserable guest? Nothing. But I might gain a few friends by putting a smile on my face.* So during that last freezing block, I made myself create a big warm orange smile. I was forcing and faking at first, laughing out loud to get those muscles going. But I walked into that party smiling . . . and three hours later, I was kissing a cute guy who wore, of all things, a pink pocket square in his suit jacket.

He programmed my number into his cell phone and told me, "I'm not letting you get away from me." I was smitten.

A week later, however, Mr. Pocket-Square still hadn't called, but I couldn't imagine why not. I was just so convinced we were meant to be. So much for his not letting me get away.

"Something must be wrong," I said to Yvonne. And it's embarrassing to admit I even thought this, let alone said it: "I bet he lost my number."

"But you said you watched him put it in his phone."

"I know," I said. "But maybe he accidentally erased it. Or maybe he forgot to put my name there, and can't remember what he put my number under. Or, *duh,*" I said. "Maybe he lost his phone."

Now we all know better than this. But crushes do crazy things to our logic. The fact was, this wasn't a complicated system that involved Missed Connections on Craigslist. Mr. Pocket-Square was a friend of a friend; it was a straightforward connection, full of email addresses and cell phone numbers. But instead of recognizing that he wasn't interested, I made Yvonne listen to me gripe about him and myself for another week after that. "I must have done something wrong," I said. "Maybe I was too straightforward. Maybe I wasn't straightforward enough. How come the guys I like never like me back? Ooh, maybe I can figure out a way to contact him and see where he'll be, without him realizing that I'm the one who wants to know . . . "

When one is feeling like the loneliest number, you're allowed to wallow for a minute. And of course, have a big sit-down with the girls and update them on the most recent turn of events—i.e., what happened before the text and after the text and what you think the smiley face *in* the text actually means. Lord knows we women like to analyze a situation until we've Sham-Wow-squeezed every mysterious drop out of it. But after one or two run-throughs, try to let it go. Because once you start trudging through all the negatives—on how you have no one, how no guys are a good match for you, how you can never get it right with anyone—you know what you'll bring: no one, no guys. This is what psychologists call "ruminating."

Ruminating translates for our purposes as "obsessing like a crazy person," and research by positive psychologist Martin Seligman, Ph.D., shows that women tend to ruminate more about stressful or depressing situations than men do. He found that when a woman and a man have a bad day at work—or, in the case of dating, get rejected by someone they like—they're likely to do two different things. A woman tends to ruminate about it, analyzing what was said and what wasn't, trying to put a finger on what went wrong and why. Men on the other hand? They tend to distract themselves. They have a drink. Or go to a sports bar. Or play video games. They take their minds *off* of what frustrates them. And you know who fares better for it? Men, who end up less depressed than women overall.

So women, do your best to stop reviewing and analyzing and neuroti-cizing every single second of every uncertain moment you have with a guy. Snap out of it, get out of it, and go *do* something that takes your mind *off* of it! See a mindless movie. Do yoga. Bake a tin of muffins. Stroll through a museum. Work out. Buy yourself a beach read no matter *what* season it is, and dive into it. Or hit a sports bar yourself. Your goal is to get out of your unconstructive and unproductive rumination and get your soul swimming in those *good* feelings about life again!

You can still have play-by-plays about the curious cases of men in your life—by all means, your best friends know you better than anyone and their input can really help. But when you start sounding like a skipping CD, don't allow yourself to ruminate about it for another single second.

This especially includes ruminating with your toxically bitter single friends. I know it *feels* like these conversations are helping, being in the trenches together, but all that commiserating and complaining isn't helping either of your cases. A toxically depressed single friend can suck the optimism out of your magnet, pulling the positivity away from you and sending your half-orange backward, away from you! So if you need to snap out of it (or you want your friend to) head to a place where people are happy. This can work wonders, thanks to a study done on the principle of "mood contagion" that found happiness is contagious. Nicholas Christakis, a professor of sociology at Harvard University, and James Fowler of the University of California in San Diego, in a study in the British Journal *BMJ*, discovered that having a next-door neighbor who is happy makes you up to 34 percent more likely to be happy yourself. Having a friend living a half-mile away who is happy increases your chances of contracting their good mood up to 42 percent. And having grumpy friends *decreases* your happy mood by 7 percent. So head to a place you know the world will be smiling, and let the mood contagion do its magic. That's what I did. It took me a few weeks to get over my crush—and an "accidentally" arranged meeting with Mr. Pocket-Square at which I learned he had a *girlfriend*—but I eventually got back to spending time with contagiously happy friends. After seven months of optimism, something good was bound to happen soon, right?

YOU DESERVE A BIG, BAD WONDERFUL LOVE

I'd like to assume that you know how great you are, and that you deserve a relationship with a man who makes you shine. But I realize not everyone gives their self-esteem high marks—and if you're one of those people, pay close attention. Parker, our resident dating pessimist, for example, has a hard time believing there's a guy out there for her. Not because of how she feels about the guys, but because of how she feels about herself. She fears she's angry inside, a little demanding, and that maybe she chooses men who will hurt her because of some feeling that she's not good enough. These are big issues, so she's in therapy working on them—and if you feel you have things that are holding you back, like a past trauma or painful relationship, please, follow her lead. Face the hard parts, don't run from them! You'll be a better half to your dream relationship when you love yourself first.

But while you're working on your issues, start the dating optimism process. Continue to focus on how wonderful it will be when you feel great about yourself and find someone who will let you *be* every inch of who you are—bunions and big issues and all. Please don't wait to think about your future love until you've "perfected" yourself. That's like saying that as soon as you're done paying off your student loans and have put a little more money into your rainy-day account, *then* you'll finally start adding to your company-matched 401K. Suze Orman might beat you with a stick for that one, and rightfully so. If you waited to put money into your 401K until you were in the black, you'd only have enough for the IKEA hot dog special by the time you retire.

My point is, don't wait to want love until you think you have resolved every single one of your issues. Everyone deserves love. *Everyone.* So stop looking for reasons or excuses for how difficult your life is or why you don't deserve love right now. And if you do have self-esteem issues or other serious problems, then for goodness' sake, take some control of your life and fix them! **Because if you don't love yourself, the right partner won't know how to love you either.** If you think your life feels out of control, pull the reins in, take charge of your work, your money, your family, and your future and get on course. If you hate your body, then either eat better and exercise more or find a way to love yourself just the way you are. If you feel unworthy for deep emotional reasons, get to a therapist and sort your stuff out. But don't wait to find love until you're shiny and fixed. Instead, ask for a love who will find your "issues" surmountable, your silly bad habits adorable, and who will see you for the stunningly beautiful person you are *right now.* You can't go forward if your head is turned back over your shoulder looking at your past. Stop digging up reasons why you don't deserve love today today. If you love yourself, you'll realize that the right man will be happy and lucky to have you.

REMEMBER: YOU'RE HOLDING OUT FOR A GREAT REASON!

I know it's easy to start doubting yourself sometimes. Are you searching for the impossible? Are you hoping for too much? Should you settle? But I want you to remember one thing: If you wanted to be with someone right now, you could be, right? There are people who like you and you know it. Come on, let's hear the list:

- The guy at work who's always asking you to lunch.
- The guy friend who's had a crush on you for a decade.
- The man at your lunch place who lights up when you walk in.
- The guy on Facebook who e-mailed you for a second date.
- That ex who still calls to "check in."

If you wanted to settle down with someone who liked you, you could.

Right now. But you're holding out for something more special—and you should. Because all those love songs aren't written about the guy you settle for who treats you pretty well and you have a good enough time with. They're written about people who fall deeply in love, because that's what we all want, and that's what we all *deserve* to have. So don't beat yourself up when you don't feel it with someone. It's a sign that you're brave enough to hold out for someone who's really right for you, who makes any amount of waiting worthwhile. "I want an amazing relationship," you should be saying. "And I can't wait to see who it'll be."

THE WRONG KEY EFFECT: IF YOU'RE STUCK, *CHANGE* SOMETHING

If you have a handful of keys and the first one you try isn't opening the lock on your front door, you try a different key. That's true of lots of things in life: If the password you typed to get into an old website isn't working, you try another one. If you can't get a taxi on one busy block, you walk to a new one. The same is true in love. If you feel stuck in your life in general, like nothing new is coming or *going* to come your way, change something. First, because sitting in a rut can put you in one depressing funk. And, second because that rut could be a sign that you're not opening yourself up to the energy the universe is providing for you.

If you're focusing—really, truly focusing—on the feelings of your dream relationship, the universe may invite you in new directions and send you signs. Open your eyes and pay attention. Is there something you're inspired to change today? Do it. **Change something. Anything. Resolutions aren't just for New Year's Day!** If someone stops you on the street today and asks you to sign their petition, maybe you should stop and read it for once. If you're surprised to get invited to a party of a coworker you're not close with, maybe it's worth going. If you get a flyer in the mail for an outdoor concert or a blood drive in your neighborhood, maybe, for once, you say yes.

The key is to create a feeling in yourself that anything can happen and that it's all leading you to your half-orange. So if you're trudging the same streets to the same job to the same drinks with the same friends and home to the same quiet house again and again and again . . . maybe it's time to change something.

CHANGE SOMETHING BIG

Alanna was a successful fashion designer in New York City when she broke up with her live-in boyfriend, leaving her depressed, lost, lonely, and uncertain about her future. But instead of giving into the funk, she sold her business, then sold her apartment, and moved to upstate New York, where she bought a small weekend house on an old ninety-acre farm. "I moved here with no job and no man and a barn that hadn't been used in fifty years," Alanna said. "I bought a sheep, a pig, a goat, and a tractor and then got to work learning what to do with them all." It was while this city girl was focusing her energy on her new life, on learning how to plow the whole farm herself, that she met Bob, a guy from the Long Island suburbs who had inherited his grandparents' farm down the road. Bob and Alana are now married and running her farm together successfully.

Leslie, a Washington D.C. editor, made a similar bold move. After living and dating in New York for a decade, Leslie had a lightning bolt moment of sorts. It flashed when a guy she'd been seeing on and off for years told her he felt they were meant to be together and wanted to make an official go of it with her. Three days later, however, he re-dumped her by email. They officially got closure at brunch soon after. "I remember sitting at this table, inches apart from the people around us, with tears in my eyes, asking him, 'How could you treat me like this?'" remembers Leslie. "And that's when it flashed before me like a movie montage that this was the *third* time I'd cried in a restaurant breaking up with a guy. I just thought, *That's it. No more break-ing up and crying in restaurants!*" By then though, she says, the city had begun to taunt her: This was the place she met that one guy she liked; that place over there was where she met the jerk. She was fatigued, weighed down by the mental deadline that she should have met someone by now, and felt like life had hit a steady plateau. "There were no big lows," says Leslie, "but there were also no highs. I was coasting." So she decided to take a big leap and lit-erally try a different key—a key to a home in a different city.

Leslie, a systematic planner, identified five cities she might like to move to, made pros and cons lists about them all, contacted all the people she knew from each one, and eventually chose Austin, Texas. "I wanted to go somewhere completely different, to get out of my comfort zone," she says. "And as soon as I made the decision, I felt more upbeat and alive than I had in a long time. Instead of just coasting, I was taking control, being com-pletely selfish, and doing something just for me." She had some naysayers: "Friends would say, 'But you know a million people, you have a great job, and you have a rent-stabilized apartment in an elevator building!' They did-n't seem to get that the rent-stabilized apartment in the elevator building wasn't making me *happy*."

So after nine months saving money to buy a car, doing a reconnaissance trip to find a place, and getting her nerve up, she finally did it. The move invigorated her: "I had to make friends and find my way." She got a job at the local paper. She took ballroom dancing lessons to learn how to country waltz. She went to a few football games, ate barbecue, and signed up for golf lessons with a group of women who quickly became a comforting girl-clique. And on her back porch at home, she soaked in her new lifestyle, "where I could crack open a Shiner [beer] and sit under my pecan tree," she says. It was great practice for Leslie, focusing on brand new things in her life, instead of ruminating about the old. "When I moved, some people said,

'You'll take your problems with you,' and it's true," says Leslie, "but you also see your problems in a new way. When you have to consult a map to figure out how to get to the grocery store, you don't have as much time to wallow in your own stuff! You're just busy living."

Six months later, Leslie met a great guy who wanted to get married and have children. Could it be true? Six months after moving, her love life was solved? Well, not exactly. Because after eight months with her boyfriend, her gut told her it wasn't right. "I realized he didn't love 'Leslie' specifically, he just wanted a wife," she says. "And if I'd still been obsessed with finding the One, I might have married him. Instead, I was fine waiting for a man who wanted *me* in particular."

So Leslie stumbled back into her singledom and dumped the details of her story as she always did on her good friend and coworker, Jeremy. The two had a platonic relationship, "but with a spark," she says. Then one night, as she dropped him off at a music venue, Jeremy—who is much more spontaneous than Leslie—leaned over and kissed her. Their courtship was off to a bold start, and Leslie felt great about it. "Here was someone who had listened to me bitch about things and seen me lose my cool in the workplace," she says. "Everyone has baggage, of course, but I'd opened my bags and dumped them out on the table in front of him! I thought, *This guy really knows what he's getting into.* And I did too." It was a far cry from how she'd always felt with men before. "When I was in New York, I got swept up in putting the most 'perfect' me out there—only telling the stories that put me in a flattering light and only talking about things that were going well. But I'd found a city with the motto 'Keep Austin Weird.' It's a place that's about diversity and showing your whole self. In Austin, I wasn't worried about the image I was putting out there. I learned that it's not only okay to be imperfect, it's *fun* to be imperfect. Accept it and celebrate it!"

Jeremy got married on the sand in Hawaii and are now figuring out the next step of their adventure together.

In the end, Leslie credits her big move—trying a different key—for putting her in a new mindset. "Just the moving itself gave me a sense of control," she says. "Like, Hey, I did this. Me. My choice. Now, I unpack." And, she says, once you get on the path of making a big move or a big change, you get better at taking control of your life. You no longer worry how it looks to other people or whether others think it's logical or whether it makes financial sense. Once you make that first leap, it makes it easier to keep going on that path and try even more new things—which includes marrying a wonderful man who is much different than herself. "He's a very spontaneous person, and I'm Miss Planning the Worrier," she laughs. "I can have fun, but it has to be *planned* fun. Also, I'm incredibly cheap and thrifty, but Jeremy knows how to splurge when the time is right. So when you think about two halves that fit together, that's definitely what we are. We work really well together."

The easiness of their match is why she agrees so strongly with the half-orange premise that you should throw away that physically specific list of what you want in a man. "We're all too close to ourselves to have the perspective to know what we want," says Leslie. "If I had done that, it would have not led me to Jeremy—in fact, that potentially could have led me to the *opposite* of Jeremy!" So do what Leslie did: Dump that list of what he looks like, and focus on how you want to feel in a relationship. If you want someone who gets you, appreciates you, and loves you even after seeing all your baggage poured out on the table, focus on and ask for that. It's not about the guy, remember, it's about you. "I was just being myself," says Leslie, "and someone who is more chill and fun than I am came and found me."

If you think you might need a change as big as Leslie's, just be prepared for some similar personal fallout. "People get weird when they think you're doing something off the map," says Leslie. "A lot of people didn't understand my choice. But they only saw the sweet exterior—they didn't know the sadness I was feeling. You have to be prepared for people who will not be supportive, and do what you need to do for yourself."

So how do you know if a change is necessary for you? Focus on the feeling you're reaching for. Rather than jumping up and making a huge change right off the bat, give yourself a few weeks or months of focusing on what you want *from* a change: a new lease on life? Excitement when you wake up in the morning? Feeling like you're jumping off the hamster wheel? Go ahead, make a huge leap, as long as you do it for you—move to Alaska because you love crisp days, not just because the male/female quotient is gender-ously tipped in your favor.

Do something that makes you nervous

You know those feelings when you first like someone? The nervous jitters in your knees, the butterflies in your stomach, the sweat collecting in your palms? If you're feeling stuck and stale, then it's probably been a while since you've felt those things—not just in love, but in life. So I say: Do something unusual that makes your body feel what it's like to have the nervous excitement again. Make your body crave that feeling again by giving yourself a taste of it.

After I met my husband, I passed on the secrets of dating optimism to my friend Emma, an interior decorator with a towering personality, a shock of curls like a hair commercial, and one of those smiles that cuts halfway through her cheeks. A mutual friend of ours said of her, "Emma is someone who deserves such happiness. I look at someone like her who I *know* is put on this earth to have a big, bad wonderful love, and I hope she never gives up hope. It will happen for her. Everyone knows it will, but she just has to continue to keep herself open to it."

Emma, for her part, felt more positive every day about finding her great relationship. One afternoon, she emailed me this note: "I'm still searching for my half-orange and trying to stay optimistic (it's hard!). But I think I may be drawing closer. I'd love to think so . . ."

A week later, however, a frustrated, thirty-nine-year-old Emma hit a wall: She was doing it all—keeping positive, imagining the relationship she wanted, and using her orange smile as much as possible. But she was feeling stuck. "I'm considering a change, along the lines of your 'trying a different key,'" she wrote. Emma just wasn't sure which key. "The other night I was looking at old pictures of myself, and I seemed so happy and free then, I hardly recognize myself," she wrote. She felt like the new version of herself wasn't in any mood to attract the right guy. "I'm thinking of moving back to Italy, where I lived after graduation for a few years."

It's an understandable instinct, and making huge moves like that can work for some people, as it did for Alanna and Leslie. But I also recognized that her panic was leading to a desire for overcompensation. When life feels flat, you think the only way to spark it up is to bungee off the Verzasca Dam in Switzerland. But not everyone needs to make such a big leap. "Are you sure you want to go to Italy?" I asked Emma, "Or do you just want to recapture that feeling you had when you were there last, when you felt daring, brave, and alive?"

Maybe you are ready for something big—for changing jobs, for a move to a new city or country, for a big month-long travel trip—but maybe you can create the same hopeful feeling in your life now. Instead of strapping on the bungee cord, maybe you can take a small jump instead, because a new something, as small as it is, can sometimes create the same rush of a much bigger change. A friend of mine from San Francisco felt so stuck in the hamster wheel of work, she took three weeks off to go on an African safari by herself. Not only did she have the trip of a lifetime, but she ended up in a love affair with her safari guide that has lasted for a year so far. "He's pretty remarkable," says Hannah. "He's different from me but we fit each other so well, it's hilarious. I've not stopped smiling and there is this feeling with him I've never had with another. No drama. Zero. Zilch. No drama."

Whatever happens, she's said, the trip and relationship have reminded her how good it feels to interact with life again—and has proven she's capable of feeling those heart-pounding, butterfly-flapping, palm-sweating feelings she thought she'd lost.

And then there's my friend Andy Clerkson, who was dating his girlfriend, Carolyn, for eleven years before they finally decided to get married. Yet before walking up the aisle at the wedding, he suddenly felt like he was going to lose his lunch. Why am I so *nervous*? he thought. For goodness' sake, they'd already been dating for a decade. But then he realized something: "All the things that are really worth doing in life," said Andy, "make you want to throw up before you do them." I live by that still today: **Anything that's really worth doing in life makes you want to throw up before you do it.**

If you want a love that sends your pulse pounding, maybe you need to remind yourself what it feels like to be high on life again. So get out there and find something that makes you want to throw up before you do it! Take an acting class for the heck of it, sign up for sailing lessons, apply to be on *The Amazing Race* with your best friend, or learn karate. And by the way, that surge of adrenaline you get when you're scared creates the same physical reaction—the increased heart rate, sweaty palms, and butterflies—that you get when you're in love. So go on, mimic the feeling. Don't wait to feel those surges of excitement when you meet him—create those feelings *now*.

Because if you find something that makes you feel new—something that makes you want to throw up before you do it—after you gather yourself and wipe off the sweat, you can capture the buzz and hold onto it. Resolve that *this* is the feeling you want to have when you meet your dream guy. Isn't it awesome? These moments are like popping the clutch in the car—they give you momentum, get you moving, and send such positivity out, it will be easier for your half-orange to find you.

After a year of thinking pessimistically, Parker made a big advance toward feeling better about herself by doing something that made her nervous—

really freaking nervous. Parker said she was becoming so scared of heights that even standing twenty feet up on a glass balcony "was like a terror in my veins!" she shrieks. So to combat her fear, she organized a skydiving trip with six of her friends for her birthday. "I felt like I had to do it, to prove I could," she says. "Plus, I was comforted by the fact that I would be strapped to someone else. I mean, worst-case scenario . . . well, I die. But you know, I was hoping I wouldn't."

Parker knew that if she sat in the slow lane and let life pass her by, she might let the same thing happen with love. Instead, she was determined to keep doing things that made her nervous, to keep the rush of living alive. And though she wanted to throw up before she did it, she jumped out of that plane at sunset and careened her way back down to a portion of earth called New Paltz. "The moment I jumped out of the plane, I was like, 'This is the best choice I ever made,'" says Parker. "It was mind-blowing. That feeling, that real elation, it lasted for a good month." According to her friends, Parker walked taller, smiled bigger, and dove into things more after her birthday. In addition to that short-term pleasure, the sensory rush that lasted as long as the two-minute fall, she also fed much more: She had conquered a fear and come out of it alive (thank goodness), kicking and proud of herself. And every time she talks about it now, that same spark comes back.

Though I don't think I have the nerve to jump out of a plane, I did find myself feeling like Parker at one point: a little stuck and cruising in the slow lane of life. I was still single and writing the same kinds of stories for the same magazines I always had, and I feared I would end up stalled and bored. So I started wishing for new opportunities. Well, wouldn't you know, an opportunity came up for me to go to Los Angeles to interview the cast of *Entourage* from HBO for *Glamour*. Though I'd done celebrity interviews before, this one scared me a little: I would have one shot at one hour of conversation with five famous guys, and it was my job to spin gold from the moment. Still, I've never been one to shy away from a challenge, and I was optimistic about it: Just as I was convinced I would find love, I was also convinced I would succeed at work.

I prepared my questions and booked tickets to fly to L.A. a month later—planning to pack my positivity right along with me. As with any new adventure, I looked forward to the fact that anything could happen once I got there. I couldn't wait to find out what.

SEE IT AS ANOTHER SCENE IN THE MOVIE OF YOUR LOVE LIFE

In the movies of our lives, we've all got our own reels going, and without the ups and downs, what kind of story is it, really? Your singledom *will* end, and it will have a *happy* ending, so now, sit back, relax, and let yourself enjoy the scenes that get you there while I chow down on a family-size bucket of popcorn beside you (if that's okay).

Bask in the fact that you don't know your whole ending, and mindfully appreciate each and every scene that gets you there. I'm telling you, once you meet your half-orange and you're melting into his bear hugs, you'll wish you had enjoyed this ride. You'll wish you had chilled out, smiled more, tried new foods, attempted new hobbies, traveled to different places, enjoyed yourself, enjoyed your friends. Knowing how you'll feel *then,* change what you're doing *now.* Inhale a big round orange breath, look up into the possibilities of your future, and relax into your life *right now.* Pour yourself a glass of red wine, cuddle up on your couch and reflect on all the ways you have it going on.

This life of yours will be different when you meet the guy who is right for you, you know. Perhaps you'll move out of the home you're in. Perhaps you'll move out of the city or state you're in. Perhaps you'll end up with a cat, a dog, a baby, a new couch, new friends or a new point of view. So do yourself a favor and luxuriate in the scene you're living now.

I promise you: Once you've met your half-orange, you will look back and find that the path leading you to your partner was clear and informed. Sure it will have taken turns you didn't expect, but, alas, *those* were the ones that led you to that sweet and delirious moment when you recognized the man you're meant to be with. So instead of thinking, "I can't take another day of not knowing if I'll ever meet anyone," have faith in your surprise happy ending. There's no fast-forward button on your life, or a spoiler review online to tell you what happens. So smile, soak in the fun of the journey, and say, "My half-orange is out there, and I can't *wait* to see how we meet."

DON'T GIVE UP . . . OR, OKAY, *DO*

The most difficult stretch of completing a task is not when you first begin, and not at the end when you can see the finish line, but when you've been working hard for a long time and still can't see the end coming soon. It's true for marathon runners. It's true when you're trying to lose those last ten pounds. And it's also true for entrepreneurs. Business writer Seth Godin writes about this rough patch in a fantastic little book called *The Dip*, in which he delves into the stress one feels in that moment after you start a new project, when it stops progressing and being fun and starts to feel like you're stalling. If you want it all, he says, you need to survive your own Dip! "The challenge is simple," Godin writes. "If the journey you started was worth doing, then quitting when you hit the Dip just wastes the time you've already invested. Quit in the Dip often enough, and you'll find yourself becoming a serial quitter, starting many things but accomplishing little."

If you feel like you've given it everything and it just hasn't worked—like you're trying to survive Godin's Dip in love—sit back and rest for a minute. But don't officially give up. Because the minute you feel like it's totally hopeless, well, that's often when the magic happens.

Joanna Withey was single, living in Toronto, and working at a corporate speakers' bureau when she decided she wanted more from life. She'd learned from a speech made by personal growth coach James Arthur Ray that she had to become very specific about what she wanted to feel in all areas of her life. She made the decision that she wanted to work in a warm climate, helping others with their personal growth. And as for love? She wanted a man she could talk with for hours on end and who she'd feel comfortable with in any social situation. "I had a habit of saying as a joke that my future husband was probably married right now and learning the ropes," says Joanna, "because relationships take work and commitment, and I wanted him to know that already by the time I met him!" Within six weeks, a job opportunity came up working *for* James Arthur Ray in Carlsbad, California, and Joanna sold her condo, her car, and all of her furniture and moved to her nice warm climate to take it.

When she arrived in California, she didn't know anyone, so she joined Match.com "as a form of social interaction," she says. She had a few bad dates and mismatches, so she gave up and took her photos off of her profile. "But right after I gave up on the dating thing," she says, "I got a great note from a man named Karl. I told him that he sounded like a great guy, but that I didn't have time to date. He was respectful but persistent," laughs Joanna, "and this was before he'd even seen a picture of me! When we finally met, the sparks flew." A year and a half later, Joanna married Karl, and the pair just celebrated their first anniversary. It turns out, Karl had been married before, just as Joanna had pictured, and he'd learned the ropes of relationships well. "I couldn't have picked a better partner for myself," says Joanna with pure tenderness in her voice. "We have a blast together and are just getting started." And she found him when she was on the brink of giving it all up. "The second I let go of finding my perfect man," she says, "he marched right into my life." They've now been married for two spark-filled years.

Well, they do say (those "they" people) that the minute you give up, that's when you find love. Well then, fine, "give up." But here's what I mean: Give up on a day or two of smiling and buzzing while you pull the duvet onto the couch and dial Dominos. It's exhausting keeping those positive feelings zipping through you, I know it is! But don't give up on your dating optimism overall—on your utterly immovable belief that your love life *will* absolutely, positively turn out okay. When you feel frustrated, I give you permission to take some time off from all of it—provided you agree to hold on, with a tiny string attached to the floating balloon of hope that you *do* think it can happen for you. Really, go ahead: Feel tired, feel frustrated, and get annoyed with me for making you hold onto this damn positivity that you just don't feel like using anymore. Just promise me you'll tie the string to your belt loop and let your hope fly up there on your behalf. Even Jessica Simpson tweeted about the power of hope after her July 2009 breakup with football star Tony Romo. "Everyone needs to know that hope floats," she wrote on Twitter. "Grab the strings and pull it back to you." She's right. Your optimism will keep working without you.

Remember Chuck, the commercial editor who taught us how to keep our heads up when we walk, so things would "keep looking up?" After a failed marriage, he told his friends he was finished physically searching for love, because he kept coming up empty-handed. At the same time, my friend Susan, a commercial producer, was saying the same thing to *her* friends. She'd reached the point of "giving up" because she was tired of the search for the holy grail of love. "I finally realized that I couldn't *make* it happen, and I couldn't make it *not* happen," says Susan. "I knew that nothing I tried to do to find the right guy would alter the path of me finding him," says Susan. "So I respectfully gave up pushing for it and decided to make myself happy instead. I figured I'd let go and let the world do its thing."

Chuck and Susan. Two single people. Two hearts that pined for love but had exhausted all efforts of making it happen. And lucky for them, they were also two talented professionals who ended up working together when Susan hired Chuck's company to edit a primetime commercial they were making. Chuck asked her out, and a month later Susan was beside herself with happiness. "I just knew, this is the man who was meant for me." They've now been married for seven years, have launched their own hugely successful commercial and film editing company, and are living happily with their three-year-old daughter Fletcher.

So go ahead and pretend to "give up" if you want. Because your heart is already invested and your optimism is helping you believe you'll find your other half. That balloon will be flying no matter what you do, so you may as well keep doing things that make you happy. "The universe won't let you get away with being alone," says Chuck. "It wants good people with beautiful hearts to be in love. It simply won't let you get away with not having it."

PHASE SIX:

Know When to Pluck: How to Recognize Your Half-Orange

USE YOUR WRONG-DAR TO WEED OUT THE WRONG GUYS

If you feel strongly about your orange seed, you won't have to go on three, four, or six dates with a guy until you finally decide it isn't right. From now on, you will be able to weed out the wrong guys with your very own radar—consider it your *wrong-dar.*

Me, I lingered too long over my crush on Mr. Pocket-Square, but I began to make man decisions more efficiently by comparing how I wanted to feel in my dream relationship with the way I felt with the guys I was meeting. Any time I felt uncertainty, neediness, or desperation or I felt a man was taking too long to decide if he liked me, I closed the door and walked away. And it really is that simple. Ask yourself the same things: *Does this guy match the feelings I'm looking for? Will I feel secure, smart, adored, fun, incredible, fulfilled, and more with this guy? Or should I move on?* Because the longer you linger with someone you're not sure about, that's the time you're not open to another—maybe right—guy who comes along.

Scientifically, there's even more reason your wrong-dar works. In 2008, scientists from the Max Planck Institute for Human Cognitive and Brain Sciences in Leipzig, in collaboration with the Charité University Hospital and the Bernstein Center for Computational Neuroscience in Berlin, measured what is happening in the brain just before we make decisions. Participants were asked to push a button with their left or right hand, and to let the researchers know when they consciously made the decision. It turns out the brain activity showed that the onset of predictive information came on *seven seconds before* the participants thought they were consciously making the decision. This points to evidence that many brain processes occur without the involvement of our consciousness.

In fact, if you rely *too* much on conscious thinking when making decisions, you may be doing yourself a disservice, which is what a study by scientists at Duke University discovered after having participants make "lottery" choices for various sums of money. The study was complex, but their findings were clear: They concluded that if you have too much time to consciously mull over a decision, your attention shifts to "information of lesser relevance" that may be getting in the way of making the best choice. Are you doing the same with men? Are you confusing your choices about guys with information of lesser relevance?

Don't force yourself into making pro and con lists of every little thing about a man. Let your brain and body work at its own pace and tune into your *new* tools to see if a man is worthy enough to be your half-orange. Simply put, this is what's happening when people say, "Don't think with your mind, think with your heart." Your wrong-dar—the unconscious of your emotional brain—will help make decisions for you.

Chesley Sullenberger, the US Airways pilot who saved his aircraft with a safe landing on the Hudson River in early 2009, made an instantaneous decision on where and how to land, but all the information he needed was already in his brain. His unconscious tallied more than forty years of flight experience for him in milliseconds. And your brain will do the same for you each time you meet a potential mate. Malcom Gladwell, in his book *Blink,* similarly refers to moments like this as "blink" moments, and they work. You've been planting the seed about what you want to feel, and your brain and your whole body will tell you how close you've come to the real thing.

My friend Yvonne had a watershed moment about reading her wrong-dar. Remember those Dream Boards we made? Well, she's the one who covered hers with diamonds and vacations as well as children and couples holding hands. One night, she brought home the guy she was seeing to her apartment, and when he saw her Dream Board, he mocked her for it.

"Oh my God, I was so embarrassed that he saw it," Yvonne told me over a glass of chilled rosé one night. "He kept making fun of all the things I wanted and laughing at me. I'm so dumb," she laughed. "I should have put it away!"

Wait, *really*? I reflected back what she was telling me: "You created a picture with all the things you want in life—your ideal dreams come true—and he *laughed* at it. Do you really think he would be a good match for your future?"

That's when Yvonne realized this guy seeing her Dream Board was a gift. And the fact that he made fun of her dreams only sped up the realization that this guy was *so* not right for her! If she had tuned into her wrong-dar, she would have seen it instantly. Use the relationship you want as a barometer of how close you are, too.

HEY, IS THAT A LITTLE GREEN SPROUT?

They say you know you're getting good at a language when you no longer think in English before you say it. Well, you'll be able to tell you're close to meeting your half-orange when you find yourself meeting people who are closer and closer to being right for you. I'm not talking about meeting the One. I'm talking about meeting even one person who exhibits one quality about them that is something you want in the One.

Before I became a dating optimist, I literally couldn't find a man I wanted to spend an hour at dinner with. But over the months, I found myself meeting more and more guys who seemed like what I was looking for long-term. I met someone I knew I could talk to for hours at a time (he ended up asking out someone else, but still). I was able to perceive the so-so looks of a great guy I'd met as kind of sexy (our tastes in life were too dissimilar to get along, but still). I kissed a guy who was goofy and smart *and* attractive (he didn't like me back, but still). Something was happening. Each guy I was meeting was getting closer to the real thing than the last.

Take note of this as it happens to you: *This is a great sign!* If you find yourself on a date with someone you're actually enjoying and want to kiss? Hallelujah! Don't get down because you learn you don't want to marry him. Stay upbeat because at least you found someone with whom, at this stage of the game, you actually want to spend time. That's progress! Maybe this guy and the next doesn't turn out to be right for you, but the fact that you're meeting people you're interested in is a serious step in the right direction!

Remember Lily, the writer who made her career happen, but worried she couldn't do the same for her love life? While working on her novel, the scales were tipped to work every single day, and they *had* to be. Though she dated a few guys while she was working on it, none of them shouted out "half-orange" to Lily, who was ready for a serious relationship and wanted to start a family. Two weeks after she handed in the first draft of her book, she emailed to tell me about her great date with a guy she'd met. "The conversation was so easy and wonderful, and did I mention he is adorable?" she wrote. Their first date went so well, in fact, he steered the conversation in a surprising direction.

"Do you want kids?" he asked Lily.

"Um, yes . . . why?"

"Oh, okay," he said, "I just wanted to check. Because my last girlfriend didn't want kids, and I really want them, so I figured it would be a good idea to put that on the table right away." Lily was dumbfounded. "You look surprised," he said, "do you not often go out with guys who want kids?"

Lily had to explain that as a thirty-eight-year-old woman, she wouldn't dare mention kids on the first date, because then a guy would think she wanted them right away "Well," he said, "I *do* want them right away."

While years of bad dates and disappointing relationships made it hard for Lily to give in to the moment and feel excited, she *was* excited. "Even if it ends tomorrow," she said, "I'll know that this is how I've been wanting to feel and deserve to feel." Unfortunately, it did end a few months later. Though the guy was very kind and wanted children, Lily didn't feel (among other things) intellectually or emotionally stimulated by him. And though they talked about just slowing their relationship down and seeing other people, Lily knew she needed to be completely open—without a "sort of, kind of still seeing him" boyfriend on the side—to leave room for her half-orange to fit in. Of course she had a good old college cry when she realized he wasn't the right match for her, but she also didn't feel like she was back to square one. Why? She was fortified by seeing the little green sprout.

"Even though he wasn't the One, he was a *huge* step closer to the right guy," Lily says with sure conviction in her voice. "I think I needed to know I could feel that giddy and excited about someone again. And I needed to see that warm, kind guys who wanted kids were actually out there." Instead of making Lily feel like she might want to settle for less, the relationship taught her she didn't want to settle at *all*. "I thought a guy wanting kids was the magic piece missing," says Lily, "but now I know I don't just want a family with any guy, I want it with the *right* guy."

As Lily's book debuts, she's optimistic that her positive energy will help get her momentum of dating optimism going right along with it. "I know I'm close," she says, "so I really, truly can't wait to see what will happen in the next few months."

And that's exactly how you should see it, too. The little green sprout doesn't always signal the One, but it means you've found someone *that* much closer to what you want in the One. If it's happening to you, too, let this embolden you! It's a sign that by putting the positive energy of your authentic real self out there, the guys you're attracting are getting closer and closer to your sweet other half.

My friend Yvonne noticed a little green sprout the night she attended a Hawaiian-themed party after work. She didn't feel like going at first, but she knew she'd have fun with her friends. Plus, she adds, "It was a free dinner, and with my bank account I figured I'd take what I can get." On the way over, Yvonne focused on her orange seed. Who knows? Maybe her other half would be at the party.

She walked in to a beautiful scene: tiki torches lining the room, orchids on the tables, leis around everyone's neck, and a room full of people she felt instantly attracted to. "I looked around and just thought, 'Wow, everyone here looks like someone I would like.'" Upon seeing so many guys she found attractive, Yvonne felt a new hope that, somehow, her love life was going to work out okay.

Then Yvonne spotted a hot man in an expensive suit. "Ooh," she said to her friend Caroline, "what about *him*?"

Caroline rolled her eyes; Horatio, she said, was the worst kind of player, hooking up with four girls at once, always seeking a new model to latch onto his arm, and only wanting what he couldn't have. He was, indeed, the type of guy I call the Rising Man. And though Yvonne used to consider a man like that an exciting challenge, she was using her new tools now. "I was tempted," she admits, and while she made her way around the room meeting new people, she *did* talk to Horatio to see for herself. But within a few minutes, her wrong-dar sent a clear signal that he couldn't provide what she was looking for in her dream relationship. "He was paying attention to everyone but me," says Yvonne. "I knew I would never get what I wanted from him, and I wanted to save up my energy for something good."

Two hours later, Yvonne and Caroline left the party and headed off for drinks. No, Yvonne hadn't met a guy at the Hawaiian party, but she felt she'd glimpsed the little green sprout. Just seeing that room full of guys she was attracted to and talking about art and travel with a few new people, she felt rejuvenated about her search. She'd seen the sprout of an orange tree: These men were closer to what she wanted than she'd seen in months! And it only meant one thing: She was also closer to finding her other half. Little did she know *how* close.

A few blocks further, Caroline spotted an old friend of hers on the sidewalk. And while Caroline got caught up talking to the friend, Yvonne smiled politely at the *friend* of that friend standing behind him. This was Sean, a handsome, dark-haired man with the most striking blue eyes. Once Yvonne and Sean got to talking, they never stopped.

"The connection was instant," says Yvonne. "I remember thinking, '*This is crazy. This is the feeling that everyone chases.*'" The group went inside to have drinks, and Yvonne and Sean sat together, leg touching leg, and talked about their families, their futures, their last relationships, their life goals—"all the real stuff," says Yvonne. And as for those feelings she had been focusing on, the ones she wanted to feel in her dream relationship? Sitting next to Sean, those feelings matched up. Using her new tools to decide if this guy had potential for her, she could tell there was a chance. In fact, she was falling harder by the hour. (And I can't help but like this part of the story, too: That guy Horatio, the player from the Hawaiian party? He came to the bar soon after. And the minute he saw Yvonne talking to Sean, he suddenly became interested and tried to charm her away. She waved the Cassanova away; she'd found her man.)

Though Sean lived in Canada, he and Yvonne began to fly back and forth to visit each other. Before they knew it, they were saying the "L" word and talking about marriage and children. Just after their year anniversary, he'll be moving to New York and in with her. By the sound of it, the diamonds on *her* Dream Board will come soon after.

You get the idea: seeing the sprout is a really big step. It's like spotting, for the first time, the finish line in the distance, the light at the end of the tunnel, the end of your Dip. It's proof that what you want for yourself *does* exist. You're drawing the guys you're interested in, and you're noticing the opportunities the universe is putting in your path. I'm telling you, *it is a great sign!*

When I got to this stage, I started believing in my gut that I was getting closer, so I said it out loud. "I'm getting closer, I can feel it," I'd tell Todd. "Seriously, I feel it. It's coming soon."

DON'T STARE AT THE SPROUT!

When you make a loaf of bread by hand, you mix the flour, salt, water, and yeast and then you let it rise. An hour later, you beat it down again, and then you walk away, *again*. You do your own thing, and you literally let the magic happen. The same goes for dating optimism: Walk away, live your life, and let the right man walk right into it.

When I put my faith in optimistic magnetism, I stopped forcing myself to go on dates. Instead, I went on a family road trip from Nice to Barcelona with my mom, dad and my sister (on a stretch of land full of foreign men with accents, not exactly a single girl's choice of wingmen, but worthy travel companions just the same). I went to the family barbecue at Grandma's that I had missed the year before because I was determined to attend the singles event of the summer instead. *No mas,* as the Spanish say. No more. From now on, I was doing what I *felt* like doing.

Remember Emma, the interior designer who considered moving to Italy to recapture the freedom she felt after graduating from college? She made her bread and let it rise—literally. And the recipe led her other half right to her. Here's how she explained it in an email to me:

"I put a profile up on JDate, but I hadn't gotten up the nerve to email anyone quite yet since I wasn't that excited about the process," wrote Emma. "I was waiting, as you'd suggested—until I felt like it would actually be a *fun* thing to do. In the pursuit of fun, I *did* really want to bake this one cranberry bread that I've loved for years and never have the time to make. So, late one Saturday afternoon, I zoomed over to the Food Emporium in my neighborhood (that I never go to) to buy flour and sugar. They'd opened a giant organic produce department since I'd last been there and I got really psyched about the place. So when I went to pay for everything I decided to sign up for one of those membership cards. I vaguely remember that there was someone behind me in line, and I told the checkout person that I didn't want to infuriate the people in line behind me, but could I fill out the form? Which I did. Then I went home and made my bread and had a great night out with some friends later. I was feeling good.

"Two days later I checked my JDate email and saw that there was a message from a guy saying, 'Hello from the neighborhood.' The first line of his email said that he'd stood behind me in line at the supermarket on Saturday and recognized my picture! He asked if I'd want to grab a drink sometime in the neighborhood. I met him for coffee a week later, and by the third date I was smitten. Greg is a photographer, exactly my age, was married for two years then divorced, and lives four blocks away from me. He is a lot like me, kind of a dreamer and creative. We often just look at each other and shake our heads and say, 'I can't believe how great you are.'"

Not only did Emma feel great about the present, but she's even happier about the future. "I even showed him my Dream Board," says Emma, "and he didn't *flinch* at the pictures of cute babies and all of the women sitting in the lotus position at the edge of the ocean." A few months after they met, they traveled to Japan to celebrate their fortieth birthdays, and they're now engaged and planning their wedding.

That, my friends, is how you do it. Emma followed the dating optimism process, and it didn't just end in a nice happy date—it brought her half-orange straight *to* her. She dreamed of him long and hard, and then one day, she stepped right into his path at the grocery store. Instead of digging for dates online when she wasn't feeling up for it, she did something she *was* feeling good about. Was love on her mind while she did it? Sure, deep in her heart. But Emma knew she didn't have to become a slave to her singleness. Instead, she embraced what brought out the most eudaimonically, authentically happy version of herself: baking bread on a sunny day.

It's exactly the point I had reached in my dating arc. I was in Montauk, chatting away with my friend Phillip, who was spending the weekend. When he asked about my love life, I told him, "I'm single at the moment, but I'm going to be in a relationship soon—I can feel it." He looked at me a little funny, and then asked me the ol' but-how-you-gonna question: "But how are you going to meet someone when you're hanging out with your gay hairdresser all the way out here?" I finally had my answer.

"I figure," I told Phillip, "that if I'm going to meet the love of my life soon, I want to be at my *best* when I meet him. And being out here, spending time with my friends and family and watching my cat chase butterflies around the backyard, is what brings out my best. I believe that the happier I am, the more likely he'll come along. And the more authentically me I am, the more I'll know for sure if he's right for me when I meet him."

The following weekend, my sister and I went home to visit my parents for Mother's Day, which meant I would miss a big party on a big city hotel terrace, sure to be teeming with single guys. The former Desperately Dating Amy would have groaned inside about missing the opportunity to go out.

But the new optimistically dating me wasn't disappointed at all, because I had learned to follow the cues my life gave me. I was going to do what made me feel warm and fuzzy and happy, and that meant spending time with my parents and sister.

When Liz and I arrived home, my mom said she wanted us to accompany her to a movie at our hometown theater. It turns out my mother's friend had a son named Mike who'd made a documentary film, and she wanted us to go with her. (The film was called *Access Nation*, about the bizarrely real people who produce their own cable access television shows.) I had only one question: "Will there be popcorn?"

When the opening credits started, I saw Mike's name. And then I saw a name that sent chills down my spine: Gustavo. The kid I watched sing "Jailhouse Rock" in grade school. The guy I ran into years later in the summer between college semesters and had a summer of innocent dates with. The guy I spent hours on the phone with. The guy who asked me to lunch and then pulled wine and a blanket out of his trunk and reminded me romance wasn't dead. I'd had no idea, but Gustavo was Mike's best friend. They'd spent six months driving around the country making the documentary film together.

My body went fuzzy and my hands got damp as I turned to the back of the theater and saw Gustavo's silhouette standing in the doorway. When the (fantastic!) film ended and the lights went up, I was as nervous as a schoolgirl. There I was, walking toward the lobby wearing jeans, flats, and a navy V-neck, plain as can be; my hair was dirty and my face hadn't a bit of makeup on it. I was grubby as heck, but glowing on the inside. As I exited the theater, I dabbed some Rosebud salve on my lips and behind my ears. Then I walked up to Gustavo in the lobby and said hello.

He was now an artist living in Los Angeles—and he was single. My stomach flipped a few times as he pulled out his phone and started showing me a slide show of the art he painted—beautiful bright-colored semi-abstract images of women dancing, trapeze artists flying, a cat fishing his paw into a pond. His art was more beautiful than I could have imagined, and it made my whole body warm. What in the world was happening? I hadn't felt this way in years.

When my mother approached us, something hit me: *Wait,* I thought, *did I just meet the love of my life while I was hanging out with my . . . mom?* After catching up in the theater lobby, Gustavo said he'd be heading back home early the next morning. "Well, if you ever come to L.A.," he said, "you should give me a call."

"That's funny," I said. "I just got an assignment to interview the guys from *Entourage.* I'm coming in two weeks."

SWEET SUCCESS: KNOW IT WHEN YOU SEE IT

Focusing on what you want in your relationship has given you a wrong-dar. But it will also give you the ability to sense when something is worthwhile for the *right* reasons.

Julianna was living in Atlanta, Georgia, and engaged to her boyfriend. Six weeks before the wedding, she crumbled with doubt. Yes, the wedding hall was booked, the dress was altered, the invites were out, and her future, should she choose to accept it, was written. But Julianna's gut was screaming that she deserved more, and she didn't want to settle. Instead of spending his days off with her, her fiancé went out for beers to watch football; instead of spending his vacations with her, he'd go on ski trips with his buddies. Julianna didn't feel loved or appreciated for who she *really* was. "I knew that if I followed through and married him," she says, "I'd be settling for less than what I wanted and what I deserved." So six weeks before the wedding, she called it off and flew to New York City to start a new life.

Julianna said the breakup gave her the strength to ask for what she *really* wanted, and she began focusing on it immediately. "I wanted a man who loved me and stuck by my side and showered me with affection," she said. "I wanted a partnership and a lover for life." A few days after landing in New York, she met Dave, a tall, lanky illustrator raised in South London who wore wacky suits and mohawks. They fell for each other immediately and married two years later. Julianna later said she knew she wanted to be with him in the first fifteen minutes. She was, she said, able to recognize him immediately, because she'd been waiting for everything that he was. The way she put it was this: "Everything I ever wanted in a man arrived on my doorstep in the most surprising package."

When you allow yourself to let go and believe in dating optimism, you can live with this faith every day. You'll know when you're settling—the same way Julianna did—and you'll know when it's right. Just remind yourself of that: "I don't know what he looks like. But I'll know him when I see him." How? You'll recognize him by the *feelings* you have when you're with him. When you meet the man you're meant to be with, you will feel a harmony with him and the feelings in your body. This is what people mean when they say, "You'll know in your gut," and "When you know, you know." You'll know because the energy around both of you will match the relationship you've focused on. You have attracted it and him right to you. After Julianna found Dave, I used my new phrase more than ever when people asked me what my ideal guy looked like, and you should use it, too. Say, **"I don't know what he looks like. But I'll recognize him when I see him."**

IS HE OR ISN'T HE?

There's a word many women use about their other halves, when they describe their first days or weeks together: that word is *easy*. They say things like, "It was so easy," "Everything between us was easy." "There's no drama, it was just . . . easy." Remember Wendi Forrest, whose mom set her up for a round of golf with her future husband Nate? She uses the word, too. "This is the easiest relationship I've ever had," says Wendi, "counting my relatives, counting my friends. It's the *easiest* one. I love him and it's just that simple." It's easy because the way you want to feel in a relationship matches the way you do feel. Harmony

> ### How to fall for a nice guy
> Find a way to see him in an environment where he feels more comfortable than you do. Maybe it's a work function or an astronomy club dinner or a basketball game with his guy friends, or a mountain bike ride on a trail he likes. Let him show you where and how he excels. You may find yourself surprised at how attracted you become to his mind, or to the way he commands the room. And, then, if you find yourself feeling a physical connection at all, kiss him. Because sometimes, as the Shoop Shoop song tells us, "that's where it is."

makes things easy. Which is why you shouldn't use your old tools to decide if he's right for you ("His face isn't what I pictured," or "He doesn't make tons of money"); use your new tools.

Part of your connection might elicit goosebumps and butterflies (that whole it-feels-like-high-school thing), but it should also make sense logically, with your thinking brain. Because the feelings you've been focusing on—that you want with your half-orange—are not about short-term, quickie pleasures. You deserve to feel a gratifying eudaimonia in your relationship, and the only way you will is if your connection is based on appreciating one another for your authentic selves.

Now, what if you do feel wonderful when you're with him, but it scares you because he's so different from what you expected? Well, maybe everything *you've* asked for has landed on your doorstep in the most surprising package. If not, though, it's okay. You don't *have* to date him just because he's smart and great and funny. You don't have to date him because you feel like you "should." You don't have to date him because your friends or family or therapist or coworker says you need to give guys like him a chance. And you don't have to date him because some other women would find him perfect. This is about how the two of you are *together*. And if you're not feeling it, let yourself off the hook.

Still, if he makes you feel all the right things, but you're just not sure you want to take it to the next level? Perhaps he just seems *too* nice. In that case, it might be worth trying the "How to fall for a nice guy" technique.

Rachel Cook, a thirty-five-year-old massage and bodywork specialist from Colorado, dated a lot of guys who looked the part she thought she wanted before she realized she was short-changing herself. "You're often not clear about what you want until you're getting a lot of what you don't want," says Rachel. "I was in a relationship with a really negative person who berated me and said I wasn't smart or good enough, and that I was lucky enough to have him—the whole bit. And I didn't realize I deserved better."

Then one day, while driving down Federal Boulevard in Denver, she figured out the true key to her happiness. "I wanted someone who was going to love me for exactly who I was as a person. Not who I could be or who they could turn me into, but for who I was right now. And I wanted to feel the same way about him." Rachel was so adamant that she wasn't going to settle for less, she said out loud in her car that day, "If I have to be alone until I'm sixty, I will find that person, and I won't settle for less ever again!"

Four months later, the perfect relationship presented itself in the form of someone she never expected: Frank, a friend she'd had since high school. "My ideal guy had always been an Abercrombie type of guy who was immaculately dressed. And Frank is really laid back and wears camo pants and concert T-shirts. He's a nice guy, but he wasn't the guy I was looking for in my mind." Though she admits she'd thought of kissing him in the years before, "every time I felt any attraction, I dismissed it, because I didn't feel he was my type and I didn't want to mess up our friendship." Still, they had hung out on and off for over a decade. They'd have dinner, vent as friends, and love each other for exactly who they were.

One night, Frank admitted he couldn't stop thinking about Rachel in a more-than-friends way and left her to think about it. A few days later, after dinner at Applebee's, they were about to part ways in the parking lot when Frank asked if he could kiss her. "The second I kissed him," she says, "I knew he was the guy. We locked lips for five minutes straight and I just knew at that moment." And for the first few months of their relationship, Rachel would look at Frank, shake her head, and say, "I'm so glad it's you."

She was careful about moving too quickly, however, as she wanted to make sure they were truly compatible before risking the friendship. "We played Twenty Questions, but about our future: kids, marriage, money. It's easy to get caught up in the moment and overlook the really important things that will stay with you for a lifetime." Well, they passed their own test, and five years later, are planning their wedding in Estes Park. "He is my best friend," she says, "my confidant, my mentor."

Frank wasn't the well-primped cover model Rachel pictured in her head, yet he's worlds above the relationships she almost settled for. And the only way she was able to see that was to recognize him with her heart first. In this case, she knew him when she kissed him. "It's funny how we settle," says Rachel. "I don't know if it's a worthiness issue or like, 'Oh, I couldn't possibly ask for everything I want, that would be too much!' But," she says with five years' worth of love behind her, "you don't get what you want until you're bold enough to ask for it."

WHEN THE TREE BEARS FRUIT

I had been focusing on what I wanted in my other half, and I felt I was on the verge of getting it. But as my airplane touched down in Los Angeles, there was one tiny issue at bay: Did Gustavo feel the same way about *me?*

I spent my first evening with Gustavo and his loftmate Johnny, but since the romance wasn't physically sparking, I worried it wasn't on his mind. The next day, I drove up to a house in the Hollywood Hills and watched as the *Entourage* cast posed near—and jumped into—the pool, with the view of L.A. in the distance. My stomach was stirring a bit as I checked both of my tape recorders in the living room and read over my questions, committing them to memory so I could have an off-the-cuff feeling conversation. Just as I shook my nerves about the interview, new butterflies crept in: Gustavo was just a few miles away in his loft. Was he thinking about me as much as I was thinking about him? I felt lighter and happier than I had in weeks, and I couldn't wait to see him again. And with this much optimism lifting me up inside, I knew my interview would go well. Heck, I was wearing my cutest heels and any minute now, we'd be sitting on comfy couches in the living room chatting away. How could it *not* go well?

A publicist waved me over. "The guys are wet from the pool," she said, "so they'd like to do the interview outdoors in the hot tub."

Um, gulp, *in* the hot tub? I was in too good a mood to let it throw me, so I kicked off my heels, rolled up my jeans, smiled big and stuck my feet in the water. And when a gust of wind swept my questions out from under my leg and right toward Adrien Grenier's chest in the tub, I took it the same way I took awkward moments in dating: The worse the moment, the better the story! I laughed out loud as I took back my pages, which were dripping with water and bleeding ink, and I suddenly felt more relaxed and optimistic than ever.

The guys were friendly and hilarious, so I knew I had more than enough for my story and drove back to my hotel by the beach with a grin plastered on my face. The verdict on the story? Done. The jury on my love life? Still out.

That night, I met up with Gustavo for dinner, and as we hunkered down for cheeseburgers, we talked for hours about what we'd done in life, what we wanted to, and what kind of future we saw for ourselves. As it started to rain, I noticed things about him I never would have fully appreciated at twenty-one, like how confident he was and how warmly he talked about his mother and sister. I wondered why I hadn't grabbed onto him for good fourteen years before.

But I knew why: Back as college kids, our two-year age difference was awkward. Sure, two years difference in your thirties and beyond is nothing—but when I was twenty-one and he was still a *teenager*? Back then, as much as I loved his company and laughed my way through our dates, and as romantic and mature as he was, I couldn't get the voice out of my head that I was dating "the little kid from grade school." But now it made *so* little difference. All the feelings I had been focusing on the past eight months matched what I was feeling with him now. And my mother was right about the benefits of a shared background; it felt safe finding someone back where I came from, who knew me when.

We finished our meal and took seats in the restaurant's empty back room next to the French doors facing the ocean. A few minutes later, someone on the wait staff accidentally turned out the lights, leaving us in total darkness, save for the subtle glow of the moon. The rain hammered the boardwalk, the water rippled the window panes, and my heart began to pound. Would he face me? Kiss me? I was tied up in nervous knots and couldn't take it. I had to say something. It was now or never.

"You know," I finally said, "If you were thinking of kissing me tonight, now would be a really good time."

He took me up on it, thank God. And after he dropped me off at my hotel a few hours later, I started to cry. I was literally overwhelmed by my emotions, and I sobbed into my pillow thinking, *Thank you, world, thank you.* The next morning, as I walked into the airport terminal, Gustavo called to wish me a safe flight. (Though I was flying high in that airport far before that plane took off.)

A week later, I had the first inkling that this was the real thing. It happened when I called him from New York and left a message. An hour later, I still hadn't heard back, so I picked up the phone and dialed again. My friend Todd was standing next to me and I saw a wave of panic cross his face.

"Wait, has he called you back yet?" he asked.

"No," I said putting the phone to my ear. "So I figured I'd call him again."

With that, Todd did what every good friend would: He dove toward me through the air in what felt like a slow motion movie moment, arms outstretched to swat the receiver from my hands, a "Noooooo!" bellowing low from his belly. *Don't you realize*, his eyes were asking, *that no respectable women calls a man twice without coming off like a desperate loser?*

I pulled the phone to safety and laughed. "It's okay!" I said. "This is different. I can't explain why, I just know it is."

Because unlike every other guy I'd ever called, I wasn't worried about playing games or following someone else's flirting rules. I wasn't worried Gustavo would think I was pushy or needy. I knew that he wanted to hear from me as much as I wanted to hear from him, and that he'd want to see me as much as I wanted to see him, and that any text or card or gift I sent him he'd be just as thrilled to get. I didn't know the term yet, but what I was feeling and what *you* should aim for, too, is the match of those two orange halves meeting perfectly in the middle: two equals, wanting the same in love.

A month later, Gustavo was standing with me beneath the bluffs on Ditch Plains Beach, watching the surfers bob on the waves—the same waves I used to smile at as I asked for love.

"It's my favorite place in the world," I said. "What do you think?"

"I love it," he said. A few days later, he said the same about me. Six months after that, Gustavo proposed, and I moved to L.A. to start our life together. He's my partner in crime, my other half, *mi media naranja*. And life feels like one big, loving journey every single day we're together. The day after our wedding, on a beach in Mexico with seventy-two of our closest friends and family, we went parasailing from a boat that rode up and down the coast of Playa del Carmen. We were holding hands, floating in the sky over turquoise water, smiling and laughing, when Gustavo gripped my hand even tighter. "What a way to start our big adventure together," he said.

Gustavo is, literally, everything I focused on, and I know, without a doubt, that the intensity of my dating optimism brought him to me. And I believe we all have that power to bring to us everything we desire. Focusing on what you want and feeling great about it can bring you everything you ask for, and then some. I need only look back at my original intention to see the path that led him to me.

You can Bring Yourself the Love You Want

Six months after Gustavo and I began dating, I came across my work calendar from 2004—two years before we'd run into each other again. I flipped through it nostalgically, remembering lunches I'd scheduled and events I'd dragged my single friends to so I could scope out the guys. On the front inside flap of the calendar, I'd posted two yellow sticky notes with names of editors my friends said I should work with. *What a coincidence*, I thought. They had both independently contacted me, and I'd already written stories for both of them.

Then I turned to the back cover, where a third sticky note was posted. It had a phone number on it and one name: Gus. The note sent a chill through my spine. I called Gustavo and read him the numbers. "Yep," he said, "that was my old number."

Seeing my handwriting brought a flash of a memory back: Two years before I ran into Gustavo again, I was at my beach shack flipping between the six channels we got on our wood-paneled television. I was about to head to the West Coast to do a travel story, and wondered, "Who do I know in Los Angeles?" I'd heard through the hometown grapevine that Gustavo had moved to L.A. And even though I hadn't seen him in more than a decade, I'd never forgotten him. But Gustavo was such a catch, there was no way he was still single . . . was there?

These being the days before Facebook—before Friendster, even—I couldn't write on his personal wall or check his tagged photos for a wife. I'd have to just dial the digits the old-fashioned way and see if I could get my voice to stop shaking long enough to ask. So I called information and got his number. But the thought of a girl picking up stopped me from going further; on that quiet night alone in a crooked little house, I couldn't get up the nerve. So I stuck the sticky note into my date book and carried on with my life. Two years later, Gustavo walked right back into it.

I tell you this because I want you to realize the power of your intentions. You *can* bring yourself the life you want, and you can attract the love you want if you give it the focus it deserves. Feed your orange seed right now. Feel what it will be like, in this moment, to close this book and then curl up into the arms of your other half.

MEETING YOUR HALF-ORANGE

Dating optimism is a process, and it doesn't happen overnight. There are reasons for this: Sometimes the world has to work out the logistics of getting you and your half-orange in the same place at the same time. And sometimes, you both need to experience something special that will make the path toward one another clear.

Parker, for instance, has not yet found her other half, but she's already jumped out of an airplane, so I know she can brave the fear of leaping toward love. And she feels she's closer than ever to believing that she deserves him; as she says herself, "I believe that when you're ready, it presents itself. As soon as I give up these not-worthy things I think about myself, it will happen. I know you really *do* have to be who you want to be before it will present itself." Parker, just know that you have a group of friends who know, like Emma's friends knew, that you deserve a big, bad, wonderful love and someone who sees you for how great you really are. The minute you see that in yourself, you'll get your half-orange. I promise you, you *will* get him.

The same goes for Lily, who sounds to me like she's closer than ever to finding her perfect match and getting that family of her dreams. I also know that love can come to Mary, who's been so grateful for the life she has now, she feels bad asking for more. And remember Shayanne, who attracted parking tickets with her negative perspective? She recently attracted her dream job running and cooking on her own organic farm, and once she focuses on the brilliant things she wants from love, she'll get that, too. When Francine is ready to give up dating three men around the world at once and tell the universe she wants the real thing, I have no doubt he'll come running. And as soon as Todd decides he wants a relationship (or, as he says, his dream "husberjack"), he'll get on the half-orange train, too. When you're ready and motivated to be a dating optimist, he will come. And you should be confident that if you believe you can have it, and you focus with every fiber of your being on how great it will be once your half-orange rolls into your life . . . your big love *will* arrive.

Do whatever you have to do to keep this picture alive in your mind, in your heart, and in your body, to make it a true part of you. Put pictures of your ideal relationship on your Dream Board, keep reading your Big Love List, write sticky notes on your calendar, and step foot into the places that make you feel whole and happy and loved—which you'll only get more of when your half-orange joins you on your journey.

Become the woman now who you want to be become in your dream relationship. If you dress the part of the happy, loving, adventurous, smart, confident woman you know you are, your other half will better be able to recognize you when you meet. If you want love—true, magical, incredible love with that guy—you can have it! And now, you know what to do:

1. Believe you can have it. (Because you can and because you deserve it.)
2. Admit you want it, to yourself and others. (And by this point, I'll bet you're finally doing that.)
3. Focus on, love-visualize, and imagine feeling yourself in the relationship you want. Do it every day—every hour if you can think of it. The more you do it, the faster it will work.
4. Openly hope for it like you've never hoped for anything before.
5. Live your happy life. Dress the part from the inside out. Be the happy, confident, optimistic, hopeful, loving woman you know you've always wanted to be.

Optimistic magnetism—the fact that you're creating a magnet of energy with all of your thoughts—is happening right now. So use it deliberately to get what you deserve. The fact that you've read this far gives me all the confidence in the world that you *will* find everything you want; your persistence is proof! Just do what we've talked about, and focus, focus, focus. And remember this: **It's not your job to figure out how you're going to bring your dream relationship to you. It's just your job to want it**. So want it. Want it *all*.

APPENDIX A:

Dating Strategies of Operation Optimism

You know how to engage your optimism in the grand scheme of love. But how do you do it on a daily dating basis? Well, you'll do it by calling on the strategies of Operation Optimism. If you feel more positive about each specific date, your energy will send out stronger calls to the universe, and you'll be more likely to attract the right guy—who, by the way, might be the guy you *think* you don't like in the first three minutes.

1. Practice changing your negative buzzwords.

People don't just want to be optimists, they want to date optimists, too. So work on changing your negative buzzwords before your date—then enforce it on your date, and pay your good mood forward. If you don't know what your negative buzzwords are, ask a friend. Maybe they often hear you say you "can't," you "hate," or you "won't." Or maybe you're always talking about how people "never" do anything right. Once you know what to listen for, you'll be more likely to catch and stop yourself. For added incentive, do what cursing-quitters often do: Put $1 in a jar every time you bring up a negative topic among your friends, to help train yourself out of bringing up negative topics on your date. Think about it. You wouldn't want to hear your date say he "can't understand people who like sushi" or "never feels like going to work." You'd want to hear that they love surfing and will try anything on the menu. The same goes for you: Nobody liked that *SNL* character Debbie Downer, so do what you can to be the most positive version of yourself.

2. Commit to complimenting your date on three things.

Making yourself search out the good *(He does have a pretty funny laugh!)* rather than the bad *(Uh-oh, he's a bit of a close talker . . .)* is the simplest way to flip the optimist switch on your date. If you focus on finding the good in the person across the table, you *will* find it. But don't stop at one—find three, and compliment him. Think about the big picture: You and your date are both per- ilously trying to survive Planet Single, and sometimes a few nice words can go a long way to making you feel more positive about the experience.

3. Get your friends involved.

When I was single, many of my coupled-up friends would say they envied the "anything could happen!" mentality that every new date brings. Hearing that made me appreciate my single sta- tus even more—which is why I decided to draw my friends in with before-and-after reports. I went on one date after meeting some married friends of mine for a cocktail. Before I left, we worked out a code that I would text them throughout the night: "C" for Cute, "NC" for Not Cute, "SC" for Super Cute, SFO for "Still Figuring it Out," etc. We had such laughs thinking about what I might find that I walked away from them and toward my date with a giddy anticipation I hadn't felt in a while. (That particular date was Super-Cute and Super-Nice, but later turned out to be Super-Weird.)

4. Ask questions.

They say you learn something new every day in life, so why not learn a little about life from your date? Try it: Make it your goal to learn something about the person sitting across from you. You may get some insight on a point of view opposite of your own, or you may find out you have more in common than you thought. Like Colleen Seifert's friend said: Everyone has a good story in them, it's your job to find out what it is. Here are four big story-starters to get you going:

• "What's the best trip you've ever taken and why?"
• "If you had to leave town tomorrow, what local meal would you miss the most?"
• "What's the scariest or weirdest thing that's ever happened to you?"
• "If money was no object and you could live comfortably doing any job in the world, what would you do?"

5. Buy a lottery ticket together.

Yes, winning the lottery with a perfect stranger would be weird, but isn't winning the lottery in the *first* place pretty insane? The lottery, you see, is the epitome of optimism: You don't pay a dollar for something you know you'll never win; you pay a dollar because you believe there is actually the slightest sliver of possibility that you *will* win. So just for fun, if you and your date are driving or walking past a convenience store, suggest popping in and picking up a scratch-off or picking some numbers on a card together—50/50. Or, if you must, buy two separate lottery tickets. Either way, before you find out if you've won, talk about all the great stuff you'd do with your shares of the money. It doesn't get more positive than that.

6. Go on you-can't-lose dates.

Nothing seems like more of a waste than having an average, predictable evening with a boring date you know you'll never see again. Instead: Find something you've always wanted to do or something you really *need* to do, and do that on your date. You can't help but be optimistic when you know that no matter what happens with the love connection, you still win! So take your date to a driving range or a kooky Thai restaurant with singing Elvises, or to the Mac store to look at laptops or to a museum gift shop to pick up a present for your dad.

Early into my dating optimism, I found a play I really wanted to attend, and though I usually went to see theater on my own, I figured, what the heck, I may as well see if the guy I'd met playing pool with wanted to spend our first official "date" seeing it with me. I loved having the company, and it was a great way to assess what he was really like as we talked about the play afterward. (There wasn't much zing, but I had a fantastic night.) So instead of putting yourself in places where you might lose on your dates, do what you can to make sure you gain.

7. Look at your short-term date as practice for your long-term relationship.

From now on, officially, no date is ever a waste of time. Because if you're not gaining a friend or getting a laugh or learning something new, at least you can use the experience to become a better girlfriend or partner when you do find your half-orange.

How? By being clear about what you want or don't want on each date, you're honing the personal growth process known as "differentiation," which Ellyn Bader, Ph.D., defines as "the ability to know what you think, feel, and desire and put that out in an ongoing way in a relationship, and to be able to tolerate and encourage your partner doing the same thing." Translation: You get good at letting a guy know, "This is who I am, and this is something that matters to me," which is what you must do to keep a long-term relationship alive. "When you're dating, you don't take things so personally, and you learn to be able to rebound from rejection," says Bader. "The more differentiated and capable you are of handling tough discussions, the more you're actually strengthening your capacity to be a better partner in a relationship or marriage."

So if you meet up with your next date and can tell in the first twenty minutes that the flames aren't sparking and probably never will, instead of just enduring an hour, practice your "skillz." If he wants to sit over in the dark corner and you'd prefer a spot by the window, speak up. If he asks if you want children and you do, practice being honest and say, "Yes, definitely." If he wants to go out again and you don't want to, politely decline and tell him why. "I would underline this advice six times," says Peter Pearson, Ph.D., Bader's husband and partner in therapy practice, who finds that couples' lack of differentiation is one of the biggest issues in fractured relationships. Take it from the marriage therapists: "It's practice in being authentic. You have everything to gain. The only thing you have to lose," laughs Pearson, "is your future ex-husband."

8. You date, you learn.

You don't rent the first apartment you see, and you don't buy the first bathing suit you try on. You sample them all, and the more you try, the closer you know you're getting to what you want. Well, it's the same with love. Sometimes the restaurant is only average, sometimes the $160 jeans stretch too much in the butt, and sometimes your date will disappoint you. But learning from each date and getting the bad ones out of the way takes you that much closer to the good ones—and more importantly, makes you appreciate the crazy twists and turns on the road to real romance.

9. Remember: The worse the date, the funnier the story.

Dating is like the opposite of Olympic figure-skating judging: Instead of throwing out the highest and lowest scores, a happy dater relishes both! And the more you can learn to laugh at your lows, the better you'll feel. That guy I took to the play with me, for example? On our way to dinner at a nice steakhouse, we were stopped by a man making balloon animals, which my date insisted he buy for me. I blushed as I carried my two-and-a-half-foot balloon doggie into the restaurant, and I immediately shoved it under my seat—not realizing I was positioned beside a heating vent. Thirty minutes later, the balloon doggie *exploded* like a gunshot, sending the entire restaurant into shock and life-threatened stares toward our table. It was mortifying and hilarious at the same time, and I thanked that busted doggie for giving me the best laugh I had all week.

And Nadine, the New York editor, still laughs about the night she was invited to a book reading by a guy she'd met. When she showed up, she saw that he had invited three *other* single women he was wooing. "At that point, I had to laugh," says Nadine. "It was a comedy. And I reached a nirvana of understanding: Everyone is trying to meet someone and we're not all doing it so gracefully. Dating is hell for everyone, so you have to just become more compassionate about it and have a sense of humor. As long as you live in the belief that you will meet the right person, you can learn to laugh that the universe is providing entertainment along the way!"

APPENDIX B:
The OrangeAid Handbook

They say that when life gives you lemons, you should made lemonade. Well, that's what we're going to do here, but with an orange twist. The goal is to get you in the habit of making dating optimism your default. You'll do this by changing your explanatory style about setbacks and fears, and turning your negative, discouragingly single thoughts back into hopeful, positive ones. So the next time you find yourself saying any of the following things, use the ammunition of optimism to fight back!

"I'm never going to meet anybody."

Boy, this strategy always works really well, doesn't it? "I'm never going to lose weight," "I'm never going to be able to do ten push-ups," "I'm never going to find parking." And it's funny, you never can do all those things when you think you can't, can you? Sheesh. Haven't you learned anything from *The Little Engine That Could?*

You're right, though, you're never going to meet anyone if you keep calling the "never" right to you. Come at your love life from a place of hope and optimism and stomp the "nevers" with the pointiest stiletto heel you own! You can be who you want to be and attract who you want to attract. You're fabulous and special, and there are men out there who would kill to meet a woman like you. But if you keep calling the "never" your way, you'll *never* find out who they are! Live your life as if you'll meet your big love soon, and the next somebody you meet might be pretty freaking fantastic for you.

"There are no good guys out there."

Of course there are good guys out . . . ohhhh, right. You just mean there aren't any of them whom you would want to date anywhere near you. Again, I hate to argue with you on this, but there *are* good guys you may want to date near you. You just haven't met them yet.

As with most things in life, I can't help but compare this to food. (It's why one of the few Spanish phrases I know is *Me gusto comer:* I like to eat—which my half-orange felt the need to teach me two weeks into dating.) Have you eaten everything your town has to offer? I don't just mean, "Have you ever tried something from that dive on the corner?" I mean, have you eaten every single dish offered from every single place? Heck, you probably haven't even had everything on the Burger King menu. Well, the same goes for the guys out there!

Sure, you've had a smattering of dates here and there, but that doesn't in any way account for the breadth of men to choose from. That guy you dated last? He has a dozen friends and quite a few coworkers you haven't met. And if you've noticed even one guy at Macy's who you'd never seen before, that's proof right there, because where did that guy come from? The place all new guys do: They fell off the "You haven't met them yet" truck! My suggestion is that you admit there are good guys out there, and then ask the world to bring one to you.

"I haven't met the right guy yet, but, whatever, I don't care."

Beware the "whatever." Because "whatever" doesn't mean "I don't care." It means, "I really *do* care, but I don't have a clue how to fix it." And let's be honest: You do care. You want love in your life, and not just any love, but a big, bad wonderful love. And you haven't come this far in the process of dating optimism to stop caring. You're closer than you've ever been, so of all times to care, this is the time!

"Whatever" is a word of weakness that means you can't bear the weight of having to come up with the words to explain how you really feel. You owe it to yourself to be honest and *say what you mean.* Maybe what you mean is, "I haven't met the right guy yet, and I'm frustrated." Or "I haven't met the right guy, and I'm scared I won't." Whatever you truly feel, say that. Then you have something real to address: real emotions, real fears, not a fake sense of "I don't care." Once you admit you care, you can focus on caring about meeting the right guy.

Also, although you haven't met him yet, your "yet" tells me you know you will. Just because you haven't done your taxes yet doesn't mean you'll never do them; it means it's on the list and it will get done. And if you haven't met the right guy yet, you'll meet him at some point, too. So stop falling back on your "whatever" attitude. Your love life is no "Rapper's Delight." You may "party hardy like you just don't care," but you'll get a lot further a lot faster if you acknowledge your authentic feelings and put caring on the top of your list.

"I don't need a man to make me happy."

First of all, good for you. It takes some people a good long time to reach that point of self-assurance and confidence to know that we are the captains of our own happiness. That said, if you think it will make you happier to be in a committed relationship with your other half, to love and be loved? That's a want. Not a need.

Think of all the other things that make you happy: A birthday present wrapped in a big bow. A frozen drink on the beach. A pair of pants that make you look so ridiculously skinny that everyone who sees you asks, "Have you lost weight?" Do you need all those things? No, of course not.

What you need, teaches Les Stroud of *Survivorman*, is water, shelter, and food. But if you're lucky enough have a life in which you get more than water, shelter, and food, then you're allowed to look at some of your wants. What are the things that will make your life not merely survivable but worth surviving for?

If your needs are being met, go ahead, meet some of your wants. Splurge on a pair of pants if they make you look skinny, because you'll beam with confidence. And if a relationship will make your day, too? Well, you may not "need" it for survival, but it can make life a lot more fun.

By the way, I'll tell you when I used to say "I don't need a man to make me happy." I'd say it when I wanted people to know that I was a tough cookie and would be just fine on my own. (Ooh, how exciting, a life of being "fine.") Part of my message was: *Please, everyone, stop worrying about me!* But when you say this, your body will look just as livid. Think about it: When you say, "I don't need a man," you may do one of a few things: Your shoulders may shrug, you may have a dismissive "You're wrong" scowl on your face, you may shake your head, cross your arms or legs, or lean back and away from the people you're saying this to. Now, look at yourself from a bird's eye view—or better, a guy's eye view. Is *that* a woman he wants a relationship with? Seriously, your guy—your dream guy—could be close. He may be in your circle of friends, he may be in the same restaurant, or he may be passing you in the grocery store aisle. And if, perchance he is, do you want him to see that side of you—the naysaying, dismissive, shrugging, scowling you?" Uh . . . no. So stop telling everyone and yourself what you *don't* need and start talking about what you *do* want.

"Maybe I should just settle . . . "

Oh, that's a good idea. Commit to something you really don't want all that much, and then spend the rest of your life resenting what you chose. Since food metaphors have been serving us well, that's like going into a restaurant with a friend who's trying to spend as much as possible on you and suggests you both get the surf and turf, the chocolate soufflé, and a bottle of the finest wine. "Nah," you say. "I mean, that sounds incredible and I'd love to eat it, but I'll just settle for some boiled chicken, a scoop of vanilla ice cream, and a glass of water." Never mind that the choice that will make your soul sing is on the menu. You're going to settle.

Well, guess what? That's lame. *Settling is for quitters.* Settling is for people who, instead of aiming for first, just aim not to be last (i.e., alone). If you're already feeling a flat-line with a guy you meet now, just imagine—imagine, really—what it's going to feel like in five years.

This isn't about settling in one small area, which plenty of people do. Settle on the small things (fine, he doesn't think *30 Rock* is funny; he's crazy but it's *fine*), but don't settle on the important things. Don't settle on how big his heart is. Or on how wonderful and smart and sexy he makes you feel. Don't settle on how devoted he is to you, how loyal, how trustworthy. Don't settle on how attracted you are to him; he doesn't have to be someone else's definition of "hot," but *you* have to want to kiss him. (If the idea of being naked with him turns you off now, I'm telling you, it ain't gonna get better later.)

Back to that restaurant meal. Picture how happy you'd be if you accepted that steak, lobster, and a heavenly dessert. You'd be patting your gut and gushing about how you'll never forget that decadent meal as long as you live. So which do you want: The meal that makes you gush, or some bland, boring chicken? That's the difference we're talking about here. One choice makes you soar with happiness and satisfaction and use words like "utterly amazing," and "crazy-great." The other makes you shrug and say, "Eh, it's okay." You wouldn't have done it to yourself at that meal, and you shouldn't do it to yourself in life.

Don't settle for less than you deserve. If you really, truly want to have an utterly amazing, crazy-great love in your life, then hold out for it! Please don't settle out of fear that you won't find it. The relationship you want is on the menu.

"I give up."

Oh, stop it, no you don't.

"No, seriously, I'm exhausted. I give up."

If you were really giving up, you wouldn't be *telling* me you're giving up. You would have just done it. I think all you need is a final push to help get through this tough time. Like the juicy sliver of orange that gets a marathon runner through her last miles, you need only give the image of your dream orange one final push.

"But why bother? It's so much easier to resign myself to a life alone . . . "

Why bother?? Really? You want to hear why you should *bother*? Fine, I'll tell you. You should bother because you *want* it. You want it more than anything else right now! You've lived a great, happy, full single life up until this point, and now you want a relationship, so guess what—you're going to get one! You're going to stop saying all those crappy negative things about yourself, and about the guys you meet, and about the town you live in, and you're going to stop saying "I give up." You're a total catch and you know it. Look, there are great guys out there looking for love *just* like you are. You're not doing anything wrong, and the world isn't conspiring against you to make sure you're as lonely and miserable as possible—even though it feels like it sometimes. You're just having a down moment, that dip before the rise. So buck up and stop talking about how scared you are that you'll end up alone, and get focused on the relationship that will make you shine. Come on, put down the pessimism. . . there you go . . . now back away.

Instead, think about all the things that make you fabulous: your talent, your jokes, your legs, your laugh, your kindness, your sarcasm, your warmth, your spirit. Inhale deeply while you accept what makes you magnificent. Then exhale slowly and let a real orange smile put creases in the corners of your eyes. See? You're too pretty to end up alone!

Your half-orange is out there and, right now, looking for you. Be the beacon and send the signal stronger than ever. For the sake of your happiness, don't give up for real. Now is the time to turn on the thrusters and give it your biggest push of all.

"I want to believe it's going to happen for me, but . . . I just don't know, you know?"

Sheesh woman, if you're really asking that in the *last* section of the whole book, then I have a question for you: What does it take to believe you deserve a great love? Because while you may not know whether or not you deserve love, I know you do. We all do. And we can be better, brighter human beings if we're given the chance to have it.

I'll tell you what it seems like to me: I think you've built a tall, thick wall around yourself that protects your heart from being hurt. The wall is keeping others away so they don't discover—*gasp!*—how picky you think you are, or depressed, or old, or bitter, or unattractive, or needy, or finicky, or boring, or whatever other preposterous negative attribute you've come up with to explain why you don't deserve an adoring, true love.

Well, it's time to knock that stupid wall down. Why? Because it's also keeping out the good people! Because if you don't knock that wall down, some other girl out there is going to take your guy! I'm talking about *that* guy, the one who is looking for someone exactly like you: someone as funny or sarcastic or nerdy or smart or unique-looking or strong or as obsessed with the Smiths as you are. And, sorry, but if he can't see you behind that wall, he's going to have to settle for some other girl along the way—someone not as right for him as you are. And are you going to put up with that?

With some other girl stealing *your guy*?

Look, I know these things take time. But the Berlin wall came down, and yours can to. We all have walls, you know. No one wants to be hurt or disappointed. No one wants to say, "I believe it will happen for me!" and then be left out there alone, unwanted. But I assure you: You're not so unlovable or broken that no one will want you. Your half-orange is going to love you for exactly who you are. He's going to be able to see through the cracks in the rock to the inner, real you—the gooey center of the Tootsie Pop. To all those things you don't like about yourself (from shaky thighs to looming bitterness), he's going to say, "Nonsense! You're perfect! I love you!"

You don't need to worry about how your half-orange is going to stumble over the chips of your crumbled wall. Or how you'll meet him. Or how he'll find you. You just need to *believe* that he will. I've said it before and I'll say it one final time: **It's not your job to figure out how to make it happen. It's your job to want it**. So do yourself this one favor. Stop saying "Well, I mean, I want to believe" and just *believe*. Believe that it can happen for you. Let the balloon of hope rise up from your belt loop and float far above those old, thick walls of yours so your half-orange will know how to find you. If you want an incredible, fulfilling, magical, compatible, loving, adoring relationship, it will come. So want it, want it all.

Acknowledgments

A big heartfelt thank you to my agent, Laurie Abkemeier, who was as optimistic as I was about this project and whose cheerleading skills she could package and sell. I'd also like to thank my fabulous editor Jennifer Kasius, for her excitement, belief and support, Josh McDonnell for the great cover design, and the rest of the fab team at Running Press.

I'd like to thank *all* the people who shared their stories, each of which confirmed that expecting a great love can bring it bigger than you dreamed. I'd also like to thank those whose insight and encouragement made the book better: Joanna Bober, Lisa Kay, Janet Ozzard, Leslie Yazel, Jennifer Syed, Kate Ayrton, Jenn Gardiner, Margie Cader, Shelley Morales, Mim Eichler Rivas, and especially Laurie Sandell, who inspired entire sections of the book and could not have believed in me more.

Thanks to Todd Bush and Yvonne Cheoun who kept me feeling loved and laughing through my single days. To Darby for the gem of Captain Dusty's. To the gang at *Glamour* magazine, for being like family to me and for giving me what turned out to be a love-changing assignment. To Mrs. Kenny, my first grade teacher who said she wanted to read my first book…ta daaa! And to the doctors, scientists, psychologists and people whose work in positive thinking, optimism and brain research continue to floor me and inspire me. Thank you Dar Meshi, Dr. Lucy Brown and Katherine Spencer for helping me get the science right.

Thanks, Mom and Dad, for being such smart, cool, loving parents, and for your forty-two-year marriage—a reminder every day of the relationship I aspire to myself. Thank you to my sister, Liz, for being my mentor, protector, friend and for encouraging me to think positive the one time I needed it most.

My deepest thanks must go to Gustavo Albero, my beloved husband, for showing me how fun and reeling love can be and for letting me make him a grand finale. Trust me, he deserves the gush. And though little Minnie didn't live to see the publishing of this book, one week before she died, she stretched across the first draft and purred before I sent it, which I took as her sign of approval.

Finally, thank *you* for reading this book. You were my ultimate push to write every single day, because I believed as much as I hope you do: Your half-orange *is* out there.